Speaking Out

Speaking Out

Tanya Serisier
Speaking Out
Feminism, Rape and Narrative Politics

Tanya Serisier
School of Law
Birkbeck, University of London
London, UK

ISBN 978-3-030-40425-3   ISBN 978-3-319-98669-2 (eBook)
https://doi.org/10.1007/978-3-319-98669-2

Library of Congress Control Number: 2018953719

© The Editor(s) (if applicable) and The Author(s) 2018
This work is subject to copyright. All rights are solely and exclusively licensed by the Publisher, whether the whole or part of the material is concerned, specifically the rights of translation, reprinting, reuse of illustrations, recitation, broadcasting, reproduction on microfilms or in any other physical way, and transmission or information storage and retrieval, electronic adaptation, computer software, or by similar or dissimilar methodology now known or hereafter developed.
The use of general descriptive names, registered names, trademarks, service marks, etc. in this publication does not imply, even in the absence of a specific statement, that such names are exempt from the relevant protective laws and regulations and therefore free for general use.
The publisher, the authors and the editors are safe to assume that the advice and information in this book are believed to be true and accurate at the date of publication. Neither the publisher nor the authors or the editors give a warranty, express or implied, with respect to the material contained herein or for any errors or omissions that may have been made. The publisher remains neutral with regard to jurisdictional claims in published maps and institutional affiliations.

This Palgrave Macmillan imprint is published by the registered company Springer Nature Switzerland AG
The registered company address is: Gewerbestrasse 11, 6330 Cham, Switzerland

For my brother, Gerrard, who never would have read a book of feminist theory on rape, but would have been proud of me for writing it. I miss you.

Acknowledgements

There are a great number of people who have contributed support and feedback for this book, in the form of informal chats, feedback on conference presentations or providing inspiration through their own thoughts and ideas. Over the long journey of this book, which began in a different version as a PhD project, they are far too numerous to mention.

Special thanks go to Nina Philadelphoff-Puren and Chris Worth, who assisted this book in its PhD stage. My work here and elsewhere owes an enormous debt to their dedication, enthusiasm, wealth of knowledge and willingness to challenge my ideas and writing to be tighter and stronger. Sharon Marcus and Tanya Horeck both offered extremely useful and generous feedback on the PhD in its final form, and this has significantly informed the final structure and shape of the book.

Numerous friends and colleagues have taken the time to engage and comment with ideas or papers that have ended up here in some form or have informed this work through wider-ranging conversations about gender, culture, sex and violence, and the connections between them. These include Mark Pendleton, Sarah Tayton, Liz Humphrys, Lisa Smyth, Véronique Altglas, Nicola Carr, Siobhán McAllister, Eoin Flaherty, Jonathan Heaney, Bob Miller, Madeleine Leonard, Paul Turnbull, Les Moran, Sarah Turnbull, Teresa Degenhardt, Steven Hutchinson, Anthea Taylor, Meaghan Morris, Zora Simic, Alex Dymock, Esther Singer, Sam Sowerwine and Dave Eden. I also want to acknowledge that I have been lucky enough in my workplaces to have been surrounded by friendly and generous colleagues who, even if they didn't contribute directly to this book, made academic life better and easier, which is itself an enormous help and should be acknowledged.

Pulling the book together has been a significant undertaking, and I am particularly grateful to those who took the time to comment on chapter drafts (often with a very tight deadline!). Each of these people is an important part of my intellectual life and the final form of the ideas in this book. In each of these cases, the specific feedback is just the most obvious manifestation of the informal conversations, reading, writing and thinking that we have done together or that they have inspired me to do. Sarah Lamble always inspires me to think more deeply about difficult questions and models a commitment to combining ethics, politics and scholarship that I find truly inspiring. Kiran Kaur Grewal has been an extremely dedicated reader and whose excellent scholarship has challenged me to think deeper and better in my own work. Vicki Sentas and I began our PhDs at the same time, and I could not imagine someone with a more generous and thoughtful attitude to scholarship as a shared endeavour. Eve Vincent is the person with whom I have had the most dedicated on-going project of reading and thinking alongside, and her influence on this book is significant. Jessica Whyte and I graduated from our PhDs together, and I can't imagine life, or my work, without her influence, thoughts and feedback.

My parents constantly surprise me with their support and generosity, even though I live very far away. My siblings have also always made me feel that they valued and were proud of me and my work.

The person to whom I have the biggest debt of gratitude is Kate Carr, who has accompanied and supported me through many years and transnational moves during the writing of this book. She has read more of it and more often than anyone else and engaged in every aspect from the core concepts to where exactly to put the commas and references. She has spoken far more about rape and stories of rape than anyone could reasonably be expected to, and she still makes me laugh and smile more than anybody else I have met, even in the final weeks of editing this book.

I have been writing on the themes of this book for some time, and earlier versions of some sections have appeared elsewhere. Earlier versions of sections of Chap. 2 appeared in 'Speaking Out, and Beginning to be Heard: Feminism, Survivor Narratives and Representations of Rape in the 1980s', *Continuum*, 32:1 (2018). An earlier version of the discussion of Andrea Dworkin in Chap. 7 appeared in '"How Can a Woman Who Has Been Raped Be Believed?" Andrea Dworkin, Sexual Violence and the Ethics of Belief', *Diegesis*, 4:1 (2015).

Contents

Part I Speaking Out, Building a Genre   1

1 Introduction: The Political Promise of Personal Narratives   3

2 Speaking Out Beyond Feminism: Public Survivors and
   Rape Narratives   23

3 'A New Literature of Rape': Storytelling, Genre and
   Subjectivity   43

4 Speaking Truth to Law's Power: Legal Judgements and the
   'Powerful Letter' of Emily Doe   69

5 #YesAllWomen and Heroic 'Silence Breakers': Online
   Speech, Collective Stories and the Politics of Belief   93

Part II The Politics of Speaking Out   117

6 Whose Business Is Speaking Out? The Bell Debate,
   Indigenous Stories and the Construction of White Feminist
   Expertise   119

7 Turning Rape into Fiction? Judgement, Genre and the
   Politics of Belief   145

8 That Which Must Be Broken: Silence and the Politics of
   Listening   177

9 Conclusion: Break the Silence, End the Violence? A Politics
   of Narrative   197

Bibliography   217

Index   239

Part I

Speaking Out, Building a Genre

1

Introduction: The Political Promise of Personal Narratives

Against Our Will: Men, Women and Rape, published in 1975 by Susan Brownmiller, became a *New York Times* bestseller and saw its author feature as one of *Time* magazine's 12 'Women of the Year' in the magazine's official tribute to feminism (*Time* 1976). The mainstream success of this feminist polemic is generally understood as 'the beginning of an era' in which feminist understandings of rape as a social problem and political issue entered the public sphere (Horeck 2004, p. 17). Brownmiller's (1976, p. 15) description of rape as 'nothing more or less than a conscious process of intimidation by which *all men* keep *all women* in a state of fear' is developed through an epic historical narrative of rape as a core feature of women's oppression. The story begins with an imagined 'first rape' by 'prehistoric man' and concludes with the birth of 1970s' feminist activism in the USA. Despite compelling criticisms of its racial politics (Davis 1983) and its historical accuracy (Porter 1986), the book remains, as Tanya Horeck (2004, p. 17) argues, important as 'a point of origin' for feminist anti-rape politics. It is a useful tool to 'inquire into the kind of work rape has done for feminism', as well as the work that women's narratives of sexual violence perform for feminism. This analysis is crucial to understanding the development, successes and limitations of feminist responses to rape and the impacts of feminist politics on cultural understandings of sexual violence, and sexuality, gender and political authority more broadly.

This is a book about the foundational role that personal stories play in feminist responses to sexual violence, from the writing of *Against Our Will* to contemporary hashtag activism such as #MeToo and #YesAllWomen. I argue that feminist anti-rape politics is founded on the belief that producing and disseminating a genre of personal experiential narratives can end sexual violence. It is a belief, in the words of the well-known slogan, that 'breaking the silence' through telling personal stories can and will 'end the violence'. The production of this genre of stories is one of the key legacies of second-wave feminist politics, as is the widespread cultural acceptance of the political and ethical necessity of speaking out as a response to rape. *Speaking Out* is concerned with the consequences, both intended and unintended, of this commitment to the transformative political potential of experiential storytelling. I suggest that understanding the 'narrative politics' of speaking out necessitates examining the relationships between survivors of sexual violence, the stories they tell and the feminist movement that has enabled these stories to be told. In this introduction, I draw out the complex relations between personal narratives and feminist politics through an exploration of the story of Susan Brownmiller and how she came to write her foundational feminist work on rape.

The 'Personal Statement' that opens *Against Our Will* makes immediately clear that the book does not arise from a direct experience of sexual violence:

> The question most often asked of me while I was writing this book was short, direct and irritating: 'Have you ever been raped?'
> My answer was equally direct: 'No'.

Brownmiller attributes the prevalence of this mutually dissatisfying exchange to a 'curious twist of logic' on the part of her interlocutor: 'A woman who chooses to write about rape probably has a dark personal reason, a lurid secret, a history of real or imagined abuse, a trauma back there somewhere, a fixation, a Bad Experience that has permanently warped her or instilled in her the compulsion to Tell the World'. She is not a survivor, although she 'may have been shortchanged here and there', and the text is not a survivor's story (Brownmiller 1976, p. 7). It is, instead, the result of five years of archival, academic and journalistic research, and draws on the traditional and impersonal authority of these discourses to tell its story.

There is, however, another story hidden within and behind the sweeping historical narrative that constitutes the majority of the book. It is the story, told briefly in the 'Personal Statement', and in greater detail in Brownmiller's (1999) memoir, *In Our Time: Memoir of a Revolution*, of how she 'changed her mind about rape' (1976, p. 9). This personal narrative provides the origin and the core of *Against Our Will*'s analysis and politics. It begins when members of Brownmiller's consciousness-raising group, 'West Village I', first suggested discussing rape in 1970. In response, Brownmiller 'fairly shrieked in dismay':

> I *knew* what rape was, and what it wasn't. Rape was a sex crime, a product of a diseased, deranged mind. Rape wasn't a feminist issue. (Brownmiller 1976, p. 8, emphasis in original)

After the group over-ruled her objections, Sara Pines, 'married, a professional psychologist, and the calmest woman in our group', volunteered to begin and told her story of having been raped while hitch-hiking (Brownmiller 1999, p. 198). To Brownmiller's (1976, p. 8) surprise, Pines was followed by other women, women who, 'when their turn came to speak, quietly articulated their own experiences' and showed that 'they understood their victimisation whereas I only understood that it had not happened to me'. She would later summarise the effects of this meeting in her memoir: 'Listening to Sara Pines was the moment when I started to change my mind about rape' (Brownmiller 1999, p. 198).

Following this meeting, 'West Village I' proposed to the larger 'New York Radical Feminists' (NYRF) collective that they hold a speak-out and conference organised around the theme: 'Rape is a political crime against women' (Brownmiller 1999, pp. 198–199). NYRF organised ten women, including Sara Pines, to tell their stories at the speak-out to an audience of about 300 women and reporters from *Vogue* and *New York* magazines.

To Brownmiller's (1976, p. 9) surprise, 30 other women from the audience also spoke and what they said 'blew her mind'. The conference, held three months later, was a 'moment of revelation' where Brownmiller (p. 7) was 'forced by my sisters in feminism' to face 'a new way of looking at male-female relations, at sex, at strength and at power'. While the conference was designed to prioritise 'objective information, statistics, research and study' (p. 9), Brownmiller's experience of it was dominated by the personal accounts that underwrote and informed this political analysis. In addition to *Against Our Will*, these stories would inspire several significant feminist texts of the 1970s. Among these was Phyllis Chesler's (1972) story of being raped by her therapist, a topic she would revisit in *Women and Madness*, a now classic text on the pathologisation of women by the psychiatric establishment. Germaine Greer (1970), in New York to promote her book, *The Female Eunuch*, spoke about being raped at the age of 18. Florence Rush (1980) recounted her experience of childhood incest, a topic on which she would later publish one of the first feminist accounts, *The Best Kept Secret*. The speak-out and conference demonstrated the epistemological primacy and political power of women's experiential knowledge around sexual violence and solidified the central tenets of feminist belief in speaking out: it promises to produce cultural change by shifting public understandings of rape to more closely reflect the experience of survivors; it assists the collective liberation of survivors by chipping away at the stigma and shame of rape; and it produces individual empowerment for the speaker by having her story heard and herself recognised as an expert on the basis of her experience.

But these events also demonstrated that speaking out is a more complex form of politics than is often presumed. While feminist politics around rape traditionally emphasises the act of speech, perhaps the most important element in constructing a new understanding of rape was through practices of collective listening or 'witnessing'. Narrative requires both an individual to speak and a collective to listen, and, ultimately, storytellers are reliant on what Walter Benjamin (2002, p. 149) describes as the 'community of listeners' who act as the 'web in which the gift of storytelling is cradled'. Women did not begin to speak of rape in 1970, but at that time their speech found new collective and political practices of listening that made their speech meaningful in new ways. Feminism did not give women the ability to speak where previously they had been silent. It provided them with an environment and a discourse in which their stories could be heard and verified through creating a community that was able to receive these stories (Plummer 1995).

This reception was in direct contrast to the failure of witnessing that has historically greeted women's stories of rape, legally and socially. As Sara Pines explained, this failure compounded, extended and could even surpass the harms of the act of sexual violence:

> The worst part of her ordeal had been at the police station. "Aww, who'd want to rape you?" an officer teased. Another said she was too calm to be credible – in his view she should have been crying hysterically. (Brownmiller 1999, p. 198)

The responses of the police officers render Pines' story untellable rather than simply untrue. As I discuss in more detail in Chap. 4, they subject her to what Jean-François Lyotard (1988) describes as a *differend*, a social process of silencing that refuses the victim of a wrong a legitimate speaking position. As feminist critics have shown, the law places contradictory and unfulfillable demands on women which prevent their stories from being heard (e.g. Smart 1998). Pines is pronounced too unattractive to be raped, where if she was labelled attractive she would be guilty of provoking the assault. She is too calm to be credible, where if she was crying she would be too hysterical to be reliable. In granting truth and authority to women's narratives of sexual violence in the 1970s, feminists not only generated a collective discursive politics that opened up new ways of speaking about and understanding sexual violence (Young 1997). It simultaneously exposed the history of legal and social suspicion of women's narratives as a form of political and social silencing that Leigh Gilmore (2017) has described as the 'tainting' of survivors and their testimony.

By providing a space in which women's stories of sexual violence could be told, feminists demonstrated how social storytelling can contest power relations and create a stream of further action and storytelling (Plummer 1995). The narratives told in forums such as the 'West Village I' consciousness-raising group and the NYRF speak-out and conference became part of a feminist 'web of stories' that could call new narratives into being by creating a space in which they could be told, heard and validated (Benjamin 2002). It is almost impossible to trace a clear beginning to this web just as it is impossible to locate an end-point. For instance, while the 'West Village I' conversation was a point of origin for Brownmiller, the group made the decision to speak about rape after reading a personal account, 'Anatomy of a Rape', in the San Francisco zine, *It Ain't Me Babe* (Brownmiller 1999, pp. 196–197). It is in this sense that I argue that speaking out needs to be understood as a form of genre creation, enabling new modes of telling, understanding, hearing and reading women's accounts of rape.

This new genre of feminist stories of rape was able to change women's understandings of their experiences by providing a new discursive framework for making the experience and its articulation politically meaningful (Scott 1992; Phipps 2016). Brownmiller initially objected to rape as a topic of discussion on the basis that it was a 'sex crime' and therefore 'not a feminist issue' (Brownmiller 1976, p. 8). It belonged under the authority of criminal justice discourse and was understood as an act of pathological and deviant individuals. On the basis of the stories she heard, she came to see it as belonging rightfully under feminist discourse and a universal gendered logic that saw her pronounce 'police blotter' rapists the 'shock troops' of patriarchal rule (Brownmiller 1976, p. 209). To use the language of Mikhail Bakhtin (1981), whom I draw on throughout this book, Brownmiller was one of the major figures in a discursive struggle by feminism to move rape and sexual violence out of the discursive orbit of criminal justice and into the domain of feminism and the politics of gender (Serisier 2005). This also redefined women who spoke about rape from objects of legal suspicion and silencing who the 'women's movement had nothing in common with' to heroic survivors whose narratives of experience were foundational to feminist activism and theory (Brownmiller 1976, p. 8).

As cultural theorists have made clear, however, the horizons of possibility for new stories are constrained by the norms and conventions surrounding existing representations (Ewick and Sibley 1995, p. 208). In other words, the discursive shift that I discuss isn't a process of absolute rupture but involves drawing on, reworking and incorporating the existing canon of stories and their discursive frameworks

(Bolter and Grusin 1999, p. 56). Otherwise, the new framework of understanding is not culturally comprehensible. In the case of Brownmiller's (1976, pp. 174–209) text, the process of accommodation with existing frameworks is made most explicit in the chapter, 'The Police Blotter Rapist', in which she uses criminal justice statistics and discourse to conclude that rapists are most likely to be poor men of colour. As Angela Davis (1983) has famously argued, in a book that otherwise sees the criminal justice system as responsible for a set of woman-blaming 'myths' about rape, Brownmiller fails to question criminal justice myths around race and rape. As a result, she reproduces what Davis labels the 'myth of the black rapist', a damaging cultural trope that sees sexual violence as a crime committed primarily by racially marginalised men against white women. Brownmiller's insistence on seeing rape solely in terms of gender makes her unable to critique the carceral politics that selectively recognises and punishes rape as a crime through racist and class-biased policing, prosecution and sentencing practices (Bumiller 2008).

In her prioritisation of gender over race and insistence on a politics of gender universality, Brownmiller paradoxically constitutes race as a generic boundary around the genre of women's stories. As Derrida (1992) has made clear, genre is both an enabling and a constraining force. It constructs a cultural space and a set of tools for telling certain narratives but marks other narratives as outside of that space and forecloses other ways of telling or understanding a story. Brownmiller locates the beginning of women speaking politically about rape in the radical feminist consciousness-raising groups of the 1970s, despite the fact that black women in the US had been speaking publicly and politically about rape from the time of slavery when abolitionists made political use of women's accounts of sexual violence (e.g. Jacobs 2000). Throughout the twentieth century, black women such as Recy Taylor and Amelia Boynton Robinson also testified to their experiences of sexual violence at the hands of white men as part of civil rights and anti-racist movements (McGuire 2010). They produced political understandings of rape as a 'conscious process of intimidation' by which white men kept all black people in a state of fear. Their narratives demonstrate that the feminist truth constructed by Brownmiller is a particular interpretation of some women's experiences rather than a universal truth that arises naturally from listening to all women's stories. It is a truth that sees only speech that is solely about gender as political speech about sexual violence, thus casting the history of black women's speech as located outside this politics of story production. As I show in later chapters, as feminists attained increasing discursive authority in relation to rape, selective recognition of stories continued this process of generic boundary-making at the same time as enabling specific forms of narrative. Relations between feminist experts on rape and the narratives of experience that provide their inspiration are marked by power dynamics that, at their most extreme, contribute to or produce the erasure of certain women's narratives or their framework of interpretation. As I explore in the following chapters, this has made the genre of stories enabled by speaking out a predominantly white genre. Within this genre, as I discuss in Chaps. 3 and 6 particularly, the stories of women of colour may be incorporated within white feminist stories that presume to speak on their behalf.

But even relations between feminists such as Susan Brownmiller and the women like Sara Pines whose stories they tell are not as automatically or naturally complementary as feminist analyses often presume them to be. In the introduction to the 1974 New York Radical Feminists' publication, *Rape: The First Sourcebook for Women*, a collection of papers and narratives from the 1971 conference and speak-out, the editors note pointedly:

> Rape as an issue didn't arise because feminist leaders decided it was 'the issue' or because it was a designated topic on a consciousness-raising list. Instead, it became an issue when women began to compare their experiences, and realised sexual assault was common. (Connell and Wilson 1974, p. 3)

Indeed, some leaders like Brownmiller had to be dragged unwillingly into recognising the political significance of rape by survivors such as Pines. Once convinced, Brownmiller spent the next four years researching and writing *Against Our Will*, a text that would establish her as the pre-eminent feminist expert on rape and largely obscure its own foundations in the stories and insights of Sara Pines and the other unknown women whose experiential narratives inspired the project. Feminist interlocutors like Brownmiller are not merely supportive listeners or even sources of dissemination and amplification for women's experiences and the understandings which arise from them. Instead, feminist texts based on women's experiential narratives simultaneously produce new understandings of rape and install themselves as the experts or custodians of these new truths (Yeatman 1993). A hierarchy can be introduced in which the narrative of experience is shaped and moulded into a political feminist story by the expert. Through this reshaping, Brownmiller, now authorised as a feminist storyteller, gains the right to make meaning from Sara Pines' story, which only reaches us through Brownmiller's mediation.

All of this speaks to the ambivalent position of survivors who tell their stories. To speak of sexual violence, and break the silence and taboos surrounding it, can be an incredibly empowering experience, a way of reclaiming subjectivity and agency after a desubjectifying experience of violence. But it is an experience that is fraught with vulnerability and risk. There is the potential response of disbelief or trivialization, as documented by Sara Pines in her experience with the police and other survivors who told stories to Brownmiller of disbelief and denial from friends, families and partners. But, these are accompanied by less obvious risks. Even sympathetic and feminist audiences may want to hear a story told in a certain way or may interpret an experience differently to a survivor and insist on that interpretation. The political model of speaking out offers political benefits to survivors but it also asks and even demands a lot from them. Feminist politics both supports survivor stories and requires survivors to tell these stories and to tell them in specific ways. This ambivalence has only been heightened with the success of speaking out as a form of discursive activism 'directed at promoting new grammars, new social paradigms through which individuals, collectivities, and institutions interpret social circumstances and devise responses to them' (Young 1997, p. 3).

Speaking of the women who spoke at the first New York Radical Feminist speak-out in 1971, Brownmiller (1999, pp. 198–199) reflected that 'their words were to reverberate far beyond the confines of the tiny church' in which the speak-out was held, and it is these reverberations that are the focus of the remainder of the book. The success of speaking out means that it has moved from feminist-defined and controlled spaces, such as consciousness-raising groups, into the wider public domain. In doing so, it has become an increasingly mediatised and mediated process. The journalists who were present at that speak-out were the first of many who would find the phenomenon of women speaking about sexual violence newsworthy. Survivor narratives can now be found as books, magazine articles, in documentaries, films and television talk shows, and, in recent years, on the internet and social media. This growing cultural influence is shown in the 2017 *Time* magazine award of 'Person of the Year' to the 'Silence Breakers' who had spoken out about workplace sexual harassment and violence, following the emergence of the #MeToo movement (Zacharek et al. 2017). This was the first time the magazine had awarded the title to a group since the 1975 'Women of the Year' edition that featured Susan Brownmiller, although by 2017 it was speaking out, defined far beyond feminism and feminist influence, that was the topic of the magazine's profile, a moment I return to in Chap. 5.

As survivor accounts have acquired greater cultural acceptance and a broader sympathetic audience, their public and cultural dissemination has come to exceed the discursive and political bounds of feminism. While many survivors and their supporters speak as feminists, not all do, and feminist claims to a natural affinity with survivor narratives are challenged by other experts and interpreters, from psychologists and therapists to proponents of law and order and victims' rights organisations. The success of speaking out has produced, I argue, a more complex set of risks, pitfalls and ethical dilemmas for feminists and survivors. All of these are underwritten by a central paradox. Breaking the silence, despite its significant cultural impact, has not ended sexual violence, nor does it seem to have significantly reduced it, or to have eradicated the stigma associated with being a rape victim. Many of the stories women tell almost 50 years after the birth of the feminist anti-rape movement contain disturbingly similar elements to those from that first speak-out, even as the cultural context in which they are told has been undeniably altered by the effects of half a century of speaking out. This paradox provides the primary context and impetus for this book.

Introduction: The Political Promise of Personal Narratives 13

Approach, Scope and Organisation

This is not a book about rape as such. Rather, it is a critical analysis of 'speaking out' against rape as a form of narrative politics. My aim is to trace some of the consequences of telling stories of sexual violence as a form of political activism. The book is framed around a central question: What are the implications of this narrative-based politics for the project of ending sexual violence, and for survivors and feminists who participate in this project? The answers to this question will necessarily be partial, based in part on the rapidly changing political and cultural landscape surrounding this issue, the most recent example of which at the time of writing is the explosion of public speech around rape falling broadly under the auspices of #MeToo. The cultural scholar John Fiske (1996, p. 13) has written that: 'Anyone who analyses change while it is in progress and is foolish enough to predict its direction must be prepared for history to prove him or her wrong'. Nevertheless, as Fiske notes, it is possible to draw out historical tendencies and legacies while being mindful of this limitation. That is what I attempt to do here.

The primary object of enquiry in this book is Anglophone Western feminist practices of speaking out and their legacies. This limits the scope of the book in several ways. First, following feminist understandings of rape and sexual violence as an act which shapes the life experiences of women in specific and highly gendered ways, when I discuss survivors of victims of sexual violence, I generally refer to women, and where relevant, I move between discussions of survivors of sexual violence and women as a social group. There is a great deal to say about other gendered experiences of survivors but that is beyond the scope of this book. The case studies discussed move between national contexts (particularly the USA, UK, Australia and Canada) but remain within what Rentschler and Thrift (2015, p. 239) label a transnational, Anglophone feminist 'discursive public' defined through shared discourses, media platforms and reference points. Within this context, feminism as a cultural and political movement is the product of both shared and nationally specific histories and understandings, as are cultures of telling stories of sexuality and victimisation. As Ken Plummer (1995) notes, the culture with the strongest history of narrative politics around rape is the USA, and this is reflected in the proportion of case studies that focus on that country.

This is an interdisciplinary work that is primarily situated in relation to debates within and among feminist scholars even as it draws on wider sociological and cultural work on the social and political uses of narrative. I follow in the tradition of feminist interpretation of representation, narrative and rape that contends that understanding and combating rape is as much 'a question of language, interpretation and subjectivity' as it is about embodied violence (Marcus 1992, p. 387). Or, as Lynn Higgins and Brenda Silver argue, 'who gets to tell the story and whose story counts as "truth" determine the definition of what rape *is*' (Higgins and Silver 1991, p. 1). Feminists have used these insights to make powerful critiques of the ways that women who speak about rape are 'tainted' by doubt and disbelief (L. Gilmore 2017), and their narratives over-written legally, socially and culturally (Ehrlich 2001), while respectable and powerful men are granted narrative 'immunity' from the consequences of the stories that women tell (Waterhouse-Watson 2013). These critiques, and the debates and discussions from which they arise, form an important foundation of this work.

The book also takes part in on-going processes of interrogation and critique of feminist responses to sexual violence, noting with Wendy Brown (1995, p. x) that 'critique is not equivalent to rejection or denunciation, … the call to rethink something is not inherently treasonous but can actually be a way of caring for and even renewing the object in question'. In producing my own critique, I draw on debates on the potentials and limitations of 'survivor discourse' as a tool for political transformation (Alcoff and Gray 1993; Naples 2003), and the investment of feminists and feminism in social stories of rape and the ways in which they are told (e.g. Haag 1996; Horeck 2004; Mardorossian 2014). In my consideration of the ways in which speaking out has become a widely accepted and even 'common sense' response to rape, I engage in a growing literature that is concerned with what Rose Corrigan (2013) refers to as the 'failures of success' in the feminist politics of rape. In engaging in critiques of 'feminism', I remain cognisant not only of the existence of multiple feminist positions but of the importance of not ceding the terrain of feminism to institutionally or discursively dominant forms. Nevertheless, following the critics above, I find it useful to retain a focus on 'feminism' as a meaningful term that can specify, variously, political commitments, institutional position or a cultural location. For this reason, I frequently discuss 'feminism' even as many of the chapters articulate and explore debates and disagreements about feminist identities and politics.

As a critical engagement with the politics of 'speaking out', this book extensively discusses, analyses and debates women's narratives of experiences of sexual violence. In doing so, I only make use of published or otherwise public narratives. Where this 'public' status is questionable, as in the case of individual tweets, I err on the side of what the Association of Internet Researchers (2012) refers to as 'contextual' privacy, recognising that simply because something is publicly searchable it is not necessarily intentionally public. Beyond this, I am committed to engaging ethically with these texts through, firstly, giving them what Leigh Gilmore (2017, p. 5) refers to as an 'adequate witness', responding to them without 'deforming' them by doubt or 'substituting different terms of value for the ones offered by' the survivor herself. I do not interrogate the 'truth' of the narratives here but accept them on their own terms, although I do explore the ways in which some of these narratives were granted or not granted belief. I accept the story and interpretation offered by the writer or speaker. For me, this does not mean simply accepting all interpretations offered and presenting them as empirical artefacts but engaging with the authors as experts on their experience. I both discuss these texts as examples and treat them as feminist literature to be drawn on, debated and considered. Following the point made by the survivor and anthropologist Cathy Winkler (2002, pp. vii–viii), I avoid terminology such as 'her rape' or 'her rapist' that linguistically connects the event to survivors' identity and decentres the responsibility of men who rape. Finally, the terms victim and survivor are subject to extensive debate. My usage reflects the dominant tendency in the survivor narratives discussed here, outlined in Chap. 3. In what I label the core narrative of speaking out, a victim transforms herself into a survivor through her act of speaking out, and that is the usage I follow, even as I seek to draw out the complexity and paradoxes of that narrative structure.

The chapters of the book are based around a series of case studies that draw out key elements of the politics of speaking out. The book does not attempt to provide a comprehensive survey or overview of the stories told by survivors of sexual violence or their political influence historically or geographically. Indeed, a focus on public texts means that the majority of acts of speech about sexual violence, told in private or semi-private forums, are not the subject of this book. Instead, it seeks to analyse moments, texts and case studies to draw out their significance for the public reception and understanding of survivor speech, and to assess the political and cultural legacies of speaking out as a form of narrative politics. Chapters 2, 3, 4 and 5 map the discursive framing and institutional and cultural positioning of these narratives, while the remaining chapters focus on the political and ethical responsibilities of feminist audiences and interlocutors of these narratives.

Chapter 2, 'Speaking Out Beyond Feminism: Public Survivors and Rape Narratives', provides an account of the increasing cultural acceptance of the ethical and political necessity of speaking out as a response to sexual violence through revisiting the late 1980s as a turning point in the public recognition of survivor narratives and 'public survivors', women who achieve a public profile through speaking about their experience of rape. Using Mikhail Bakhtin's (1981) work on the 'competition' between discourses to draw words and concepts into their 'orbits', the chapter traces the way that the growing cultural authority of speaking out has seen survivor narratives become discursively separate from feminism, focusing particularly on the competing discourse of criminality and 'law and order'. The chapter explores this through consideration of two early 'public survivors', Nancy Ziegenmeyer in the USA and Jill Saward in the UK, ordinary women who became public figures through speaking out about their perspectives of rape, although not, as I argue, from a straightforwardly feminist perspective.

Chapter 3 uses the proliferation of book-length 'rape memoirs' in the late 1990s to explore the effects of genre formation and the existence of a recognisable core narrative of speaking out mentioned above. While feminists and survivors believed that speaking out would enable all survivors to speak and to tell a diverse range of stories, this chapter describes a clear set of generic boundaries around the kinds of stories that are tellable: primarily narratives of stranger rape told by educated white women. The chapter also explores the ambivalent effects of speaking out as described by the women who tell their stories. While the promise of speaking out is that it can produce individual empowerment and collective liberation, the survivors in this genre describe it as an act fraught with risk and vulnerability as well as recognition and empowerment.

Chapter 4 considers the complicated relationship of the criminal law to women's speech about sexual violence. It discusses the Victim Impact Statement of Emily Doe, produced for the criminal trial of Brock Turner, and then distributed publicly as a political statement condemning both Turner and the legal system that minimised his actions (Baker 2016a). Doe's statement helps to elaborate the ways in which speaking out has worked to contest the law's self-proclaimed ability to determine the 'truth' of rape by revealing legal investments in rape myths and its refusal to grant women's speech a just hearing. Simultaneously, as I argue in the second half of the chapter, Doe's story reveals a continuing commitment among survivors and many feminists to speaking through and within legal domains. The chapter concludes by asking whether speaking out offers a means for moving 'beyond' the law as a site for the judgement of women's speech about rape.

The first half of the book concludes with a discussion in Chap. 5 of the significance of social media as a forum for the production and dissemination of women's narratives of sexual violence. Recent years have seen an upsurge in public and publicly accessible survivor speech, accompanied by claims that social media has produced a new era of speaking out, in which it is far easier for women to speak, and to find a 'community of listeners'. This chapter begins with a discussion of the effects of the collective storytelling of hashtag activism, and the ways it has enabled increasing forms of speaking out. I argue, however, that social media does not eliminate the problems discussed in previous chapters, of a lack of control over the framing and reception of narratives; of generic boundaries that exclude certain stories; or of being disbelieved and refused a hearing. Instead, I suggest that it changes the terrain on which these conflicts happen. Finally, I ask whether, if social media represents a logical extension of the politics of speaking out, it might also offer insight into its political limits.

The focus on feminist politics in relation to survivor narrative begins with an attempt to think through the relationship between the experiences of survivors and their representation by feminist experts. This is examined through the lens of a significant controversy in Australian feminism, the 'Bell debate', which centred on the right of Diane Bell, a white American anthropologist to 'speak out' about high levels of sexual violence in remote Aboriginal communities. Revisiting this debate, the chapter insists that postcolonial analyses of power relations between and among women are crucial for understanding the political and ethical responsibilities of feminists in relation to narratives of sexual violence. The Bell debate demonstrates, I argue, the importance of subjecting the actions of feminist interlocutors of women's experiences to critical scrutiny.

The following chapter discusses the ethical and political responsibilities of feminist interlocutors through a discussion of the politics of generic judgement and belief. I argue that rather than enacting a politics of universal belief, the politics of speaking out shifts the boundaries of belief and disbelief, and the basis on which this boundary is drawn. The chapter begins with an analysis of the ways in which the controversial radical feminist, Andrea Dworkin, was unable to obtain belief from feminists in response to her story of being raped in a Paris hotel room in 1999. I suggest this was because she failed to adhere to generic requirements of credibility. I then introduce the problem of authenticity through a discussion of Katie Roiphe's (1993) *The Morning After: Sex Fear and Feminism*, a text that asserted that the generic conventions that structure survivor narratives render them insufficiently authentic and therefore unworthy of belief. Finally, I consider Laura Kipnis' (2017) *Unwanted Advances: Sexual Paranoia Comes to Campus* and her argument that the genre of speaking out is an inappropriate genre for telling specific and general stories of sexual harassment on campus. I contend that these examples are united in drawing attention to the inevitability of generic judgement and the vulnerability it produces for survivors.

Chapter 8 revisits the opposition between speech and silence that underwrites much of feminist and survivor discourse in this area. The chapter argues for a more complex understanding of speech and silence that recognises, following theorists such as Foucault, Lyotard and Brown that both speech and silence are components of discourse and that neither are inherently liberating or oppressive. The chapter explores survivor narratives for more nuanced understandings of silence, from Louise Armstrong's (1994) critique of storytelling as a silencing of the political to Nancy Venable Raine's (1998) depiction of silence as an essential part of the process of speaking out. Finally, I argue that silence is an essential component of listening, and in this way, may constitute an essential part of any ethics of feminist responses to survivor speech.

The book concludes with a consideration of the relationship between narrative and politics that asks what it is that speaking out can do through a brief discussion of the 'politicisation' of speaking out in the 2016 US Presidential election. Drawing on arguments made throughout the book, I propose that a transformative narrative practice around violence must insist on the need for open narrative possibilities and reject a form of narrative closure that sees telling stories of rape as an inevitable part of our political future.

A Personal Statement

Before continuing the arguments of this book, I want to pause and provide a 'personal statement' echoing that made by Susan Brownmiller in *Against Our Will*. Like Brownmiller's opus, this book is built on a foundation of women's personal narratives of sexual violence but is written in a language of impersonal authority and expertise which can obscure the relationship between personal experience and feminist politics.

Like Brownmiller (1976, p. 7), I have found that claiming this authoritative position does not dispel the presumption that women's writing about rape is always the product of an experience of sexual violence. For Brownmiller, this was an irritating and inaccurate assumption that prefigured a combative exchange with her interlocutor. In contrast, I have predominantly experienced a solemn silence or a comment about the 'importance' of this work, and a change of topic. While colleagues are frequently questioned as to their motivations for working in a particular field, my choice of topic is heard as a personal revelation that does not require further explanation. I read this response as a solidification of the assumptions faced by Brownmiller and a shift in sensibilities. The questions she faced are largely deemed irrelevant in a culture in which the link between personal experience, writing and activism around sexual violence are largely presumed, but they are also deemed insensitive in response to the cultural dominance of narratives that see women as inevitably and irretrievably traumatised by rape (Gavey and Schmidt 2011; McKenzie-Mohr 2014).

Rather than irritation, I find myself ambivalent about these exchanges and their meaning. The link between experience, writing and activism doesn't only arrive from the internalisation of dominant discourses. It is connected to ethical and political claims made by survivors and directed towards feminists and others who use their experience as a kind of emotional raw material for their academic discussions. The ethics and politics of these relations is one of the central concerns of this book. Further, it remains the case that to speak publicly about experiences of sexual violence carries significant risks and entails substantial vulnerability, even within feminist spaces and among feminist audiences. An ethical engagement with the texts produced by survivors who have faced those risks as part of their activism against sexual violence means, at the very least, challenging the binary between experience and expertise that sees those texts labelled as personal and this book labelled as theoretical or political.

On the other hand, I am sceptical about the continuing imperative to speak confessionally as a precursor to writing or speaking politically about sexual violence. To accept and further the expectation that survivors must or should confess the violence that has been done to us in order to authorise our speech is itself a highly compromising position. Critiquing the effects of tying feminist politics so closely to experiential narratives and the authority of 'experience' is therefore also one of the central tasks of this book. For these reasons, I have prevaricated over what role, if any, my own personal narrative should play within this book.

The story of how I came to write this book is not Brownmiller's story of the transformative impact of listening to others' experiences. It is a story that includes my own experience of sexual and domestic violence. More importantly, this book arises from my experiences of, frustrations with, and commitment to, feminist anti-rape politics, and this is something I share with many of the texts discussed in this book. One of the phenomena I discuss in this book is the frustration, anger and hurt produced among survivors by feminist imperatives to tell one's story and to ascribe certain meanings to it. These negative emotions can sit alongside a deep commitment to the political project and narrative genre of speaking out and to the feminist project of ending sexual violence. Of all the elements of my personal story, this complicated relationship to feminist politics, and the attitude of immanent critique it inspires, most accurately reflects my motivation in writing this book, and is most closely related to the analysis performed within it.

2

Speaking Out Beyond Feminism: Public Survivors and Rape Narratives

In October 1989, Nancy Ziegenmeyer was awaiting the trial of Bobby Lee Smith, the man who had broken into her car, kidnapped and then raped her a year earlier while she was studying for a real estate exam in Des Moines, Iowa, in the USA. During this time, she attended a public panel on media treatment of victims of crime where she found herself increasingly frustrated listening to 'experts' talk about 'theoretical victims' and so, she raised her hand, stood up and began to speak: 'There, standing in front of about a hundred people I didn't know, I heard with astonishment the words coming out of my own mouth. "I am a rape victim."' For Ziegenmeyer, this was a moment of revelation, where she began to discover the power of public speech about her experience:

> As I told them, from beginning to end, what had happened, and how everything having to do with it had made me feel, they listened. I was unsure of myself and my role here, and I rushed the words out… I knew that what I was saying was important for them to hear. And I knew it was important for me to say it. (1992, p. 109)

After she sat down people began to applaud. This was the beginning of a career as a public rape survivor which would culminate in providing testimony to the US Senate Judiciary Committee on 'Legislation to Reduce the Growing Problem of Violent Crime Against Women', or what would eventually become the 'Violence Against Women Act' (United States Senate 1990). For a brief period, Ziegenmeyer became a well-known figure. Her story was syndicated internationally and was even made into a television movie, all because she spoke publicly about her experience of rape (Ziegenmeyer 1992; Plummer 1995).

Writing 15 years earlier, Susan Brownmiller (1976, pp. 396–397) described the ridicule early feminist activists faced in their attempt to change cultural understandings of sexual violence: 'When just a few years ago, we began to hold our speak-outs on rape … the world out there, the world outside of radical feminism, thought it was all very funny'. However, as she notes, it wasn't long 'before the world out there had stopped laughing'. Those 15 years mark a cultural chasm between a grudging acknowledgement beginning to be given to 'women's libbers' and their political preoccupation with rape, and the authority granted to Ziegenmeyer on the basis that she was a survivor of rape. In this chapter, I provide an account of this shift, its causes and its consequences.

Ken Plummer (1995, p. 49) argues that the period from the 1970s to the early 1990s saw 'stories of sexual suffering, surviving and surpassing', including narratives of rape, grow 'from being insignificant to widespread'. These stories prefigured 'major social changes as a result of being retold and replayed', and it is this relationship between storytelling and social change that concerns me here. I am interested in the cultural shifts that enabled and preceded ordinary women being able to publicly tell their stories of rape and claim cultural authority on the basis of their experience. The first half of the chapter considers the 1990 *Des Moines Register* serialisation of Nancy Ziegenmeyer's story that ran as front-page news for five days, and ultimately saw her address the US Senate. The second half discusses the case of another white working-class woman who built a public profile out of speaking out about rape. Several months after the *Des Moines Register* series, Jill Saward (1991) published her memoir, *Rape: My Story*, and became the first British rape victim to waive her right to anonymity. Saward was the victim of a 1986 crime, widely referred to as the 'Ealing Vicarage Rape', in which a group of armed men broke into the vicarage and raped Saward and physically assaulted her father, the

Vicar, and her then boyfriend. The violence of the case, its setting, and Saward's status as virginal 'vicar's daughter' led to a media frenzy. Public debates about media sensationalism were soon matched by outrage against the trial judge who gave a lighter sentence for rape than burglary on the basis that 'the trauma the girl suffered was not so very great' (Saward 1991, pp. 58–59). I propose that the emergence of these two prominent survivors, and the response that they received in terms of media coverage and public support, marks 1990 as a turning point in the history of speaking out.

Both women were deeply committed to speaking out but neither considered themselves a feminist. Ziegenmeyer, as I show, made use of feminist analysis but within an overall framing within a 'victim's rights' and criminal justice discourse. Saward, on the other hand, was openly hostile to feminism, interpreting her experience through law and order politics and socially conservative Christianity, and unpacking this seeming paradox is the focus of the second half of the chapter. These examples show the politics and narratives of speaking out as becoming increasingly separate from their feminist origins and, instead, open to the competition between different discourses seeking to attract 'words and forms into their own orbit' (Bakhtin 1981, p. 290). The examples of Ziegenmeyer and Saward show that increasing public acceptance of the tenets of speaking out often resulted in incorporation of this political practice within criminal justice discourses rather than promoting feminist understandings of sexual violence. The idea of a politics of speaking out that was not associated with feminism would have been unthinkable to Susan Brownmiller in 1975, but it is, I argue, an important if unintended consequence of the success that second-wave feminists had in making the world stop laughing and start taking rape, and the experiences of rape survivors, seriously.

Nancy Ziegenmeyer, Feminism and Criminal Justice

On Sunday, February 25, 1990, the front page of the *Des Moines Register*, the newspaper of record for the state of Iowa, USA, was dominated by a headline, 'Staring Down the Cruel Stigma of Rape', and a photo of Nancy

Ziegenmeyer standing in a car park. Above the photo was a title that would remain on the cover for the next five days: 'It Couldn't Happen to Me: One Woman's Story'. As a sidebar, 'How This Story Came to Be', explained, the *Register* would, over the course of the week, recount a 'victim's story' of rape, from the day that she was attacked in 1989 to the conviction of the man who raped her just over a year later (Schorer 1990d). The unprecedented series, based primarily on extensive interviews with Ziegenmeyer, was reproduced in newspapers internationally, including the *New York Times*, *The Guardian* (UK) and *The Age* (Australia). Jane Schorer, the journalist, received a Pulitzer Prize, while Ziegenmeyer and the paper's editor, Geneva Overholser were awarded prizes by the National Organisation of Women (Ziegenmeyer 1992).

The origins of Ziegenmeyer's story are to be found in the cultural changes brought about by feminist 'discursive activism' around rape in the 1970s and 1980s (Young 1997). From the late 1970s, rape began to feature more frequently in popular culture, particularly in cultural formats, such as day-time television and magazines, marketed towards women (Cuklanz 2000; Horeck 2004). These new representations accepted and reproduced important feminist claims that rape was common, harmful and a social problem that affected ordinary women and deserved to be taken seriously. As the decade continued, these representations found their way into increasingly influential media forums, such as prime time television and major newspapers (Cuklanz 1996, 2000). Jodie Foster's Academy Award for her portrayal of gang-rape victim Sarah Tobias in the 1988 film, *The Accused*, can be seen as a watershed moment in this cultural shift. Although aspects of the film have been criticised, it was the first major Hollywood release to challenge victim-blaming myths through a sympathetic portrayal of a 'disreputable', working-class woman as a rape survivor seeking justice (Horeck 2004).

As the production and reception of the *Des Moines Register* series shows, these changes contributed to a growing interest in survivor narratives and acceptance of the importance of speaking out. In July 1989, Geneva Overholser, the *Register's* editor published an editorial titled, 'American Shame: The Stigma of Rape'. She argued that the 'public testimony of courageous rape victims' was the only thing that could end the stigma surrounding rape, and she spoke admiringly of the actor Kelly

McGillis and Democratic party activist and law academic, Susan Estrich, for speaking openly of their experiences of sexual violence. McGillis (1988), Jodie Foster's co-star in *The Accused*, had published an account of being raped by two men who broke into her apartment in *People* magazine in the lead-up to the film's release. Estrich (1987), the 1988 campaign manager for Democratic Presidential candidate, Michael Dukakis, was also the author of *Real Rape*, an important work of feminist legal critique that begins by recounting and analysing her own experience.

Ziegenmeyer was motivated to contact the paper by Overholser's plea for more women to come forward and her insistence that 'we will not break down the stigma' that surrounds rape 'until more and more women take public stands'. She had also come to believe that survivors had a unique authority to speak about rape, and this belief propelled her intervention at the public panel. Speaking out gave her a sense of individual empowerment and the belief that she had imparted a necessary perspective to the audience. It was only after her story appeared in the newspaper, however, that she realised that her speech had another audience:

Women who had never told anyone, not even their husbands, or their doctors, or their mothers, or their ministers. Women who'd lived in silence with their secret, and had believed that they were alone, and somehow to blame. Every day, more phone calls, more letters, from farther and farther away. They were all out there someplace, and they were all talking to me.

'It was', she concludes, 'the most amazing thing I had ever seen' (Ziegenmeyer 1992, pp. 148–149). The response to her speech fulfilled the three promises of speaking out: individual empowerment, wider attitudinal change, and inspiration and support for other victims.

Despite this, Ziegenmeyer's experience was not entirely positive. When, for example, she asked to review the *Register* series prior to publication she was informed that, as a 'news source', this was impossible: 'So that's what I've become, I thought. First a victim, then a survivor, then a witness, and now, a news source… I simply couldn't believe that I didn't have access to something I basically saw as mine. My life, my family, my rape. How could the story not be mine?' (Ziegenmeyer 1992, p. 145). In a very real way, Ziegenmeyer's role was reduced, as Alcoff and Gray (1993) caution, from the owner of and authority over her own narrative to the provider of 'raw experience' in a story told and interpreted by others. But, as Alcoff and Gray also note, this was not an absolute experience. It would be just as wrong to say that the paper completely removed Ziegenmeyer's control over her story. Her story was framed by others but her authority to speak within it was not entirely eclipsed. Most of the analysis or 'editorialising' in the series came in the form of quotes from Ziegenmeyer, including the final summative paragraph: 'A statement that has been made about rape – that rape is just short of murder – is in fact an understatement... The person that I was on the morning of November 19, 1988, was taken from me and my family. I will never be the same for the rest of my life' (Schorer 1990a, p. 9). Her expertise and authority, in short, was both recognised and contained, and it was her definition and understanding of rape that was put forward.

The definition of rape as a crime equivalent to murder is repeated in Ziegenmeyer's subsequent memoir and in her contributions in other forums, such as the Senate Committee. It reflects, I argue, a competitive intersection between feminism and criminal justice discourses, or, more precisely, the continuing influence of criminal justice discourses in defining the meaning and reality of rape (Serisier 2005). As Susan Brownmiller (1976, p. 8) testifies, prior to feminist consciousness-raising around rape, understanding it as a 'sex crime' seemed to be simply common sense. As she notes, the natural consequence of this was that it 'wasn't a feminist issue', but rather was located within the linked discourses of criminal justice and psychology. The discursive claims made by feminism that rape should be understood as a social problem of systemic gendered violence were simultaneously claims of discursive ownership or influence, although in practice, feminist analyses have diverged as to whether the problem of sexual violence is located in the 'normal' functioning of dominant forms of heterosexuality, and therefore a cultural and gendered problem, or an issue of violence and not sex (Gavey 2005). These understandings produce different relations to criminal justice discourses and institutions. The former suggests that targeting 'deviant' acts and individuals is a mistaken strategy, while the second allows for the possibility that criminal justice solutions, properly and fairly applied, might help to combat sexual violence. These different discursive understandings produce, therefore, different relationships to the criminal justice system, and the issue of law reform (Heath and Naffine 1994; Serisier 2005). As I discuss in detail in Chap. 4, defining the problem of rape as one of inadequate or selective punishment critiques legal responses and simultaneously recentres them as the appropriate institutional venue and discursive framework for defining and responding to sexual violence. In other words, it suggests that an appropriate response to rape might be for the law to take it as seriously as crimes such as murder.

The *Register* series also enacted this double movement of support and critique, discursively centring the criminal justice system through arguments for the necessity of reform. Three of the five headlines focused on the trial, all in ways that emphasised the inefficiency of the legal system and the difficulties and harms that it caused for victims: 'Months Drag On; No Trial: "Is This Really Worth It?"'; 'Learning to Cope – With Pain and the Legal System'; and 'And Finally, the Trial Begins' (Schorer 1990a, b, c). The overall message, articulated primarily by Ziegenmeyer, concerned the 'lenient treatment of criminals' in contrast to the indignities suffered by victims: 'He has a criminal record, but he's the one with all the rights. I haven't even had a parking ticket. What about my rights?' (Ziegenmeyer, quoted in Schorer 1990b, p. 6). These complaints do not primarily evoke feminist critiques of the legal system, but rather emerging discourses of 'victims rights', 'penal populism' and 'law and order' politics which see the rights of offenders and victims as counterpoised (Newburn and Jones 2005; Rentschler 2011).

Ziegenmeyer consistently made use of this framing in describing the harms of rape and linking it to pre-existing support for punitive criminal justice measures such as the death penalty. As Nancy Naples (2003) contends, the experience of rape does not necessarily produce feminist consciousness or alignment with feminist discourses. Survivors are more likely to make use of the discourses that they already use to explain their experiences, unless doing so produces a profound disjuncture. The criminal justice system and the discursive position of victim of crime offered Ziegenmeyer an explanation for her experience that matched her existing worldview, but did not capture the specifically gendered elements of her experience. And so, Ziegenmeyer supplemented the criminal justice framework, and her complaints about her treatment as a crime victim, with elements of feminist analysis to make sense of the particularly gendered nature of rape. For instance, she objected to the use of the word 'panties' by lawyers and expert witnesses, insisting that the less sexual word 'undergarments' be used instead. This implicitly draws on feminist arguments that rape trials can undermine women's testimony by reconfiguring it as a 'pornographic vignette' that '*gives pleasure* in the way that pornography gives pleasure' and precludes it from being heard as a narrative of violence and harm (Smart 1989, pp. 88–89). While for Smart, this observation forms part of a systemic critique of the law and its capacity to respond to rape, for Ziegenmeyer, it was part of the indignity that she suffered as a victim of crime who required the criminal justice system to be more oriented towards her needs.

For Ziegenmeyer, feminist insights provide a complementary but minor discourse within a broader criminal justice logic where the primary aim of speaking out is to have rape recognised as a serious crime, legislatively, culturally and socially. The culmination of this was her testimony in support of what would eventually become the 'Violence Against Women Act', a federal US law that increased resources for the prosecution and punishment of gendered violence by placing it more securely within the framework of 'serious' violent crime (Bevacqua 2000). As in the trial, she incorporated elements of feminist analysis within the overarching criminal justice discourse that she deployed, so that the two merged into an argument for a criminal justice system that could be sensitive to gendered dimensions of criminal violence. She was careful to note that her experience differed from the majority of victims of rape because the man who assaulted her was a violent stranger. Drawing on Estrich's (1987) distinction, she noted that the fact that she experienced a 'real' rape, as opposed to a 'simple' rape by an acquaintance or romantic partner, meant that she did not feel blamed, ashamed or stigmatised, either by family and friends or by the criminal justice system (United States Senate 1990, p. 35).

Ziegenmeyer's testimony not only drew attention to the compatibility of elements of feminist and criminal justice understandings of rape, but also to the limits of this combination of discourses. While she noted that her rape was unusual in being a 'real' or stranger rape, she omitted an even greater statistical anomaly in her experience. She was the white victim of an inter-racial rape committed by a black man. As numerous scholars have made clear, in the USA, stereotypes of 'real' rape are intimately connected to racialised notions of criminality (Davis 1983; Taslitz 1999). Susan Estrich (1987, p. 1) writes, for instance, that the first question she was asked by police was whether the man who raped her was a 'crow', slang for African-American. Further, in the late 1980s, the enduring power of what Angela Davis (1983) labels the 'myth of the black rapist' had been clearly demonstrated. As mentioned above, Estrich managed the Democratic candidate Michael Dukakis' campaign in the 1988 election. Dukakis was the favourite and frontrunner until a series of attack ads by the Republican candidate George H. W. Bush portrayed him as 'soft on crime'. The ads featured Willie Horton, an American offender released on temporary leave while Dukakis was Governor of Massachusetts. While on leave, Horton escaped and committed a series of crimes, the most significant of which was the rape of a white woman, before being recaptured. This election, only recently concluded at the time of Ziegenmeyer's public prominence is widely considered a foundational moment in the trans-Atlantic embrace of penal populism by parties across the political spectrum (Newburn and Jones 2005). It was also a symbol of the on-going relationship between fear of rape, support for 'tough on crime' politics, and racism in white America (Bumiller 2008).

The *Des Moines Register* series mentions the 1988 election at several points, but not Willie Horton. As with Ziegenmeyer's testimony, it largely omits race in its description of the sexual assault. The article's initial description of Bobby Lee Smith, the man who raped Ziegenmeyer, is of 'a man, probably in his late 20s, wearing a navy pinstriped suit', and notes that 'he smelled of alcohol' (Schorer 1990d, p. 1). Race is introduced on the following page, but only through the reported speech of Smith, who is portrayed as fixated on race: 'He talked about white people, and about how his father had been killed by a white man. He talked about how his sister had been raped by a white man. He talked about slavery and the things that white people did to black slaves'. Smith is described as asking Ziegenmeyer if she has ever had sex with a black man, and in a highly coded conversation, responds to Ziegenmeyer telling him she voted for Bush in the recent election by saying, 'It figures, because you're a white bitch' (Schorer 1990d, p. 6). Smith's defence is also based on race. His lawyer suggests that Ziegenmeyer may have misidentified him on this basis, pointing in his closing address to other well-known cases of wrongly-accused black men (Schorer 1990b). Race is only ever introduced in the series by men and is associated with attempts to deny or derail Ziegenmeyer's speech and its effects.

In contrast, Ziegenmeyer only ever discusses race to assert that the case, and rape generally, have 'nothing to do with race' (Ziegenmeyer, quoted in Schorer 1990b, p. 6; Ziegenmeyer 1992, pp. 73, 117). A similar perspective was adopted by Geneva Overholser in an editorial introduction that accompanied the first instalment of the *Register* series. She devotes most of the column to the importance of talking about rape and defending the 'straightforward' language used to describe it, before ending with 'one final point': 'One of the sad facts of this rape case is that the woman is white, the man black. This, unhappily, perpetuates a stereotype that is utterly contrary to fact'. The editorial concludes that while 'race was an issue in this particular crime, as some parts of the story show, there is no truth to the cruel stereotype' (Overholser 1990, p. 19). Given the framing of the series, Overholser's inference is that race was an 'issue' only because Smith made it so through his constant reference to it. Or, as Ziegenmeyer (1992, p. 117) says in her memoir: 'I'm not the one who brought race into this... He did'.

The reluctance to narrate race directly, or to accept it as a legitimate element of the narrative, can be read within a history of feminist tendencies to remove race from the history of rape and a history of the criminal justice system's attempts to portray itself as colour-blind (Bumiller 2008; Alexander 2010). Race, and racism, in both discourses become unnameable, because it undermines feminist attempts to assert that rape is a 'universal' experience for women and criminal justice attempts to portray itself as protecting all women equally (Richie 2012). Just like the distinction between real and simple rape, racial politics assist in the construction of divisions between 'legitimate' victims of rape as crime and victims who continue to be denied support and sympathy, a process I explore in more detail in the following section.

Despite the wishes of Ziegenmeyer and Overholser, race was not so easily rendered irrelevant. The *New York Times* reported that at least one newspaper had abandoned plans to reprint the series due to its racial politics (Margolick 1990). Several letters to the editor, published at the conclusion of the series, also addressed race. One complained that the paper 'too easily dismisses the under- and overtones of this black on white rape', noting that Georgia had executed 'more than 400' black men convicted of raping white women (but no white men convicted of raping black women) and that incarceration rates of black men in the USA came second only to those in South Africa, fuelled in part by 'the myth of black men as rapists'. The letter concluded with a reference to the recent election campaign: 'Given that politicians like George Bush can win office by making Willie Horton a household word, it looks like we've got a long road ahead of us…' (Brown et al. 1990). Ziegenmeyer's story is significant, but, as the letter writers quoted here insist, it is a story of race as well as gender. To deny that obscures the functioning of discourse that continues to limit and constrain social recognition of the realities of sexual violence. It also demonstrates the ways in which the discourses that are mobilised by survivors determine the political significance and meaning of their stories, both in progressive and conservative ways, a theme that is made even clearer in the case of Jill Saward.

Jill Saward's Conservative Anti-rape Discourse

Seven months after Nancy Ziegenmeyer's story was serialised in the *Des Moines Register*, parts of Jill Saward's autobiography were serialised in the *Daily Mail* as part of promotional efforts for the book. *Rape: My Story* revisited what was then the UK's most notorious rape trial, giving a name and identity to the woman who had until then been known only as the 'Ealing Vicarage Rape Victim'. The book detailed what it had been like for Saward to experience a violent sexual assault followed by invasive media coverage, which she described as a 'second violation', and a trial that dismissed her suffering (Saward 1991, p. 59). Saward's story received extensive media attention, including a BBC documentary which was later used in police and judicial training. She remained a public figure, and an advocate for victims' rights and criminal justice reform, until her death in 2017 (Veitch and Boydell 2017).

Like Ziegenmeyer, Saward's story was a product of social changes of the 1980s. Increasing public interest in rape saw a number of prominent trials in the UK, USA and elsewhere that received extensive and highly sensational media coverage (Benedict 1992; Cuklanz 1996; Lees 1997). As Helen Benedict (1992) has famously argued, the decade solidified media practices of dividing rape victims into a small number of innocent 'virgins' deserving of outrage and public sympathy, and a larger number of 'vamps' who were uniformly treated as untrustworthy and to blame for their own victimisation. Saward's case demonstrated that being a 'virgin' didn't necessarily equate to better or more respectful treatment by the press, even if it did make the overall tone of the coverage more sympathetic. Lisa Cuklanz (1996) proposes that prominent rape trials of this period are most effectively understood as 'symbolic trials' that provided a focus for widespread public debate about changing legal and social norms around sex and sexual violence. While much of the news reporting of these trials fit into the traditional patterns of victim-blaming identified by scholars such as Benedict, Cuklanz documents the ways that they also opened media space for feminist and progressive perspectives in opinion pieces, current affairs programming, longer features and other 'issue-oriented reporting'. These new voices helped in some instances to galvanise public support for reform and increase public awareness and sympathy towards the experiences of victims of rape. For instance, Saward's treatment in court and by the press had already resulted in legal reform by the time she published her book, and the spaces opened by media debates about her treatment enhanced her authority when she came to speak publicly.

Saward shared Ziegenmeyer's commitment to speaking out and her faith that it could simultaneously produce individual empowerment, benefits for other survivors and cultural change through dispelling myths and replacing them with experiential truths. She told the *Independent* newspaper that she had written the book so that 'other women will know that their feelings are not unique, and that they can also get through it. I also hope it conveys to the general public some idea of what happens to a woman who has been raped' (Wroe 1990, p. 16). At the conclusion to the book, she advised other victims to 'TALK, TALK, TALK', for their own benefit, and to improve public understanding and attitudes (Saward 1991, p. 150). Saward's experience of the cultural authority that some survivors may obtain from speaking out was more extensive and long-lasting than Ziegenmeyer's, but similarly constrained and curtailed. As a representative victim, and representative of other victims, she remained a prominent figure throughout her life. She was involved in and founded a number of organisations, she campaigned and lobbied politicians for legal reform, and she even ran, unsuccessfully, for parliament (Veitch and Boydell 2017). Despite this long career, she was simultaneously authorised and trapped by her identity as a rape victim, an issue I explore in more detail in the following chapter. She commented in an interview in 2006, 'I don't for ever want to be Jill Saward, the Ealing Vicarage Rape Victim. Something different would be nice. But it's not going to happen now' (Grice 2006). This comment would seem prescient and even more poignant when in 2017, the BBC (2017) among others reported her death with the headline, 'Ealing vicarage rape victim Jill Saward dies'.

Saward used the authority that was granted to her by this identity to assert some unconventional, or, more accurately, hyperconventional, positions in relation to rape. In other words, while her interpretations challenged feminist understandings, they drew on dominant and traditional modes of framing and speaking about rape. Her understanding of herself was, like Ziegenmeyer, primarily as a victim of violent crime, but without Ziegenmeyer's incorporation of feminism within her understandings. Through her activist career, Saward (2000, p. 26) increasingly positioned herself against those she described as 'hardline feminists', while she maintained a commitment to speaking out as a victim of violent sexual assault. Her embrace of the logic of criminal justice discourses in opposition to feminism was most explicit in her campaign in the latter half of the 1990s for rape law reform. Saward wanted to legislatively distinguish between 'rape' and a lesser charge of 'Forced Sexual Entry'. She explained her logic through examples such as this:

> Consider this scenario: a young woman dressed in a tiny and provocatively transparent dress, which would in a more restrained age have been worn as a slip, goes out to a nightclub. There she allows a young man whom she has never met before to kiss and caress her.

It would not be 'extraordinary if the man then made the perfectly logical conclusion' that the woman wanted to have sex with him. Further, 'if the man coerced the girl into having intercourse and was later accused of rape', it would not be 'reasonable' for him to be 'charged with exactly the same offence as a brutal sex offender' (Saward, in Cooper 1997, p. 2). Saward acknowledged that 'both sets of circumstances are traumatic for the victim' and 'usually accompanied by violence', but that regardless, they were most certainly 'not the same' (Saward and Atkins 1999). In drawing this distinction, she was, as date rape survivor Jemima Harrison argued (1997), insisting on the classic distinction between 'real' and 'simple' rape, and, indeed, insisting that 'simple' rape was not quite 'real'. Further, her emphasis on women's 'provocative behaviour' was highly reminiscent of classic victim-blaming, and, given her repeated use of statements such as 'happened to me', she was differentiating herself as an innocent and blameless victim of real rape from 'vamps' who were to blame for, or at least provoked, their own victimisation (Benedict 1992).

Saward began her campaign in a cultural context in which feminist attempts to expose and undermine the legal and social distinctions between 'real' and 'simple' rape were facing a backlash in both the USA and the UK (Sanday 1996; Lees 1997; Bevacqua 2000). What was relatively unique about Saward's intervention was that it undermined the general feminist presumption that enabling survivors to tell their stories would help to diminish the myths and distortions that construct date rape as either 'just sex' or something that women bring upon themselves (Gavey 2005). This is an extension of the tenets of speaking out that survivor speech not only empowers individual survivors but enables others to speak and undermines rape myths and victim-blaming in the wider community. For many feminist commentators, Saward's identity as a rape victim and her political perspective on date rape were essentially contradictory (Cooper 1997). This contradiction has been explained by some as the result of fear and denial (Harrison 1997) or as a product of trauma (J. Gilmore 2017). I argue, however, that to attribute Saward's position to trauma or some other kind of 'psychological' reading is to insist that she remain trapped in an imposed identity, that of a 'feminist rape victim'. Instead, I suggest that her positions are consistent within the discursive framework within which she understands her experience. Her campaign for legal reform shows that the presumed solidarity between survivors can only function if survivors see themselves as having an experience in common. And how survivors define that commonality or lack of commonality depends on what discourses they mobilise to make sense of their experience. Saward's framework saw victims of violent crime by strangers as in a separate category to women who are assaulted by actual or potential sexual or romantic partners, due to her mobilising conservative understandings of criminal justice and of gender and sexuality to make sense of her experience.

If feminist critics tended to label Saward's perspective as incoherent, she presented it as 'common sense' or non-ideological. This self-conception was most fully articulated in a lengthy column she wrote for the *Daily Mail* in 2000 where she announced her, ultimately temporary, retirement from campaigning against rape, following the refusal of the Blair Government to enact her reforms. In the piece, she described herself as 'one of the very few people involved in rape campaigning who isn't an extremist' (Saward 2000). Instead, she portrayed herself as a pragmatist confronting political correctness and engaging with the reality of social attitudes. Saward argued that juries would simply not convict men accused of date rape of the crime of 'rape' and that a lesser charge would therefore enable greater conviction rates. What remains unexpressed in this construction is the fact that, as indicated above, Saward herself did not see the two types of violence as equivalent. Her insistence on a distinction between 'real' and 'simple' rape was enabled by neoliberal framings of 'victims' and 'responsibility' and by heteronormative conceptions of gender and sexuality. These frameworks were obscured by her presentations of herself as simply speaking 'truth' based on her own experience of violence and her representative status as a survivor of rape.

This status enabled her to characterise the Blair Government's refusal to label acquaintance rape a 'lesser' crime as a betrayal of survivors generally: 'everything I – and the countless other women who have been raped – have been through has been in vain. No one will ever understand how that makes me feel' (Saward 2000, p. 26). She claimed that the Blair Government were 'too preoccupied backing vocal and trendy campaigns' like the repeal of Section 28, the notorious legislation introduced under the Conservative Thatcher government that prohibited the 'promotion' of homosexuality by local government authorities. She argued the Government should have been 'putting the safety of women above eye-catching, vote-winning campaigns that will make very little difference to the lives of ordinary people' (Saward 2000, p. 26). These statements begin to make clear how Saward's framing works to exclude others from the category of 'ordinary people' deserving of sympathy. LGBT communities are not ordinary people in Saward's understanding in the same way that victims of acquaintance rape were not 'really' victims of rape in the way that Saward was.

The discourses deployed by Saward are also made clear in the 'scenario' introduced above, in which a 'young woman' wearing a 'provocatively transparent dress', which 'in a more restrained age' would have been underwear, goes to a nightclub. Her description combines a socially conservative yearning for a more 'restrained' and even pre-feminist age, and a very contemporary form of neoliberalism, where a commitment to victims' rights sits alongside a political insistence that individuals take responsibility for managing their own risk. Her commitment to conventional discourses of safety, criminality and responsibility was made clear in her articulation of the kinds of situations that constitute 'real' rape and warrant a criminal justice response: 'a man who premeditatedly goes into woods or a country lane armed with a knife or other weapon and grabs at an indiscriminate victim who just happens to be walking past'; 'a man who breaks into his victim's home at random with the express purpose of committing rape'; 'a man who follows his victim along the street until they are in an isolated area and commits rape' (Saward and Atkins 1999). Each situation includes a deviant stranger who is 'premeditatedly' looking for a victim to rape. The victim 'just happens' to be walking in the wrong place or has the misfortune to have her home chosen 'at random'. She is 'innocent' of any risky behaviour or wrongdoing. Her precise reiteration implies that for Saward all elements must be present for this to be 'real' rape, as opposed to acquaintance rape, or 'forced sexual entry', which does not meet any of these criteria. The idea of a 'victims' rights' and 'rape survivor' advocate excluding women from the category of real victims might appear contradictory. However, as scholars of victims, crime and neoliberalism have shown, victims' rights discourses co-exist with broader discourses of risk-management and responsibility, so that individuals who fail to act on their own behalf to manage risk are not deserving of state protection, just as individuals who fail to look after their own health are not deserving of public healthcare (Garland 2001; Harvey 2005; Rentschler 2011). These undeserving victims are disavowed so as not to damage or sully the status of real victims. This neoliberal logic fits easily into older strategies of victim-blaming around rape and legitimises the notion of 'victim precipitation' and women's responsibility for managing risk (Mardorossian 2002; Stringer 2013). A victim who risks wearing revealing clothes or goes to a man's apartment for a late-night drink voids the right to state protection, and to public sympathy, by failing to take proper responsibility. As Saward put it, women who 'push it right to the extremes and kind of go and sell their wares on the street, invite people in, go all the way and then turn around and say no' were not her concern as an activist against violence. 'I don't feel I ought to be defending those people. I think they must be more responsible' (Hall 1997, p. 14).

In Saward's case, neoliberal logics of risk and responsibility are accompanied by a socially conservative version of Christianity. She told the *Independent* in 1990, for example, that her memoir was, among other things, a 'thank-you letter to God' (Wroe 1990, p. 16). In her campaign for the new legislation, this manifested in disapproval of promiscuity, and her belief that women who engage in sexual behaviour with a man provide implicit permission for men to engage in further sexual behaviour. 'Rape by someone you have kissed and got into bed with is not', she insisted, 'the same thing as being dragged into bushes and raped at knifepoint, or, as happened to me, by a violent intruder'. In these situations, the blame does not rest with the man but with the 'society our liberal predecessors created for us' where it is now 'the norm for a man to meet a skimpily-dressed girl in a nightclub, and end up in one of their homes indulging in heavy petting with a degree of nakedness. If the girl then says that is as far as she wants to go, but the man forces intercourse, he has committed rape' (Saward and Atkins 1999, p. 52). These examples presume a heteronormative dynamic where men have an automatic or unstoppable sex drive and women must act as sexual gatekeepers (Gavey 2005). It also uses a neoliberal logic to justify sexual moralism that refuses sympathy to promiscuous women.

For Saward, promiscuous sex, without the moral anchors of marriage, love and commitment, had created a realm of danger and radical indeterminacy. She told the *Daily Mirror* in 2002 that 'we have got to the stage where nobody knows the rules' of sex and romantic intimacy, and that therefore 'drastic' solutions were required (Sayid 2002, p. 6). Saward was not unrealistic enough to suggest a return to older forms of morality. Instead, she proposed that neoliberal logics might provide a solution. In addition to her legislative reforms, she had another suggestion to which she had 'given a lot of thought'. This was that 'condom companies should put a consent form with every condom' and this would 'need to be signed by both parties prior to sex'. The moral morass of a liberal society had created a situation in which women were able to accuse men of rape based on a misunderstanding, but also one in which there's 'too much scope for a man to say: "She came to my room and took her clothes off. I thought she meant Yes"' (Saward 2000, p. 26). The solution was to be found in aggressive criminal justice responses to 'real rape' and a contractual framework around casual sex to prevent 'simple rape' (Estrich 1987). Saward's decades-long commitment to improve 'appallingly ineffectual rape laws' combined Christian morality and neoliberal politics to assert an absolute distinction between legitimate victims of stranger rape and the irresponsible and morally compromised women who allow themselves to fall into the murky situations that lead to date rape (Saward 2000, p. 26). She claimed her authority to propose solutions on the basis of the political assumptions and promise of speaking out but framed this politics within and through profoundly anti-feminist discourses.

Success and Discursive Drift

It has been a long time since the world 'out there stopped laughing' at the political tenets of speaking out. Nancy Ziegenmeyer and Jill Saward show that by the late 1980s the idea that the experience of rape conferred a form of public authority had achieved widespread acceptance in the USA and the UK. Both were working-class women whose right to speak on rape generally was accepted in media forums and in political and legislative domains. Their authority as public survivors of rape challenged the cultural limitations placed on women's speech, and the historical refusal to deny, minimise or ignore the narratives of victims and survivors of rape. In that sense, their stories are victories for feminism as a form of discursive politics and as the producer and enabler of a genre of women's stories.

At the same time, their stories did not make use of feminist definitions or understandings of rape. Feminism was a minor presence in Nancy Ziegenmeyer's discursive framework, essentially a supporting discourse to her primary conception of herself as a victim of crime. For Ziegenmeyer, feminism enabled a criminal justice understanding of rape, exemplified in her support for the Violence Against Women Act, in which gender is a meaningful category to define victims and offenders, but race is only a distraction. This is a theme that will arise repeatedly in the following chapters, but the consequences are discussed in greatest detail in Chap. 6. In contrast to Ziegenmeyer, Jill Saward was openly hostile to feminism and refused feminist conceptions of sexual violence as a phenomenon of gendered power. This feminist understanding rejects criminal justice and social distinctions between 'real' and 'simple' rape, a distinction that Saward insisted upon, and which she campaigned to enact in criminal legislation. For Saward, this distinction was important and necessary, reflecting neoliberal conceptions of responsibility and risk and conservative discourses of gender and sexuality.

Survivor speech is not always or necessarily feminist and the public success of speaking out has not universally resulted in the promotion of feminist understandings of rape. Indeed, as the central tenets of speaking out have become more widely accepted, it has become increasingly divorced as a political project and practice from its feminist roots. Both Saward and Ziegenmeyer, for instance, frame their narratives within these discourses in ways that legitimate and centre the criminal justice system as the primary discursive and institutional site for understanding and responding to rape. I explore the paradoxical relationship of feminism and the criminal justice system in more detail in Chap. 4.

It is important to note that Ziegenmeyer and Saward were able to make use of criminal justice, neoliberal and Christian discourses because of their status as 'real' rape victims, legitimate victims of crime by violent criminals. As I discuss in more detail in the following chapter, those women who have traditionally had the most sympathetic treatment in the courts and by the media, white victims of 'real' rape by violent strangers, are also those who have achieved the greatest access to the cultural authority of speaking out. Survivors, in other words, who are able to access discourses other than feminism to validate their stories and legitimise their speaking authority, are more likely to be heard and granted the cultural authority to speak about their experiences of rape. The examples of Ziegenmeyer and Saward, alongside the other case studies in this book, show that the promise of speaking out has been fulfilled in partial and selective ways. Some women are able to achieve individual empowerment through public speech and their speech helps certain other women to speak about their experience, and this speech challenges select cultural myths and assumptions about rape.

Survivors narrate and interpret their experience using a wide range of discourses, including conservative frameworks. If, as feminists have argued, women's narratives of rape are inherently challenging to dominant social and legal orders, it is unsurprising that narratives which cleave to at least some dominant constructions and meanings of rape, particularly in relation to hegemonic ideas of criminality, are more likely to find an audience. The question is whether these narratives ultimately function to chip away at these dominant structures, paving the way for a wider variety of stories and tellers behind them, or if they work to reify the boundaries between tellable and untellable narratives. The following looks in more detail at the types of stories that have been enabled by the narrative politics of speaking out in order to consider these questions. Examining a collection of rape memoirs published in the 1990s and later, it asks what insights might be gained by conceptualising feminism as a genre that both enables women's stories and imposes boundaries around what kinds of stories count and are tellable within this genre.

3

'A New Literature of Rape': Storytelling, Genre and Subjectivity

In May 1999, Patricia Weaver Francisco (1999a) published 'Out of the Darkness', an article on *Salon.com*. Ostensibly a review of Jamie Kalven's (1999) memoir, *Working with Available Light: A Family's World After Violence*, the article provided a personal reflection on Francisco's discovery of Kalven and his book shortly after the publication of her own autobiography, *Telling: A Memoir of Rape and Recovery* (Francisco 1999c). Both were autobiographical responses to rape. Francisco's book describes her experience of being raped by a man who broke into her home while she was asleep in bed and the impact of the experience on her life. Kalven wrote about the rape of his wife by two strangers while she was out jogging and its effects on their family. In her review, Francisco describes attending the book launch and meeting Kalven again shortly afterwards at 'You Are Not Alone', a day of 'testimony and pride' held in Los Angeles to honour rape survivors. There, they also encountered Nancy Venables Raine (1998), author of *After Silence: Rape and My Journey Back*, and Charlotte Pierce-Baker (1998), author of *Surviving the Silence: Black Women's Stories of Rape*. Francisco (1999a) writes that they 'met one another like shipwrecked sailors staggering out of caves, squinting in the light of recognition'. They had each, she wrote, made 'the choice to treat the experience of rape as a literary subject… with the knowledge that such a thing had not been done before', and their coming together represented the 'flowering of a new literature on rape'. It was a literature she believes was sorely needed in a world 'simultaneously starving for the material and trying to ignore it' (Francisco 1999a).

This chapter is a critical elaboration of Francisco's claim about the flowering of a new literature on rape and its relationship to the political promise of speaking out: that narratives of experience can produce individual empowerment, collective liberation and social change. I argue that the genre of rape memoirs offers an insight into the type of stories and storytelling practices that are enabled by the politics of speaking out and reveals some of the tensions within that politics. Where the previous chapter explored the public position and reception of survivor narratives in terms of competing discourses, this chapter looks more closely at these texts as a genre of stories and asks about their political possibilities. Following Francisco's depiction of herself and her fellow authors as 'shipwrecked sailors' producing stories for a world that simultaneously desires and rejects these stories, I suggest that the politics produced by this new literature has a series of ambivalent and paradoxical effects, both for the survivors who tell their stories and in terms of its potential to enact social and cultural change.

One of the key contentions of this book is that the politics of 'speaking out' has produced a genre of experiential rape narratives. The existence of a genre encourages and enables stories, providing them with a cultural location that allows them to be heard and understood. It also connects individual acts of speech or writing to a collective practice of narrative in a way that can produce political effects. But, as Derrida (1992) makes clear in his discussion of genre, this positive and enabling function is accompanied by the production and enforcement of a set of rules, norms and constraints. In constructing a set of recognisable narrative features and practices that enable texts to be included within a genre, a set of boundaries and limits are also established. These define certain stories, by certain people, told in certain ways, as outside of that genre, and can reproduce the same racial and class boundaries that restrict survivor speech in other forums. Genre also shapes reader expectations in ways that not only disallow certain stories but mean that stories are only heard, read and understood through specific conventions, even where a survivor seeks to tell a different story or to tell their story in different ways. The multiple effects of genre construction are the focus of this chapter. In constructing a genre, feminists have simultaneously enabled the telling of stories and shaped the ways in which these stories are told, creating a set of generic expectations and rules recognised by both audiences and tellers. In this way, the telling of some stories precludes the possibility of telling others, and it is with this paradox that the chapter begins.

Genres also produce generic plots, forms and structures which influence how stories are told, shaped and understood. In the second and third sections, I explore in more detail the generic shaping and attribution of meaning to personal stories of sexual violence. I am interested in what these narratives, taken collectively, look like, and what kinds of understandings of sexual violence and of speaking out they produce. I argue that authors occupy a dual role within the genre. They are, at the same time, storytellers taking control of their narrative, and a character within it who is unable to prevent her victimisation. I consider each of these roles in turn, beginning with the story of the heroic speaker before complicating this with the narrative of the victimised woman trapped in the story. The chapter finishes with a consideration of the potential benefits of thinking of speaking out as a form of 'literature' in which a story is constructed and shaped by its author. This chapter suggests that thinking about speaking out through the lens of literary production and criticism can provide new critical insight into the tensions and paradoxes inherent in the political project of speaking out.

Constructing a Genre

My research locates the first published English-language rape memoir as Jennifer Barr's (1979) *Within a Dark Wood*, published in the UK. While this makes Francisco's claim that she and her fellow authors were writing literary accounts of rape in the 'knowledge that such a thing had not been done before' a slight exaggeration, it is nonetheless true that only about eight of these memoirs were published before the mid-1990s. From that point on, this 'new literature' has indeed flowered, with at least 40 published in the period from 1995 to today without considering the growth in recent years of self-published and 'print-on-demand' texts available solely as e-books or online. This 'flowering' occurred in the aftermath of the growing interest in rape and survivor narratives in the late 1980s and 1990s discussed in the previous chapter (Bevacqua 2000). The books also participate in a more general 'memoir boom', with a particular focus on stories of suffering and overcoming, that took place in the latter years of the 1990s (Rak 2013). Despite arguments that this boom ended in the 2000s, rape memoirs continue to be written and consumed, with at least 15 published in the five years from 2013 to 2017. While several insightful analyses exist of individual memoirs (e.g. Plummer 1995; Grewal 2016; Kilby 2018; Crawley and Simic 2018), there has not been any scholarly attempt to discuss them collectively or as a genre. This omission seems to arise in part from a general perception that there are only a 'few first-person accounts of sexual assault that have been published', in the words of Keith V. Bletzer and Mary Koss (2004, p. 121), and that these are a disparate collection of texts with few commonalities. This chapter challenges that perception.

This chapter uses my on-going mapping of this genre to explore the narrative structures and practices enabled and foreclosed by the politics of speaking out. I undertake a generic analysis that is heavily indebted to Derrida's (1992, pp. 224–225) account of the 'law of genre', mentioned above:

> As soon as the word "genre" is sounded, as soon as it is heard, as soon as one attempts to conceive it, a limit is drawn. And when a limit is established, norms and interdictions are not far behind: "Do," "Do not" says "genre," the word "genre," the figure, the voice, or the law of genre… Thus, as soon as genre announces itself, one must respect a norm, one must not cross a line of demarcation, one must not risk impurity, anomaly, or monstrosity.

I look for the outlines, limits and interdictions he describes through the commonalities and absences in this collection of texts. But I also look for what Derrida describes as the inevitable 'principle of contamination', 'law of impurity' and 'parasitical economy' that is the 'law of the law of genre' (p. 227). As he explains, 'participation' in a genre 'never amounts to belonging' because the 'trait of participation itself' requires that a text 'mark' itself generically, and this 're-mark' is, by definition, external to the genre (p. 230). Put another way, the attempt to construct a pure, clearly demarcated genre is bound to fail because it is impossible for any text to fully belong within a genre. But that does not nullify the effects of the limits and boundaries that are also an intrinsic part of genre. To give the kind of account I undertake means being attentive to both elements.

I define 'rape memoirs' as autobiographical accounts of the experience of rape and its aftermath as the defining event of the story, as opposed to autobiographical works that include discussion of rape as one element in a life narrative. I include collections of these stories such as Pierce-Baker's (1998) *Surviving the Silence*, where the author tells her own story alongside the stories of others. In categorising a text as 'about' rape I rely primarily on the title and its use of the word rape, as in Francisco's (1999c) *Telling: A Memoir of Rape and Recovery*, or a direct reference to it. For instance, the title of Kathy Dobie's (2003) *The Only Girl in the Car* refers to her experience of gang rape as a teenager by a group of boys in a parked car. Read collectively, there are clear generic features, similarities and absences. The majority (40) of the books are by American authors, but there are also texts written by survivors from Australia, the UK, Canada, South Africa, Pakistan, Iceland and Norway. Some tell stories of already notorious cases, such as Jill Saward's (1991) autobiography discussed in the previous chapter, or Trisha Meili's (2004) *I Am the Central Park Jogger* about the infamous 1989 rape case where Meili, known only as the 'Central Park Jogger', was found comatose after being violently physically and sexually assaulted. A few texts are by otherwise well-known authors such as Alice Sebold (1999) or Beverley Donofrio (2013). The majority, however, are texts by relatively unknown authors describing otherwise obscure or only locally known crimes.

This is overwhelmingly a collection of white, heterosexual, educated women telling stories of stranger rape, and, among the US memoirs particularly, a disproportionate number of inter-racial rapes committed by black men. Even where the narratives do not tell stories of assaults by complete strangers they are generally what might be described as 'near strangers', somebody that the author has only just met or a meeting in which the author is severely intoxicated. The only stories by women of colour are a memoir by Mukhtar Mai (2006), a Pakistani activist and survivor of a gang rape committed as a form of traditional village justice, Pierce-Baker's (1998) collection of black women's stories, stories in Mattilda Bernstein Sycamore's (2004) collection of writing by queer survivors, and Annie E. Clark and Andrea Pinto's (2016) anthology of activists involved in the American student survivor movement. The latter two are the only texts that include non-heterosexual narratives, and, alongside Kalven's (1999) book and a single memoir by a male survivor (Douglas 2016), the only texts to include stories not told by cis-gendered women. Most of the stories are told by people who are tertiary-educated, with a high proportion of people who write or speak professionally: writers, academics, journalists, counsellors and psychiatrists. As discussed in the previous chapter, and contrary to the hopes of feminists and the promises of speaking out, the genre appears to have primarily enabled the kind of storytelling that has historically been most able to be heard and recognised as 'real rape' and which is most assimilable to criminal justice and other normative discourses.

This underlines a core argument of the book: that even with the growing influence of speaking out, certain stories remain easier to tell than others. Those who have historically been rendered culturally 'unrapable', or whose narratives have been rewritten as romance, revenge or madness, continue to struggle to find a hearing. In Pierce-Baker's (1998) collection, contributors, identified by first names, discuss the relative lack of stories of rape by African-American women, and the reasons behind it. These speak to on-going social refusal to hear black women's stories. Jennifer (p. 199) writes that she was not believed by police who told her she seemed 'very calm', while Yvonne (p. 124) simply states that 'where I had lived… any time a black woman said she had been raped, she was never believed'. But they also speak to a sense that the genre of speaking out is primarily for and about white women. Jacqueline (p. 149) talks about the perception that 'when you compare a *sister* to a white woman, the sister is stronger'. For Adrienne (p. 161), 'white people feel that black women shouldn't be upset about rape', while several contributors express the belief that black communities see rape primarily as a 'white' issue. The most common reason given by survivors, however, almost all of whom were victims of intra-racial rape, for not speaking publicly was that they would not be able to control the meaning of their stories and they did not want to, in Pierce-Baker's (p. 64) words, 'confirm the white belief that all black men rape'.

As Danielle McGuire's (2010) study of African-American women's testimony about sexual violence reminds us, the feminist-enabled genre of speaking out is not the only genre of speech about rape. There are many memoirs, autobiographies and testimonials by women of colour that speak about rape within wider life stories and within testimonials about experiences of racism, colonialism or war (e.g. Holiday 2006; Hayslip 1989; Nannup et al. 1992; Angelou 1993). Women of colour and Third World women have also pioneered different forms of telling personal stories which reject the memoir or autobiography's presumption that a life story is best told through the linear narration of a singular subject (L. Gilmore 1994). For instance, Latin American women have developed practices of *testimonio*, stories of collective life experience best known to Western audiences through the story of Guatemalan woman Rigoberta Menchú (1984). These forms of narrative complicate what it means to tell an autobiographical story of rape and disrupt dominant 'trauma narrative' framings of rape as a singularly and incomparably traumatic event that dominates a life story (Gavey and Schmidt 2011; McKenzie-Mohr 2014). While critics have focused on the way that this narrative form limits the kinds of stories it is possible to tell, my research suggests that it also works to generically marginalise the stories of women for whom rape sits alongside other experiences of trauma and violence and reduces the possibility of telling or understanding rape as a causal factor in narratives that nonetheless remain irreducible to it. To enact a 'rape trauma' narrative on Roxane Gay's (2017) *Hunger*, for instance, is to make it only a story of the consequences of the sexual violence enacted on her body rather than, as the subtitle indicates, *A Memoir of (My) Body* in which rape plays a central role but is not and cannot be the beginning and the end of the story. As Gay and other authors make clear, in many women's life stories the harms of rape sit alongside and interact with structural harms such as racism and colonialism as well as interpersonal and familial histories and dynamics.

Processes of generic inclusion and exclusion in the politics of speaking out remain important even if they don't correspond absolutely to the presence and absence of stories. They can determine whose stories are heard, and whose are recognised as shaping cultural understandings of rape. As I argued in the previous chapter, feminism has had significant success in granting increased cultural authority to practices of speaking out, and stories that are clearly and unambiguously marked as stories of rape play a far greater role in the cultural process of deciding what rape is, how it is understood and what social responses it calls forth. It matters, therefore, that there is a dominant type of story told in these texts of 'real' or stranger rape. It should, perhaps, not be a surprise that stories that are easier to tell in other domains, such as the law, are also dominant within the genre of speaking out. These stories are still important to tell, but there are important questions that remain about the absences inherent in this genre. Thinking in terms of these absences can offer an entry point for understanding the processes of generic inclusion and exclusion. Read alongside the generic features discussed in the following sections, they also provide insight into the benefits and risks of speaking out, and what precisely it is that telling experiential narratives of rape is imagined to do.

The Heroine's Quest for Subjectivity

The question of genre and literature is not solely a question of what kinds of stories are told but how these narratives are shaped and the meanings that they make of the events and experiences that they recount. As Hayden White (1980, p. 24) argues, plots give stories momentum, provide a 'moral' and produce characters with designated roles. In this section, I explore how the texts in this genre give 'truth the shape of a story', to quote Francisco's (1999b) description of her project, and thereby construct themselves as characters in a narrative with an overall moral purpose or message. A sense of this purpose can be gained through a survey of the titles. While most include the word 'rape' or 'violence', these are more likely to appear in the subheading than the heading itself. More common as in the title are terms associated with speech and silence, such as *Telling, Surviving the Silence, Kill the Silence,* or *Words Can Describe* (e.g. Francisco 1999c; Smith 2001; Kørra 2015; Grant 2010). The books tell the story of speaking out as a political act of 'telling' in order to break, 'kill' or 'survive' silence. Many titles speak of this act as part of a 'journey' taken 'through sexual assault' (Phillips 1994) or 'beyond rape' (Joseph 1998), while others speak of a 'search' for 'truth' and 'justice' (Winslow 2016; Seccuro 2011). The final theme is that of 'coming out of the shadows' (McCreary 2004), 'remaking' a self' (Brison 2002) or 'the making of me' (Wagner 2007).

In many ways, to refer to these texts as 'rape memoirs' is a misnomer. Rather than books about rape and its effects, they are books about speaking out about rape, its necessity and its consequences. They are written to change social responses to rape through fighting the silence that surrounds and enables it, to help other survivors and to produce individual healing and empowerment. For instance, in her book about being raped while studying at a military academy, Lynn K. Hall (2017, p. 248) writes that 'by telling our stories we can end the shame put upon survivors' or, framed in the opposite way, Charlene Smith (2001, p. 190), author of *Proud of Me: Speaking Out About Sexual Violence and HIV*, claims that survivors must speak out because our 'silence cloaks the barbarity of the crime'. They are written so that other victims 'might find comfort from a sister victim' and so that 'future victims' will find their 'struggles... made easier by an aware and understanding society' (Barr 1979, p. 5). While the authors firmly believe in these collective benefits, what the books most clearly document, and provide evidence of through their existence, is an individual journey or act of reclamation. As Trisha Meili (2004, p. 3) asserts, her book 'is about reclaiming a life; *my* life' (emphasis in original). They recount a 'journey' or quest to remake a damaged self through the power of speech and speaking out. The rape, and the rapist, act as the narrative prompt which marks the beginning rather than the centre of the story. The actual story is, in the words of Trisha Meili (2004, p. 3), survivor of the 'Central Park Jogger' rape, 'about something I did, not what was done to me'. Or, as Alisa Kaplan, author of *Still Room for Hope: A Survivor's Story of Sexual Assault*, writes, as she came to tell her story publicly, she realised that 'the most interesting part about my own story – to me, anyway – was the story of my recovery' (2015, p. 197).

This story of recovery shares important characteristics across the genre, as has been recognised by some authors. In her philosophical memoir of rape, *Aftermath: Violence and the Remaking of a Self*, Susan Brison (2002) writes of her dissatisfaction with what she calls the 'standard narrative' present in most memoirs of rape. She describes it as a 'reverse conversion' narrative, where a 'perfectly good, intact, life was destroyed, then painstakingly pieced back together again' in a psychologised and individualist model of trauma and recovery (p. 110). Brison argues that these memoirs idealise a 'pre-rape past' and fail to acknowledge that 'life can be hard, in various ways, both before and after a rape' (p. 111). This echoes academic critiques of the dominant 'trauma narrative' surrounding rape experiences which acts as a constraining force on individual narratives (Gavey and Schmidt 2011). While I agree with Brison that there is a clear core or standard narrative in these texts, I don't agree that it is reducible to a 'reverse conversion' narrative, even if elements of this characterisation are true. In pointing to the conservative and conservatising elements of this structure, Brison misses the elements with more political and narrative possibility. In my reading, these texts do not tell a purely individual depoliticised story. Instead, there is a tension between individual empowerment and collective politics that is largely unacknowledged within the texts but reflects a wider tension in the politics of speaking out.

The books are less about 'piecing a life back together' in a straightforward recovery narrative than they are, to use Brison's own framing, about 'remaking' a self who is different to the self from before the rape. Kaplan, for instance, tells a story of becoming 'the person I was meant to be. Not the person I was meant to be before the rape – that girl is gone – but the woman who had survived it' (2015, p. 162). The story of becoming the 'woman who survived' can be understood as a feminine, or feminist, version of the archetypal 'hero's quest' narrative or classic 'stock plot' of Western culture. The most well-known summary of this plot comes from the literary scholar Joseph Campbell:

> A hero ventures forth from the world of common day into a region of supernatural wonder (*x*): fabulous forces are there encountered, and a decisive victory is won (*y*): the hero comes back from this mysterious adventure with the power to bestow boons on his fellow man (*z*). (2008, p. 23)

While dominant masculine versions of the hero's quest tend to emphasise force and physical skill, feminist literary critic Marilyn Jurich (1998) argues that there is an alternative tradition of feminine heroes, beginning with Scheherazade, narrator and protagonist of the *1001 Nights*, who make use of language and stories to win their victories: 'The story is more than entertainment, more than truth; it intervenes to prevent loss, destruction and violence at the same time it restores faith and transforms narrative' (pp. xiv–xv). The quest narrative of these books continues this tradition. Paraphrasing Campbell, the authors are violently pulled from the world of the 'common day' into a region of horror following their experience of sexual violence. They encounter the social forces of silencing and shame before achieving a decisive victory through speaking out. This victory is personal, as they construct a self who is a survivor, storyteller and hero from an experience of desubjectifying violence, and collective, as they 'bestow boons' on their fellow survivors and on women generally by disrupting the political and social power of rape. As Leigh Gilmore (1994, p. 25) writes in her study of women's self-representation, 'the autobiographical subject is produced not by experience but by autobiography' and this is particularly true when storytelling is designed to regain subjectivity after violence. Unlike the traditional hero's quest, these texts don't merely recount the heroine's journey. They enact and form part of it. In other words, the books produced are simultaneously a description of the quest, a product of its successful outcome, and a key part of the 'boon' that is provided to other women, and, especially, to other survivors in that they provide a resource for their own quest. As Charlotte Pierce-Baker states: 'I write for those women who never have their day in court... I write for the women who lie alone awake at night... I am a black woman wounded, and because I kept silent for so long, my voice is still emerging... I write now for those who must make the same journey' (1998, pp. 17–18).

The elements of this journey are worth elaborating in some detail as they help to explain the political and narrative logic of what it is that speaking out is believed to do. Brison is right that the world of the 'common day' is typically presented as a peaceful existence, a 'good intact life' that is disrupted by violence. This is the opening of her book, *Aftermath*:

> On July 4, 1990, at 10:30 in the morning, I went for a walk along a peaceful-looking country road... It was a gorgeous day... I sang to myself as I set out, stopping to pet a goat and pick a few wild strawberries along

the way. About an hour and a half later, I was lying face down in a muddy creek bed at the bottom of a dark ravine, struggling to stay alive. (Brison 2002, p. 2)

Charlene Smith's (2001) *Proud of Me*, begins with a similar juxtaposition: 'The day I was raped... began before dawn with my son and me warbling "Happy Birthday" down the phone... It ended with me – naked but for a thin gown... arguing with a doctor in a crowded emergency room' (p. 1). This construction is a precondition of the 'rape trauma' narrative that sees the world of the everyday as safe and secure rather than marked by violence, and it functions, as I note above, as a form of generic limit that privileges life stories in which rape occurs as an unprecedented act of violence with no biographical parallel. In these rape memoirs, rape disrupts a secure and peaceful existence rather than existing among and within other forms of structural violence.

Rape casts the victim into a new and foreign world, a 'region of supernatural wonder'. Tegan Wagner begins her book with the statement that this 'is the story of one night that changed my life forever' (2007, p. 4). Jana Leo writes that when an intruder entered her apartment, 'I realized that my everyday life was over. This was ... the last day of my present life' (2011, p. 3). The experience of rape marks a permanent shift from an old life to something else. In her attempt to make sense of this feeling, Patricia Weaver Francisco quotes the feminist author Susan Griffin's (1979) *Rape: The Power of Consciousness*:

> [O]ne of the untold burdens of the survivor of rape is what she has come to know. She has been left holding the truth.... For her the world has changed. And in this understanding she is isolated, because for us who have not been raped the world remains the same. We keep the fact of rape at the periphery of consciousness and do not let it bear on our vision. (Griffin, in Francisco 1999c, p. 52)

Brison also describes this 'unimaginably painful' existence where rape becomes central to one's consciousness. News stories, for instance, of gendered and sexual violence that 'friends found distressing in a less visceral way ... triggered debilitating flashbacks in me' (2002, p. 15).

In this new life, the survivor encounters the main enemy she must overcome in her quest, the force of silence and denial. Martha Ramsey writes that the 'greatest harm to me lay in the silence that hung in all these experiences, the silence fed by the inability of those around me to speak in any intimate way about rape' (1995, p. 109). Social denial and the pressure to be silent, Cathy Winkler writes, 'resulted in the same impact as the rape' (2002, p. 87). Silence prevents victims from constructing a new subjectivity, based as it is on a failure to confront the reality of their new existence. For Pierce-Baker, her silence grew into a 'secret' that gradually turned into a 'lie' (1998, p. 47). This lie is not only individual but social, as it operates to transform a social problem into one that is understood as only personal, as Karyn Freedman argues: 'Keeping our rape stories secret lowers the decibel level on the magnitude of the problem and perpetuates the idea that rape happens somewhere else, to someone else. It makes us complicit in the act of covering up the realities of sexual violence' (2014, p. 77).

As she finds her voice, the author shifts from being a victim of violence to a heroine who can achieve victories on her own behalf and on behalf of women generally. The story becomes focused on the political potential of narrative rather than the effects of rape. Liz Seccuro states: 'I found myself thinking less and less about the case and more about the fact that I should be proud to have opened my mouth and said something… I stood up for what was right. As the mother of a little girl, that was the best gift I could ever have given her' (2011, p. 208). This is a process, as I described above, of becoming somebody else, different, and even better. In response to concern from friends and family that she is not 'herself', Jennifer Barr writes in her diary, 'I don't want to be the "old Jennifer Barr"… I don't like her' (1979, p. 109). Similarly, Charlene Smith writes: 'In the beginning I thought the rapist had taken the Charlene I loved the most with him; in part he did, but I really like the person she is now' (2001, p. xiv). The boon that is gained from speaking out is posited as personal and political. For the individual it is about recognising that life can be better if not the same: 'Not "better" in the sense of having a life that's more coherent, in control, predictable. But "better" in the sense that comes from acknowledging that life is a story in the telling, in the retelling, and that one can have some control over *that*' (Brison 2002,

p. 115, emphasis in original). The transformation into a heroine, however, comes not only from reclaiming control over the telling and retelling of one's life, but in being able to use that telling for others. As Laura Gray-Rosendale writes of her first experience of speaking out in a public meeting about being raped by a stranger during her years at college: 'What my mouth's been saying... was never just about me. It's about us. Us, who have survived sexual violence, told it's better to keep quiet, just move on, not make a fuss. Us, who love them, know what they've been through, that their voices must be heard' (2013, p. 122). The hope, ultimately, is that of collective change arising from storytelling: 'I kept writing because I want rape to be unacceptable, not in polite conversation but in our lives' (Francisco 1999c, p. 3).

The vision of speaking out as seamlessly and simultaneously producing individual empowerment, collective liberation and transformative social change obscures the tension that I mentioned above between these elements. This tension manifests most clearly in the characterisation of the heroic speaking survivor as both representative in her experience of gendered harm, and exceptional in her heroic response to it. For instance, Abi Grant writes that her 'story's not exceptional, it's ordinary, which is the point – it could happen to anybody' (2010, p. 233). But, if it were purely ordinary it would not be worth reading about, which is also the point of an individually heroic narrative. These texts are not collective stories of suffering and liberation. They are 'representative' stories of individual suffering combined with inspirational stories of 'exceptional' overcoming through the heroic act of speaking out. This logic can be seen in the South African journalist Charlene Smith's claim that she 'wanted my story to be the story of every raped woman speaking out. By speaking about me, I would hopefully speak for many' (2001, p. 26). The heroic position of 'speaking for' is, as Gayatri Spivak (1988) has pointed out, worlds away from speaking with or to. To want one's own story to be the story of every woman is not the same as moving towards a world where every woman can speak. It is to maintain a position where those who speak embody an exceptionally heroic subjectivity. Jessica Stern, an academic who writes about her experience of childhood rape, makes an ironic observation on the temptation of this position. Thinking about why she is writing a book about such a traumatic experience, a 'grandiose thought comes to me: 'This is why I have to write this book, to speak out for those who cannot speak'. She immediately moves to 'push the thought away', acknowledging that it is an act of self-aggrandisement even if it is also motivated from the desire for political change (Stern 2010, p. 173).

Charlene Smith's determination to speak for many echoes and reproduces the power differentials that can exist between feminist experts and survivors discussed in Chap. 7, particularly where these relationships operate across other vectors of power, such as race. Writing as a white woman in South Africa, the women Smith calls 'my survivors' and imagines herself speaking for are predominantly black and brown (Smith 2001, pp. 124–158). As Kiran Grewal (2016) has argued, there is a racial politics that underlies which women are able to occupy the paradoxical position of being both representative victim and heroic survivor. Women of colour are far more likely to be understood simply as representative victims with the position of heroic survivor reserved for white women. These perceptions reinforce, and are reinforced by, the racial absences and limits of this genre of stories, and the tendency to narrate them only in terms of shared gender identity and not in terms of racial difference, a point discussed in the previous chapter and extended in the two following chapters. However, even those women who are able to access the position of heroic speaker still find themselves in a position of vulnerability as they tell stories of themselves as victims of male violence. It is to the paradox of the victim at the centre of the heroic narrative that I turn in the following section.

Narrative Vulnerability and the Storyteller's Dilemma

The transformation of a story of rape into a heroic narrative of speaking out, described in the previous section, has clear benefits. It replaces a story in which women are victims, passive objects acted on by men, and rewrites them as agentic and even heroic subjects, making the men, and their violence, largely irrelevant to the story in the process. This core narrative recounts a promise or a commitment that in telling one's story, rape survivors participate in a heroic narrative in which they rebuild a life shattered by violence and partake in a form of activism that has collective political benefits. In short, the promise is that a heroic subject can be built through telling a story of victimisation. Such an endeavour is inherently paradoxical, placing an experience of victimisation and violation at the centre of an attempt to construct a heroic subjectivity.

Storytellers in this genre are expected to occupy multiple, and paradoxical, subject positions. The difficulties of this are outlined by Martha Ramsey in her book about her experience of being raped by a stranger when she was a teenager:

> One day I'm the hero, girl martyred but still able to respond to rape with an imaginative power of her own. The next day I'm the victim, the girl sentenced to a stunted, damaged life. I know I need something more down to earth. I am myself, not these images. I am not a character in a book. (Ramsey 1995, pp. 202–203)

To tell the story of herself as a hero she must tell the story of herself as a victim, and as Ramsey explains, writing oneself as a victimised hero or heroic victim while still retaining a sense of a self who is more than a character in a book can feel like an impossible task. This is what I label the 'storyteller's dilemma', articulated by Dorothy Allison as the struggle to speak of her history of sexual abuse and its effects on her life without being subsumed by that story: 'But where am I in the stories I tell? Not the storyteller but the woman in the story, the woman who believes in story. What is the truth about her?' (1996, p. 201). As Allison implies, to tell autobiographical stories of sexual violence is, inevitably, to produce oneself as a character in a book even as one is also a storyteller. This is true of both the 'victim' and the 'hero' position.

As Lacy Johnson (2014) points out in her memoir, *The Other Side*, which tells of her experience of being abducted and raped by her ex-boyfriend, survivors do not have exclusive ownership over the single story of rape:

> There's the story I have, and the story he has, and there is a story the police have in Evidence. There's the story the journalist wrote for the paper. There's the story The Female Officer filed in her report; her story is not my

story. There's the story he must have told his mother when he called her on the phone; there's the story she must have told herself. There's the story you'll have after you put down this book. It's an endless network of stories. (p. 177)

This is the other side of the 'web of stories' that Walter Benjamin (2002) describes. While he sees it as an enabling force, a web is also a trap, and it can feel that way for survivors trying to tell their stories. Although the survivor is not uniquely in control of her story, she is uniquely dependent upon it, and, therefore, uniquely vulnerable to it: 'This story tells me who I am. It gives me meaning. And I want to mean something so badly' (Johnson 2014, p. 177).

Control is also limited by the 'community of listeners' or readers that storytellers require for their narratives (Benjamin 2002). As Smith and Watson write, readers have strong 'expectations about what stories derived from direct, personal knowledge should assert' and this may be even more true for stories of rape (2010, p. 36). Raymond Douglas, raped as an 18-year-old by his local priest, explains that 'expectations have always been high for rape victims, much more so than for those who have attacked them' (p. 41). 'The requirements', he writes, 'for the male victim are no less stringent' (p. 61). To receive a sympathetic hearing, the male victim must tell a story of violent resistance to the assault and narrate a violent and stoic response in the aftermath. He:

> must personally assume responsibility for visiting an equivalent level of non-sexual violence upon his attackers, without notifying the authorities... This accomplished, he must quickly return to a state of full physical, psychological, and psychosexual functioning. Lastly, he must never afterward speak of his victimization to anyone. (2016, p. 62)

As Douglas goes on to note, these expectations, in which rape becomes a narrative of revenge with no articulated cause, are impossible to fulfil, and so work to silence male survivors, a fact seen in the very small number of personal narratives available.

For women, these expectations can also produce silence but, perhaps, even more fundamentally, they assert, as Susan Brison describes, 'pre-existing meanings that situate the raped woman as either martyred hero or, more often as damaged victim':

> Using the word "rape" would have conventionalised what happened to me, denying the particularity of what I had experienced and invoking in others whatever rape scenario they had already constructed… People would think they knew what had happened if they labelled the assault that way. (2002, pp. 90–91)

While all narratives require a stock of conventionalised meanings to be tellable, there is a sense in these texts that the meanings associated with rape narratives are especially strong and the experience of having them imposed on one's story is particularly damaging for survivors who are attempting to construct a new subjectivity through their stories. The cultural narratives that surround rape make the storyteller a character in a story that her listeners already know, or believe they do. Alice Sebold, raped while walking home to her dormitory at an American university, writes: 'Magically I became story, not person, and story implies a kind of ownership by the storyteller' (1999, p. 97). She explains her struggle against this process, a struggle that was necessary even if it seemed impossible to succeed: 'I was trying to prove to them and to myself that I was still who I had always been. I was beautiful, if fat. I was smart, if loud. I was good, if ruined' (p. 29).

Sebold's sense that the identity of a rape victim can prohibit or disallow any other identity recurs throughout the genre, as does the fear that speaking out might reify this identity even as it offers the possibility for overcoming it. The dilemma is signalled in several titles in the genre, such as Laura Gray-Rosendale's (2013) memoir, *College Girl*, which references her sense that, once her story became known, others saw her only as 'the girl' from the story. This sense is even stronger in Samantha Geimer's (2013) autobiography, *The Girl: A Life Lived in the Shadow of Roman Polanski*. Geimer, writing decades after Roman Polanski raped her at the age of 13, testifies to the fact that moving states and constructing an entirely new existence has not been sufficient to displace this teenage experience from the centre of how she is defined and understood. These titles speak to the way survivors struggle to define the limits of the story of rape in relation to their lives and identity. To be a 'martyred hero', 'damaged victim' or 'the girl' may be to find oneself reduced to this character, with it defining all other areas of life. Speaking out cannot change or disrupt the rape scene, and it may not be equipped to stop that scene from becoming the defining moment of the survivor's life. The feminist philosopher Adriana Cavarero (2000) argues that all attempts to narrate a life story have a tendency to replace the diverse conglomeration of moments and events that constitute a life with a singular and linear narrative that is unable to capture the complexity of our stories or identities. For Cavarero (2000, p. 44), the 'hero's story' is the most extreme example of this. The hero's whole narrative is crystallised around a single event or act of heroism and her subjectivity is bound irrevocably to that event. The same thing happens to victims of rape through dominant cultural narratives that position rape as an irreparable and singular trauma that reduces a complex subjectivity to the experience of victimhood. Rather than contesting that reduction, speaking out may merely reverse the value. Even when survivors such as Shari Davies, whose memoir tells the story of how her experience of a near fatal sexual assault inspired her to become a victim's rights advocate in Queensland, Australia, insist that the book 'isn't my life story' but a 'story about one event and the implications of that event' (1998, p. xv), the implications of that event risk being read as determining the meaning of the life story in its entirety.

There is also a concern that the attempt to assert control through telling one's story of rape might contaminate and disallow one's authority to tell other stories. The crime novelist Emily Winslow writes in her autobiographical account of rape that 'I worry, though, that people will read my novels differently now and, when coming across any sexual or violent scene, look for me there, look for the rape seeping in' (2016, p. 67). Telling the story of rape is seen as potentially depriving her of the authority to tell stories that are not about rape or not derived from her own experience of victimhood. The figure of the 'raped woman' is a strong archetype. The Canadian author Jane Doe has maintained her anonymity in part to avoid being trapped in this identity, because she knows that raped women 'cannot display their rage or joy or sexuality. They cannot be glamorous or successful or funny. They certainly cannot be agents of social and political change' (2003, p. 118). However, as Dorothy Allison concludes, paradoxically, the solution might be to continue to speak and to tell stories:

> I tell my stories louder all the time: mean and ugly stories; funny, almost bitter stories: passionate, desperate stories – all of them have to be told in order not to tell the one the world wants, the story of us broken, the story of us never laughing out loud, never learning to enjoy sex, never being able to love or trust love again, the story in which all that survives is the flesh. That is not my story. I tell all the others so as not to have to tell that one. (1996, pp. 71–72)

Even with the risks and vulnerability of speaking out, the promise outlined in the previous section remains a potent one, as Samantha Geimer indicates in her explanation of why she chose to write her book. She wanted, she says, to 'take back ownership of my own story from those who've commented on it, without rebuke, for so long. Because my story is not just pure awfulness. It's crazy and sad, but yes, sometimes funny, too. It may have been messy at times, but it's my mess and I'm taking it back' (2013, p. 9).

The relationship of these storytelling-survivors to their narratives is complicated. For Lacy Johnson, her story is 'a trap, a puzzle, a paradox' which offers the hope of defining the meaning of one's own story alongside the risk of being reduced to a character in a story told by others (2014, p. 186). It is, as Dorothy Allison suggests, 'a tool that changes every time it is used and sometimes becomes something other than we intended' (1996, p. 3). This tool can, at times, threaten the subjectivity it was meant to enable, but it remains a powerful tool for exerting control over the story of one's life and rebuilding a self. It is for this reason, perhaps, that the process of authorship can leave one like Francisco's 'shipwrecked sailors' desperate for contact with others who might assist in developing the political potential of this paradoxical tool. It is to the question of the relationship between survivor literature and feminist politics that I turn in the final section.

'Not the Only Truth': Feminism and the Politics of Survivor Literature

In this final section, I turn to the relationship of this new literature of rape to feminist politics, from the perspective of the authors in this genre. Following my discussion in the previous chapter of the late 1980s and early 1990s as a 'turning point' in the politics of speaking out, there is a clear distinction between descriptions of feminism in this genre before and after that point. The earliest text in the collection, Jennifer Barr's (1979) *Within a Dark Wood*, describes feminism as a revelatory force that enabled her to understand her experience through a new knowledge about gender relations more broadly. This is a classic tale of 'coming to consciousness':

> I see women so differently, I understand their role much better. I understand why women have been expected to be submissive and passive, why they "agreed" to it, how it is perpetuated, what its effects are, and what the obstacles and disadvantages are now in trying to overcome these bonds. I really was not aware of how male dominated our thoughts, and even language, are. (p. 186)

Writing 20 years later, Patricia Weaver Francisco finds these same feminist insights inadequate and unsatisfying. When she turned to Susan Brownmiller's *Against Our Will* after being raped, 'it was not what I needed. I was looking for someone to name what had happened to me. Without this naming, I remained alone with a terrible knowledge' (Francisco 1999c, p. 207). Shortly after she was raped she went through what she describes as a 'radical feminist period' during which she viewed 'the world through the narrow lens of rage' (p. 115). Everything she understood in this period was true, she writes, but it was not the only truth, and, again, it was not what she needed: 'Powerful, unmediated truths are like straight gin; they can kill you, kill the "you" in you' (pp. 115–116).

The distance that Francisco feels from feminism is replicated and reproduced in many other texts in the genre. This gap reflects the historical and discursive shifts that I traced in the previous chapter, raising the question of how these shifts should be understood. Most feminist analyses have tended to focus on survivor narratives themselves, arguing that they have become 'depoliticised' and 'individual' rather than expressions of collective politics (Armstrong 1994), that their transgressive potential has been increasingly recuperated (Alcoff and Gray 1993), or that they are increasingly told through and with 'neoliberal life narratives' which reject discussions of systemic harm in favour of stories of individual resilience and overcoming (L. Gilmore 2017). As I suggested in relation to Brison's criticism of these narratives above, and as Francisco has suggested in relation to the discursive framing offered by feminism, while elements of this critique might be true, it is not the only truth, and it may not be the truth we need.

I argue, drawing on Bakhtin (1981), that these changes also have to do with changes in the cultural and political status of feminism. When Jennifer Barr (1979) wrote about feminism it was, using Bakhtin's formulation, a purely 'internally persuasive' discourse, denied and refused authority in the wider world. As Joan W. Scott writes, second-wave feminists contested this refusal of authority, asserting the authority of feminist knowledge and truth in order to change the 'way stories would be told' (2004, p. 10). One part of the success of that project is that both survivors and their feminist advocates are granted significant authority in cultural understandings of rape. But this has also resulted in feminism and feminists increasingly occupying positions of institutional authority so that when survivors interact with feminism it is not as a purely internally persuasive discourse but one with significant authority in determining how their experiences are understood and how they should make sense of them, whether this be in terms of the dominant 'trauma narrative' or, as Francisco describes, through a lens of rage. But feminism still seeks to position itself as telling and speaking for the experiential or 'internally persuasive' truths of survivors. Bakhtin cautions, however, that 'the authority of discourse and its internal persuasiveness may be united in a single word … despite the profound differences between these two categories of alien discourse. Such unity is rarely a given – it happens more frequently that an individual's becoming, an ideological process, is characterized precisely by a sharp gap between these two categories' (1981,

p. 342). Where survivors encounter feminism not as a way of articulating previously inexpressible truths, but as part of the forces which impose external meanings and definitions on their story, they are likely to experience a 'gap' between feminism's authorised truths and their own internal experience. It may be a sign of political and cultural becoming, for feminism, and for survivor politics, to attempt to incorporate feminist insights within life stories rather than allowing them to 'kill the you in you'.

Rape narratives are written in a 'heteroglossic' context in which multiple discursive frameworks are available to them and multiple meanings of their experience are possible. This was far truer for authors writing in the late 1990s and beyond than it was for Jennifer Barr writing at the end of the 1970s. While rape has always been surrounded by competing discourses, the majority of these historically have, as feminists have shown, denied or delegitimated women's experiences, labelling them liars or insane. In recent decades this has changed, as Susan Brison indicates: 'At different times and for different purposes, I have identified myself as a crime (attempted murder) victim, a rape survivor, a hate crime survivor, a person with a disability (PTSD and some other, stress-triggered neurological malfunctions), among other categories' (2002, p. 94). Each of these identities is tied to different socially significant discourses: criminal justice, feminism, human rights and medical, respectively. She continues, 'for me to remember – and to narrate – my assault, it has to be remembered under *some* description or other, and not under all possible ones at once'. Or, as Bakhtin (1981, p. 295) would say, to make meaning from experience, consciousness must 'actively orient itself amidst heteroglossia, it must move in and occupy a position for itself within it, it chooses, in other words, a "language"', although this choice is not necessarily fixed or permanent.

For Bakhtin, modern literature is characterised by the ability to incorporate a 'diversity of social speech types' drawn from the complex and internally stratified discursive environment of modern societies:

> Concrete socio-ideological language consciousness, as it becomes creative – that is, as it becomes active as literature – discovers itself already surrounded by heteroglossia and not at all a single, unitary language, inviolable and indisputable. The actively literary linguistic consciousness at all times and

everywhere (that is, in all epochs of literature historically available us) comes upon "languages," and not language. (1981, p. 295)

Literature, at its best, allows language to become 'fully human', depriving it of sacrosanct truth status and revealing its underlying forms and limitations. Seen in this way, the narrative and political potential of a new literature of rape is precisely in its ability to navigate different discourses and enable those who make use of it to produce 'fully human' subjectivities that incorporate the experience of rape without being defined by it or being restricted to a single discursive framing of themselves or their experience.

This sense of political possibility in the artistry of literature resonates throughout the genre, and is clearly expressed in Toni McNaron and Yarrow Morgan's classic collection of writing by survivors of child sexual abuse, *Voices in the Night*:

> To tell orally is the first step… To write these same stories as narrative is a second and huge step because we put form around what has seemed so chaotic, we make public to strangers the most intimate truths about ourselves… When we write a poem or letter or story about the impact or centre of that narrative, we take a third leaping step – we dare to make art out of our female experience – to fly in the face of all expectations for what is acceptable in such forms. (1982, p. 19)

As Francisco argues, there is a possibility of transformation of 'alchemy' in 'all tales that are relished by the teller' (1999c, p. 3). She provides an example of this alchemy and of its potential to change the meaning of the story when she writes of her decision to engage the man who raped her in conversation that it is her 'most deeply held belief … that, by talking, I saved my life' (p. 17). She is aware of the possibility of other narrative interpretations: 'The conversation that I believed saved my life may also have given him confidence. He'd sized me up, too, found me desperate to live, willing to bargain' (p. 28). But it is the interpretation or the truth she needs, and, more than that, it is the truth she wants: 'I like this part of the story. In fact, I have become committed to it. In this part, I look cagey and victorious and well worth saving' (pp. 17–18). To see oneself as shaping a story out of a violent experience like rape raises new possibilities of agency, and even desire. It allows authors, as Martha Ramsey (1995, p. 202) puts it, to ask, 'In my story, what did I want to say the rape had really meant?'

The promise of creative authorship is not unlimited. It does not erase or preclude the 'law of genre', the generic demands of audiences, or the vulnerability of the teller. To be read and understood, one must choose from available discursive frameworks and meaning. As Kalven writes of his own narrative dilemmas, the truth must be shaped 'through the conventions by which we recognise and understand stories' (1999, p. 291). While these conventions may allow for different readings of core moments, he says they 'are poorly adapted to the task of rendering that which is strenuously ongoing', like the process of rebuilding subjectivity after rape: 'I'm aware of a tension between fidelity to our experience and the temptations of plot, aware of a danger that I will falsify our experience by overplotting it' (pp. 291–292). Not all experiences are equally amenable to literary alchemy, but, even for Kalven, the possibility remains that narrative can offer a way through these dangers if the author is cognisant of them and able to navigate them creatively. Success, however, is not guaranteed.

Ability and comfort in engaging creatively with language are not evenly distributed, but rather are often a product of education, cultural capital and a subject position that enables facility with a variety of dominant and oppositional discourses, as well as language and the processes of writing. Brison's ability to make use of multiple discourses is connected to her status as an academic philosopher. An anecdote told by another survivor and professional philosopher reinforces this point. Like Brison, Karyn Freedman's experience of rape has led to a scholarly interest in feminist philosophy and understandings of trauma. In her memoir, *One Night in Paris*, she describes attending a survivor group where she was the only one to have the 'valuable' 'dual point of view' of an academic knowledge of trauma theory as well as the insight of lived experience (Freedman 2014, p. 130). She became a resource for the other women in the group, but she was unable to share the ability to navigate various discourses that enabled her to write her book. If literature can provide a 'fully human' accounting of rape with unique political possibilities, it can only be within a cognisance of the structural barriers that restrict access to these possibilities.

Questioning and contesting these barriers, politically and creatively, must be part of a literary politics. In the following chapter, I examine the existence of similar processes of contestation and their limitations in relation to women's speech about rape in the context of criminal justice institutions. The characteristics of successful legal speech, and successful witnesses, are similar in many ways, I argue, to the structural and generic boundaries that shape the political possibilities of the new literature of rape.

4

Speaking Truth to Law's Power: Legal Judgements and the 'Powerful Letter' of Emily Doe

In March 2016, Stanford student Brock Turner was convicted of the January 2015 sexual assault of an unconscious 21-year-old woman who would come to be known publicly as Emily Doe. On June 2, he was sentenced to six months in jail, three years of probation, permanent registration as a sex offender and compulsory participation in a sex offender rehabilitation programme. The judge was reported as stating that he 'feared a longer sentence would have a "severe impact"' on Turner. The following day, Doe released her Victim Impact Statement, which she had read aloud during the sentencing hearing to *Buzzfeed* news. The statement begins with a direct and confrontational address to Turner: 'You don't know me, but you've been inside me, and that's why we're here today'. It then recounts Doe's experience of the night she was raped, the aftermath of her assault and the trauma she experienced in the court. By the end of the statement, however, she is no longer addressing Turner or the court, but 'girls everywhere', to whom she says, 'on nights when you feel alone' or when 'people doubt or dismiss you', 'I am with you'. And, she says, 'I believe you'.

In this chapter, I use Emily Doe's statement to explore the complex relationship of public speech around rape to women's speech in the courtroom and the trial process. Doe's statement was originally written for, and read within, the trial, but found its greatest influence once it became an 'extra-legal' document. Both legal and public speech, I argue, are political in that both aim at producing real effects in the world. The concluding section of Doe's statement, where she speaks to other young women within and beyond an address to the court, shows that survivors may aim to speak to and within the law at the same time as speaking out publicly. It also demonstrates the way that legal speech can enact the quest narrative introduced in the previous chapter where a victim transforms herself into a hero through her speech. Quoting the author Anne Lamott, Doe writes, 'Lighthouses don't go running all over an island looking for boats to save; they just stand there shining'. She continues:

> Although I can't save every boat, I hope that by speaking today, you absorbed a small amount of light, a small knowing that you can't be silenced, a small satisfaction that justice was served, a small assurance that we are getting somewhere, and a big, big knowing that you are important, unquestionably, you are untouchable, you are beautiful, you are to be valued, respected, undeniably, every minute of every day, you are powerful and nobody can take that away from you. (Doe 2016)

Doe's heroism lies in her determination to speak truth to legal power, and her commitment to act as a 'lighthouse', signalling hope and a way forward to other women and survivors. Speaking through and to the law can, at times, seem not only compatible with but simply another avenue for speaking out.

She told *Buzzfeed* her releasing the statement publicly was a protest against the 'gentle' sentence and Turner's refusal to admit his guilt: 'I want the judge to know that he ignited a tiny fire. If anything, this is a reason for all of us to speak even louder' (Baker 2016a). The 'fire' was far from 'tiny'. Doe's statement was viewed over eight million times in the 24 hours after it was posted. It was read aloud in the US Congress and on CNN by anchor Ashleigh Banfield (Pallotta 2016). A week after posting the statement, Doe received an open letter from the then vice president, Joe Biden, in which he told her that she had 'shaken untold thousands out of the torpor and indifference towards sexual violence that allows this problem to continue' and 'helped to change the world for the better' (cited in Namako 2016). The furore led to the introduction of 'mandatory minimum sentences' for sexual assault cases in California and a successful campaign to recall Aaron Persky, the trial judge, the first judicial recall in California in 80 years (Astor 2018).

As I noted in the previous chapter, speaking out narratives are generally less about the experience of rape itself than they are about the aftermath. The experience of seeking justice and redress through the law has been a major part of this experience and of the tradition of speaking out. It is the law that has historically established the 'truth' of rape that second-wave feminists and survivors have contested. Feminists exposed these legal 'truths' as stereotypes and myths which deny the reality of women's experiences and refuse women the status of truth-tellers. Instead of validating women's stories, the law has rewritten their testimony through stock plots of romance, revenge, misunderstanding and hysteria, recasting survivors as fictional archetypes such as the 'Scorned Woman' or the 'Woman who liked it that way' (Grix 1999, pp. 89–90). Even where the law considers rape to be 'real', women's experiences are rewritten as myths of virginal white women who are ravished by brutish or bestial 'sex fiends' (Estrich 1987; Philadelphoff-Puren 2005). Feminist and survivor speech has, on the one hand, exposed these legal fictions and disputed the law's authority to judge the truth of rape. At the same time, the institutional and discursive positioning of rape as a 'crime' remains a dominant influence on the development of survivor speech, feminist politics and the practice of speaking out. Speaking out, like much feminist politics around rape, thus has an ambivalent relationship to law. It can simultaneously dispute the authority of law to determine the truth of rape and seek to reform the law so that it will make more just use of its authority when it comes to rape (Heath and Naffine 1994; Corrigan 2013). Even damning feminist critiques of the law frequently accept that a reformed criminal justice system and rewritten criminal justice discourse is the most appropriate site for stories of rape to heard, evaluated and responded to (Serisier 2005).

Doe's statement thus sits firmly within the history and legacy of the narrative politics explored in this book. Like Nancy Ziegenmeyer, discussed in Chap. 2, the story that Doe tells is aimed primarily at the law and its treatment of women who are victims of rape. She speaks truth to law, exposing it as a site that produces unjust harms rather than just truths. This is the focus of the first section of the chapter. However, she also uses the law as a platform to speak and she states, as quoted above, that Turner's conviction demonstrates that 'justice was served' and that 'we are getting somewhere' (Doe 2016). The second section of the chapter analyses the attractions and promise of the law as an institutional and generic location for some women's narratives. I discuss the ways in which other women are precluded from speaking in the legal domain, and the ways in which this domain shapes and constrains women's speech, even when they are considered 'good witnesses'. I argue in the final section that these attractions and promises, even though they remain illusory for most victims and survivors of rape, keep the law central to the politics of speaking out. The criminal justice system and its framework remains largely presumed and unquestioned within narratives of speaking out even as they speak to the harms and inadequacies of the law as venue for women's speech about rape. Responses to rape that do not involve the institutions, perspectives and assumptions of the criminal law remain largely unthought and unspoken within this politics, even as there remain large numbers of women who are unable to find recognition of redress through legal institutions and processes.

Speaking Truth to Law

Emily Doe's Victim Impact Statement is a classic speaking out text, which replicates the core narrative described in the previous chapter. Doe (2016) begins by recounting the 'quiet Saturday night' she was having and her decision to accompany her sister to a 'dumb party ten minutes from my house' before the idyllic world of the 'common day' was permanently disrupted. 'The next thing I remember I was in a gurney in a hallway'. Going to the bathroom Doe went to remove her underwear and felt 'nothing. The thin piece of fabric, the only thing between my vagina and anything else, was missing and everything inside me was silenced. I still don't have words for that feeling'. It was only then that Doe, who had been unconscious when Turner raped her, began to realise what had happened. She was thrown into a new nightmarish existence where she must overcome forces that seek to silence her and deny her story and her subjectivity. Her fight against these forces culminates in the statement eventually released to *Buzzfeed* and her reclamation of a heroic subjectivity.

While Doe's statement speaks to more general experiences of trauma resulting from the attack, the nightmare world that she describes is primarily the criminal trial in which she is a witness. The forces that seek to delegitimise her story and undermine her attempts to rebuild her subjectivity are the questions of defence lawyers and the pronouncements of the judge and other court officials. Her account testifies eloquently to the mechanisms by which she and her story are denied and devalued:

> I was pummeled with narrowed, pointed questions that dissected my personal life, love life, past life, family life, inane questions, accumulating trivial details to try and find an excuse for this guy who had me half naked before even bothering to ask for my name. After a physical assault, I was assaulted with questions designed to attack me, to say see, her facts don't line up, she's out of her mind, she's practically an alcoholic, she probably wanted to hook up, he's like an athlete right, they were both drunk, whatever, the hospital stuff she remembers is after the fact, why take it into account. (Doe, in Baker 2016a)

In her descriptions of the cross-examination, Doe evokes long-standing feminist and survivor critiques of the trial as a second violation. She must combat attempts to render her mad, drunk or a sexual aggressor, and her testimony unreliable and irrelevant. The trial is a forum in which she is attacked for daring to question male sexual prerogatives, and the means of doing so is to undermine and rewrite her narrative as a deliberate lie or hysterical fantasy (Young 1998; Grix 1999; Russell 2016).

The archetypal example of the legal system's construction of women who testify to rape is the seventeenth century jurist, Matthew Hale's caution that rape, although 'a most detestable crime', is 'an accusation easily to be made and hard to be proved, and harder to be defended by the party accused, tho never so innocent' (Ferguson 1987, p. 89). Variants of the caution remained in use across many common law jurisdictions until the feminist-inspired legal reforms of the 1980s (Larcombe 2002a). A particularly illuminating articulation of the law's suspicion of women's testimony is found in the following ruling by the Chief Justice of the South Australian Supreme Court:

> The danger of fabrication in sexual cases is greater than in other cases precisely because the allegations are sexual in character. Sex is prone to excite the imagination and the emotions, thereby creating a danger of false accusation resulting from hysterical or vindictive motives. Thus, the "good fame" or "evil fame" of the woman bringing charges, the promptness of her complaint or her concealment of her "injury for any considerable time after she had opportunity to complain," and her outcry or her silence become the central elements for scrutiny. (*R v Sherrin (No 2)* [1979] 21 SASR 250)

In essence, this logic means that in a rape trial it is the complainant rather than the alleged perpetrator who is on trial (Matoesian 1993; Taslitz 1999; Schulhofer 1998). Despite significant feminist-inspired legal reforms in the 1980s and 1990s, women like Doe continue to report that their reputation and behaviour before and after the assault continue to be subject to legal scrutiny and distrust (Philadelphoff-Puren 1997; Russell 2016).

Doe was constantly told that she was a 'best case scenario': 'I had forensic evidence, sober un-biased witnesses, a slurred voice mail, police at the scene. I had everything'. Even though she had substantial supporting evidence she was warned to be 'prepared in case we didn't win' (Doe 2016). And she still had to face the attempts of defence lawyers to turn her from a woman of 'good fame' into one of 'evil fame':

> What were you wearing? Why were you going to this party? What'd you do when you got there? Are you sure you did that? But what time did you do that? ... Did you drink in college? You said you were a party animal? How many times did you black out? Did you party at frats? Are you serious with your boyfriend? Are you sexually active with him? When did you start dating? Would you ever cheat? Do you have a history of cheating? What do you mean when you said you wanted to reward him? (Doe, in Baker 2016a)

The reality of her experience of trial, combined with the police and prosecution's refrain that she was 'lucky', was like, she says, 'being checked into a hotel room for a year with stained sheets, rancid water, and a bucket with an attendant saying, *No this is great! Most rooms don't even have a bucket*' (Doe 2016).

Rape trials, as feminist critics have shown, are less an adjudication of evidence than legal judgements of the credibility of competing narratives (Ehrlich 2001; Matoesian 2001). In most rape trials, including this one, it is not the 'facts' that are in dispute, but the 'narrative glue' that combines factual elements into a story of either 'rape' or 'consensual sex' (Brooks 2008, p. 417). The strategy of the defence is to rewrite the story told by the complainant into a different genre with different characters. To turn a crime story into a romance or, as in this case, a story of young 'party animals' drinking too much and partying too hard and having regrettable but consensual sex. As Alison Young (1998) has shown, the goal of the kinds of defence questions faced by Doe is to rewrite her testimony as a different story that belongs in a different genre. In Doe's case, the defence took advantage of her lack of memory to attempt to insert Turner's story into and over hers: 'Do you remember any more from that night? No? Okay, well, we'll let Brock fill it in' (Doe, in Baker 2016a). Because Turner knew she had no memory of the assault he was able to 'write the script'. 'I had no voice, I was defenceless… His attorney constantly reminded the jury, the only one we can believe is Brock, because she doesn't remember' (Doe, in Baker 2016a).

Within these constraints of memory, the court was called upon to judge the relative credibility of the narratives produced by Turner and Doe. Turner's narrative was, writes Doe, a 'strange' story which 'sounded like a poorly written young adult novel with kissing and dancing and hand holding and lovingly tumbling onto the ground', and 'most importantly', there was 'suddenly consent' (Doe, in Baker 2016a). It is a common practice for defence narratives to be modelled on normative popular culture narratives of 'romance'. A 'poorly written young adult novel' fulfils conservative ideas about normal and therefore 'credible' romantic heterosexual behaviour (Taslitz 1999). As Doe points out, the narrative offered by Turner was, in fact, highly implausible: 'Even in his story, I only said a total of three words, yes yes yes, before he had me half naked on the ground' (Doe, in Baker 2016a). The narratives of romance and sex that populate literature and popular culture are full of stock female characters who only ever say 'yes', or if they say 'no' don't mean it, and this is where the law looks for its understanding of narrative plausibility (Larcombe 2005; Philadelphoff-Puren 2005). It is in part for this reason that Nicola Gavey (2005) describes these ubiquitous popular culture plots as the 'cultural scaffolding' of rape. Julia Grix (1999, p. 90) has described her own experience of cross-examination and the stock figures that the defence constructed from her testimony: 'The scorned Woman. The Woman who wanted attention. The Woman who changed her mind afterwards. The Woman who imagined the whole thing. The Woman who deserved it. The Woman who liked it that way'. As she writes, even as they are clearly caricatures and stereotypes, these figures 'had currency. I had heard of such women. I had read about them. I had seen them in movies'. But, as she says, 'I had never met one of them'. The fact that, as Doe points out, these women 'never really existed' does not erase their very real presence and effects within the trial.

The construction of men in rape trials is similarly one-dimensional. Since the rapist of the public imagination is a 'hyperviolent hypersexual' stranger, any evidence that a man is not a stereotypical predator is taken as 'proof' that he is not a rapist (Taslitz 1999, p. 8). Doe (in Baker 2016a) wrote of a news article about the assault, which 'listed his swimming times' at the bottom. Her comment that 'the end is where you list your extracurriculars to cancel out all the sickening things that've happened' echoes Deb Waterhouse-Watson's (2013) analysis of the 'narrative immunity' to accusations of rape that is granted to football players in the Australian press and legal systems. Doe's comments highlight the absurdity of this process, but they also demonstrate the opposite functioning of the legal narratives in relation to victims and offenders. While victims are continually and constantly reduced to stock characters, the law accepts any evidence of 'extracurriculars' to insist that the defendant cannot be reduced to the identity of a rapist or assailant. Doe (in Baker 2016a) describes her 'disbelief, consumed by anger which eventually quieted down to profound sadness' as she witnessed this process occur in the report of the Probation Officer. The report discussed in detail Turner's youth, bright future and previously clean record, while her statements were 'slimmed down to distortion and taken out of context'. The entire trial, she writes, was premised around how much Turner had 'at stake' and the 'really hard time' he was having. One of the main functions of her statement was to reverse, contest and refuse the narrative reality constructed in the court: 'I am not just a drunk victim at a frat party found behind a dumpster, while you are the All American swimmer at a top university, innocent until proven guilty, with so much at stake' (Doe, in Baker 2016a).

As she later told *Glamour* magazine, her most demoralising moment came after she had read out her statement. Victim Impact Statements are a direct response to the concerns of victims' rights movements and to associated critiques from feminists and others of the treatment of victims in court. The Impact Statement is the law's attempt to institutionalise the rights of victims to speak and be heard about the impacts of their experience (McCarthy 1994). The response to her statement only confirmed to Doe that she did not fully exist as a speaking subject within the trial: 'I yelled half of my statement. So when it was quickly announced that he'd be receiving six months, I was struck silent. Immediately I felt embarrassed for trying, for being led to believe I had any influence' (Doe 2016). Without referencing her statement, the judge reiterated his sympathy for Turner, explaining that a harsher sentence would 'have a severe impact' on his future. It is at this moment, more than any other in the trial, that Doe's account evokes the feeling of the *differend*, the term Lyotard uses to describe the harm that occurs when a plaintiff is deprived on their ability to attest to the harm that has been done to them, and their speech is deprived on any authority:

> [T]he "perfect crime" does not consist in killing the victim or the witnesses (that adds new crimes to the first one and aggravates the difficulty of effacing everything), but rather in obtaining the silence of the witnesses, the deafness of the judges, and the inconsistency (insanity) of the testimony. You neutralise the addressor, the addressee, and the sense of the testimony; then everything is as if there were no referent (no damages). (Lyotard 1988, p. 8)

In this way, he says a 'plaintiff', someone who is wronged but has a means of redress, is transformed into a victim, someone whose harm is compounded by their inability to achieve any recognition. The force of the *differend* renders Doe effectively mute even before she is 'struck silent' by the realisation that yelling her experience of harm has only resulted in the 'deafness' of the court, neutralising her testimony as if there were no 'referent' for her speech. This is compounded by the fact that the only damages that appear to register are the harm of the sentence on Turner, as though he were the plaintiff rather than the one responsible for the harm.

The contrast of the impact of Doe's statement outside the courtroom dramatically highlights the failure of women's speech to register in the domain of law despite over three decades of legal reform (Russell 2016). Beyond the context of the trial, the same words became a 'powerful letter' when released in the genre of public rather than legal speech (Baker 2016a). As Francesca Polletta (2006) argues, stories are differently intelligible, useful and authoritative depending not only on who tells them, but for what purpose and in what setting. A document designed to speak within the institutional and discursive framework of the legal system became, when recontextualised, an indictment of that system and its imposition of a *differend* upon survivors, even in the context of a 'best case scenario' and a successful prosecution. It transformed Doe from 'just a drunk victim at a frat party' into the 'lighthouse' of her letter, signified, among other ways, in her being named one of *Glamour* magazine's 'Women of the Year' for 2016. In her acceptance of the award, Doe stated: 'The world should know every survivor has a story. Every story is our power. Together, we are louder than any system or person who threatens to silence us. Together we are countless and unstoppable. Now, we are indignantly rising' (Mallon 2016). The recall of the trial judge 18 months later seems to demonstrate Doe's point.

Even as it enacts a compelling indictment of the law's capacity to deliver justice for survivors of sexual violence, Doe's statement does not represent a turning away from the law. Rather, the evidence offered by Doe that 'we are getting somewhere' is that 'justice was served' in a common and automatic equation of justice with criminal convictions. Campaigns in response to the statement focused on increasing the punitive capacity of the law, through removing judicial discretion to grant low sentences in sexual assault cases and recalling Judge Aaron Persky. According to the campaign website for Persky's recall, 'we need judges who understand sexual assault and violence against women and take it seriously', because our 'legal system must protect every woman from violence' (Committee to Recall Judge Persky 2016). For many survivors, and those who wish to support them, the criminal justice system remains the primary forum for officially validating women's narratives through prosecution and conviction and for taking them seriously through punishment and criminal sanctions. Even as survivors testify to the *différend* they experience, some are able to navigate and manipulate the narrative structures that work, in general, to deprive women's speech of authority. These less explored aspects of the relationship between speaking out and the law are considered in the following section.

Good Witnesses and Legal Speech

I argue above that Emily Doe's statement sits within a feminist tradition of speaking out against the law's treatment of rape survivors and the law's capacity to justly and appropriately determine the truth of rape. This critical tradition exists alongside an equally strong tendency to see reporting to, and engaging with, the legal system as a crucial part of speaking out and the primary domain within which women's speech may have a concrete effect. Reporting and testifying are, of course, forms of narrative, and for many survivors of rape, testifying in court is their main opportunity to be heard in relation to the harms of sexual violence and to have their narratives responded to and acted upon. The criminal justice system offers the chance of official validation, social condemnation of the harm suffered by survivors and accountability or at least punishment for the perpetrator of that harm, even if that offer is largely illusory. An ability to make use of criminal justice tropes gives some women constrained but recognisable agency within the criminal trial. In this section, I draw on Doe's story of the law, alongside other narratives, to explore what it is that the law offers some survivors and under what conditions.

Trials offer the same promise of individual empowerment and catharsis as speaking out publicly, although as the case of Emily Doe shows, the risks of this speech are extremely high. Charlotte Pierce-Baker, raped by two men who broke into her house, found the experience of testifying in court incredibly difficult. As a black woman, she felt conflicted about her role in helping to obtain the conviction and imprisonment of two black men. Nonetheless, she concludes that 'finding answers' and resolution in the legal domain was an essential element to her recovery (Pierce-Baker 1998, p. 78). The promise of catharsis offered by legal testimony is also discussed by Patricia Weaver Francisco. Although the man who raped Francisco after breaking into her apartment was never caught, she participated in a witness support programme that allowed her to obtain a vicarious experience of testifying. The trial, she argued, performed 'the function of theatre', and the 'structured telling' of stories in the trial enabled 'an imaginative transaction' that was 'deeply emotional and personal', and unavailable in any other forum (Francisco 1999c, p. 173). Although some scholarship exists on the rape trial as theatre, it tends to assume along with much other feminist literature that the theatre of the trial is only and necessarily experienced as a 'burden' (Rayburn 2006). While this is undoubtedly the experience of the majority of women, it is not, as the examples discussed here demonstrate, universal, and there exists a record of testimony attesting to more positive or successful experiences with legal speech.

Doe's statement is interesting because of its multiple addresses and registers. Even when spoken within the courtroom it is simultaneously addressing the judge, Turner, Doe's family and friends, those who helped her, and 'girls everywhere'. This multiplicity is a potential function of any open trial but is particularly characteristic of public or symbolic trials that attract media interest. As Lisa Cuklanz (1996) notes, public trials have been one of the major forums through which survivor voices have been provided with a public platform. Thus, testimony or statements within court can be simultaneously aimed at a wider audience. The journalist Charlene Smith, for instance, became in 1999 the first rape victim in South Africa to choose to testify in an open court so that her speech would be heard and disseminated publicly. She writes in her memoir that a week before the trial a woman from South Africa's Department of Justice called her and said, 'Charlene, you are in court for every woman, they will be watching to see how you cope' (Smith 2001, p. 167). In a newspaper article describing her decision, she wrote that the 'more eloquently we describe that suffering, the more deliberately we use it as a sword in the courts or in public places, the more certainly we will vanquish the oppressor' (p. 185). For Smith, the court is simply another venue within which to tell her story and destroy the 'silence that allows society to victimise survivors of violent crime – and surrender power to criminals' (p. 183). She even goes so far as to argue that criminal law is a better and more democratic forum for speaking about and determining the truth of rape than 'decades-old imported feminist rhetoric' and practices, as it offers the chance of a clear condemnation of sexual violence and the punishment of perpetrators in the case of a conviction (p. 190).

Legal convictions can authorise survivor speech, enhancing its legitimacy and giving it a wider public platform. Even as Doe's statement testified to the law's failings, her story would not have had the chance of being so universally shared and acclaimed without her participation in the legal process and without Turner's conviction. Nancy Ziegenmeyer and Jill Saward, discussed in Chap. 2, stepped forward publicly only after the convictions of the men who raped them. If they had not had this legal confirmation of their stories, it is highly unlikely that they would have spoken publicly, been given a platform or found an audience. This was also the case for Tegan Wagner, one of the victims in a series of racially charged gang rape trials in Sydney, Australia. Following the conviction of the four Pakistani-Australian brothers who had raped her and three other young women, Wagner spoke publicly about her experience (Grewal 2016). Again, it is unlikely that she would have done so without the validation of a conviction. As she writes in her memoir, the conviction transformed her sense of herself: 'They'd made me feel powerless, but now I had power and used it to bring full weight law down on their heads' (Wagner 2007, p. 169).

Wagner's story of her experience in court reflects Doe's ambivalence. She has called in interviews for reforms to end 'victim-blaming' in court, describing her experience of cross-examination as 'three days of hell' and 'like being raped again' (*Sixty Minutes* 2017). While she sought to assert her identity as a survivor testifying to the harm committed against her, she described in a television interview the ways defence barristers consistently and repeatedly attempted to label her a 'slut' and a 'liar' (*Sixty Minutes* 2017). Echoing the criticisms made in the previous section, she has written that when 'you're a victim in a rape trial, what you're experiencing is an argument about what kind of person you are'. This experience is traumatic and 'the argument is hard to win' (Wagner 2007, p. 241).

Even while Wagner is adamant that survivors should not be placed in the position of having to defend their identities in court, her experience shows that it is possible to win, and this legal validation enabled her to counter the victim-blaming she experienced from friends and family. For Wagner, the experience of 'winning' the argument about who she was in court meant that she won the argument generally, and that she 'couldn't be called a liar anymore' by anyone (p. 229). As Wagner's experience highlights, legal attempts to 'taint' a survivor and her testimony are not always successful. They do not, in the words of Leigh Gilmore (2017), always 'stick'. When they don't, the experience of legal testimony may enable other acts of speech and further political interventions, including attempting to reform the conditions under which women give testimony.

Wagner's assessment of the trial as an argument about 'who' she was and her criticisms of 'victim-blaming' and 'slut-shaming' highlight another important element of the relationship between survivor speech, feminism and the law. Decades of feminist critique of the functioning of rape trials, many of which have, to varying degrees, been incorporated into popular culture and mainstream public debates about persistently low reporting and conviction rates, function as a resource for at least some survivors during their trials. Survivors such as Emily Doe and Tegan Wagner may be shocked and traumatised by their experience, but they are not completely unprepared for it or without any tools to combat the narrative tactics arrayed against them. Indeed, prosecutors and feminist organisations train survivors, helping them to construct narratives that will 'work' in legal settings (Trinch 2003). In analysing the methods that the law uses to silence women's testimony, feminists have provided women with discursive tools to combat that silencing, making it more possible for them to 'win' the argument about who they are in court and compel belief in their story within this setting.

An example of successful manipulation of legal tropes and stock plots is provided by the American author Alice Sebold in her memoir, *Lucky*. She writes that she was determined, in her performance as a witness, to become the worst 'nightmare' of the man who raped her one night as she was walking home to her college dormitory (Sebold 1999, p. 172). For Sebold, the trial helped to restore her sense of agency by allowing her to become an 'opponent' in a strategic battle (p. 160); a plaintiff rather than a victim, in the language of Lyotard. To win the battle, she mobilised her understanding of the narratives and semiotics that the court would use to define her character, and through that, the outcome of the trial. On the day of her testimony she prepared and dressed for her performance as 'an eighteen-year-old virgin coed … dressed in red, white and blue' (p. 172). Describing her interaction with the defendant she told the court, 'he was very interested in the fact that I was a virgin. He kept asking me about it', thus providing the prosecutor with an opportunity to repeat and emphasise the fact of her virginity (p. 174). Following her testimony, the bailiff told her, 'I've been in this business for thirty years… You are the best rape witness I've ever seen on the stand' (p. 198). In the book, Sebold writes that she 'would hold on to that moment for years'. Her successful performance at the trial represents a significant turning point in the narrative. The following chapter in the memoir begins: 'That summer I began my makeover' as the trial enables her to begin to move forward from her experience of rape (p. 202).

Sebold's performance is clearly enabled through an awareness of feminist critiques of the narrative strategies that the law uses to 'taint' women's testimony. Rather than adopting or asserting these critiques, Sebold uses them as a tactical resource. In a system where women continue to be defined as 'virgins' or 'vamps', Sebold makes it impossible for the court to define her as anything other than a virgin. Her successful performance relies on regressive discourses of gender that are not available to most women, and, as I discuss in more detail below, racialised semiotics of 'All-American' identity that implicitly highlight her whiteness and the blackness of the man who raped her. Even though I argue that Sebold's ability to successfully manipulate legal tropes implicitly relies on feminist critiques, in the memoir, 'feminism' embodied in Tricia, a representative from the local rape crisis centre, fails to offer Sebold any of the benefits that she obtains from her participation in the criminal justice system. Tricia defines her story through 'generalities' and statistics, insisting, in terms of the analysis used in the previous chapter, that Sebold's story is simply 'one of a group' of victims of rape, collectively understood and defined. This representation 'blindsided my sense that I was going to survive'. While the trial gives Sebold the opportunity to do battle, 'Tricia prepared me for failure by saying that it would be okay if I failed' (Sebold 1999, p. 133). Feminism, in the figure of Tricia, forecloses narrative possibilities that Sebold is able to open through her manipulation of the narrative expectations of the trial.

In the courtroom, Sebold is able to reject the 'stock characters' that defence lawyers attempt to impose on women by turning herself into a different character, that of the 'good witness', a survivor who is able to make use of legal discourses and the conflict of narratives within the courtroom to achieve her goals and win her case. The 'good witness' is not co-terminous with the ideal victim, as Wendy Larcombe makes clear in her study of successful rape complainants. Rather than being dependent on criteria such as virginity and sobriety, which are used to categorise women as 'virgins' rather than 'vamps', Larcombe (2002b, p. 144) argues that the key to success for rape complainants is the ability to contest the narrative constructions made by the defence:

> She has a strong sense of herself and takes overt offence at (rather than being taken by surprise or accepting as all too familiar) alternative and derogatory constructions of her character and credibility. She will need to be reasonably familiar with and experienced in managing power-loaded situations so that she can be polite but not compliant, co-operative but not submissive. She is not prone to exaggeration or embellishment but seems to talk straight. She answers questions quickly and precisely and speaks fairly frankly and without shame about sexual acts and activities.

As Larcombe makes clear, 'success' in the legal forum is determined by being a strategic opponent. The ability to access this position is, as Sebold's case shows, reliant on class and racial identities, but also on facility with narrative and the ability and determination to manipulate it, in a similar manner to that discussed in the previous chapter. This is made clear in Sebold's memory when her best friend, Lila, is raped. Whereas Sebold has struggled to be a 'good witness', Lila is unwilling or unable to adopt a similar performance. She does not pursue a conviction or speak out publicly or privately about her experience. The contrast between their responses ultimately makes their friendship untenable, illuminating the pressures placed on survivors and the relentless processes of legal and social judgement (Sebold 1999; Kilby 2018).

Consequently, as mentioned above, one can prepare for trial by building these skills. Migael Scherer (1992), like Sebold, writes in her memoir of the way in which she was complimented for her trial performance, and described by police as 'one of the best witnesses we've got' (p. 25) and 'sent to us from heaven' (p. 156). Scherer saw herself 'as part of a team' engaged in a narrative contest with the defence (p. 142). In this team, she was directly confronting the man who assaulted her with 'words as my only weapon' (p. 146). Her role was to tell her story under direct examination as 'naturally' and spontaneously as possible, so she undertook only minimal rehearsal and preparation (p. 136). Under cross-examination, she directed her answers to the jury rather than the defence barrister, making them as simple and straightforward as possible in her effort to convince them that 'not only that I was certain but that I could be trusted to tell the truth' (p. 160). The trial of the man who raped Scherer occurred before the widespread adoption of Victim Impact Statements, but Scherer wrote her own letter to the judge detailing the impact of the rape upon her. She later learnt that the judge exceeded the prosecutor's sentence recommendation for the first time ever 'due to her letter' (p. 185).

I would suggest that Scherer's letter was able to influence the sentence in her case in a way that Doe's statement was not because of their differential access to the position of the 'good witness', not because Scherer's letter was necessarily 'better' than Doe's eloquent statement. Scherer, like Sebold, was able to leverage a relative rather than an absolute social position. The man who assaulted Scherer was white, but he was poor and had a previous criminal record. He was not given the 'narrative immunity' granted to Turner on the basis of his bright future and talent. For this reason, Scherer did not face the same barriers as Doe to having her narrative heard successfully and being able to tell a story that was accepted by the court. To be a 'good witness' relies on telling a story that the court finds credible, and this depends not only on the identity that the survivor can project of herself but also on her ability to position the defendant as a 'rapist' within her narrative. The importance of this relational positioning is described by Abi Grant, a British survivor, in her memoir. Grant had to testify twice about the sexual assault she experienced, and in the first testimony it became clear that even though she had fought and struggled during the rape, the defence was trying to introduce a narrative framing of consensual sex. Like Sebold, Grant prepared carefully the second time to refute that characterisation. She organised her outfit weeks in advance, deploying semiotic symbols of the British class hierarchy, 'to say, one cashmere jumper and discreet gold earring at a time, that not only wouldn't I fuck Strachan, I wouldn't even mix socially with him' (Grant 2010, p. 193).

Grant (2010, p. 193) understandably declared that she didn't care if she was perceived as a 'snob' if it led to the conviction of the man who assaulted her. Other survivors, however, may make use of these tools reluctantly simply because they are the most effective, and maybe even the only, weapons in their narrative arsenal. Sebold, for instance, described her discomfort during cross-examination when the defence lawyer attempted to infer that the white All-American co-ed character that Sebold had created for herself would live in a mainly white world and so may have misidentified his client. Sebold was forced to calculate and report the number of young black men she interacted with on a regular basis to counter his implication. This, she said, 'wouldn't be the first time, or the last, that I wished my rapist had been white' (Sebold 1999, p. 198). Similarly, Jana Leo (2011, p. 95), a white architecture student who was raped by an unemployed black man who broke into her New York apartment, writes in her memoir that 'I hoped that detective work would lead to his arrest, and I was happy and relieved when I learned he was in prison, but I was angry that he fit so neatly into these stereotypes'. As I have argued, as uncomfortable as it may be, these stereotypes enable or increase the likelihood that the man who raped her went to prison. One of the most effective ways to avoid being trapped in a sexist characterisation as a 'vamp' or a 'victim', or having one's testimony denied and rendered meaningless through a *differend*, is to successfully mobilise a different stock plot, and the majority of these rely on class and racial difference. While Sebold writes that she wished the man who assaulted her was white, her performance was highly racialised and made more effective by racial difference. The myth of the vulnerable white virgin in the USA is, as Angela Davis (1983) argues, simultaneously the 'myth of the black rapist'. The two characters rely on each other for their meaning and power, as the novelist Emily Winslow (2016, p. 13), a white woman who was also raped by a black stranger while in college, acknowledges: 'I know that my experience after rape is what it is in part because of biases that reward my race and class and religion'. As she states, 'I was the perfect victim, not in the sense of attracting harm, but in the sense of the world being indignant on my behalf'.

My analysis is not about condemning the women who make use of these narratives, but to recognise that certain stories are more potent because of the assumptions that are made about the tellers (Polletta 2006). The criminal trial is an institutional and discursive framework within which the most effective, or even only, way for women to counter a narrative of them as liars or blameworthy for the violence enacted on them is to make use of other harmful narrative tropes, even where, as in the cases of Sebold and Leo, they would rather not. Scherer, Sebold and Grant are all white, middle-class and educated and occupy a higher social position than the men who assaulted them. These factors make it more likely that they will have the skills and the social capital to engage in a contest of narratives with defence lawyers, to understand what discourses will aid them in developing an effective counter-narrative, and to have this counter-narrative recognised. The race and class positioning of complainants grants them different access to narrative resources, and means that their use of these resources will be read differently. While some women may be compelled to mobilise narratives of racial and class bias in order to succeed in court, these narratives are simply unavailable to many and even most survivors.

The final criterion of a good witness is somebody who accepts the discursive framing of the law as the dominant and appropriate location for defining and responding to rape. She may seek to reform or manipulate criminal justice narratives, but she accepts their right to adjudicate and determine the truth of rape. She must, in other words, accept and make use of the law's definition and understanding of experience. In order to harness the authority of legal discourse, she must, Susan Heinzelman (1990, p. 90) contends, 'erase or invalidate her own experiential truth' and replace 'her own story with one that echoes dominant narratives of the law, inadvertently legitimating the myths that the law has put at the centre of its truth of rape'. While Heinzelman is right in many ways, I would caution against presuming that women's own experiential truth is always or necessarily opposed to that offered by the law. As the stories here and in Chap. 2 indicate, not all women experience the law as an alien discourse, even if many do. A more difficult point to grapple with is, as I have argued, that even where dominant narratives of law reflect or validate experiential truth, they still work to legitimate the myths that the law has put at the centre of its truth of rape.

Legal Grammars and Women's Stories

This chapter is concerned with a seeming paradox in relations between feminism, survivor speech and the law. The criminal justice system is both a target of and an audience for women's speech about the injustices of sexual violence. Women such as Emily Doe have testified repeatedly and eloquently to the inadequacies and failures of the criminal law as a venue for their stories. At the same time, Doe and many others continue to speak to the law, petitioning it for a hearing and for justice. In the final section, I continue to ask what it means to speak within and to the law and why it is that the law retains such a central presence in the politics and stories of speaking out. Perhaps the most important point is that, like the previous chapter, these legal stories are a genre with clear boundaries of participation and exclusion. The majority of victims of rape do not tell their stories in court or even tell their stories to the criminal justice system in any form. And yet, the criminal justice system retains its status as a taken-for-granted point of reference in many stories and the politics which supports and enables them.

A way of understanding the function of the law in these stories is provided by Stacey Young (1997, pp. 1–2), who suggests in her work on feminist discursive activism that liberalism operates as a 'grammar' for feminist discourse and narratives. What she means by that is that while liberalism is rarely named or discussed, it is largely taken for granted that it frames the limits of what is tellable and thinkable within this politics and the stories it produces. It is a grammar that works to broaden the appeal of mainstream feminist discourse and politics by narrowing its agenda. Thinking in Bakhtinian terms, it would be possible to understand mainstream feminism as a discourse or socially significant language that does not compete with but is contained by liberalism as a more powerful discourse. Young is clear there are important marginal and critical voices that contest liberalism's framing, but its grammatical function means that within mainstream discourse it is largely presumed, unseen and therefore uncontested. I suggest that the criminal justice system operates in an analogous way for feminist politics and speaking out about rape. While there are important voices and movements that contest the taken-for-granted status of the law within rape politics and stories, these remain marginal within mainstream feminism (e.g. Incite! 2001; Richie 2012). As Young (1997) notes, these critiques, in relation to both liberalism and the law, arise most clearly from feminist subjects who do not find themselves in liberalism's racialised notion of the citizen-subject, or are unable to access the position of the 'good witness' due to their racial or class position.

Understood through Young's framework, the logic of this carceral grammar works, like the liberal grammar, to broaden the appeal of anti-rape politics by narrowing its agenda. Following from the discursive and cultural shifts discussed in the first chapter, the mainstream politics of speaking out has become the kind of politics that, as Clare Hemmings (2011) puts it, 'everyone' can agree on. The wide appeal of Doe's statement, to the Vice President and CNN, among others, is in part a result of this broad appeal and narrow agenda, and its acceptance, alongside much contemporary feminist speech on rape, of a carceral horizon. Her statement critiques the law's imposition of a *differend* upon her while assuming that Turner's conviction is a sign that 'we are getting somewhere'. The movements in response to her statement have continued this logic, campaigning for the imposition of mandatory minimum sentences, a classic 'law and order' form of politics, and the repeal of an overly lenient judge. The presumption is that increasingly punitive measures are the only way in which rape is or can be taken seriously, and, in our current social context, this is arguably true.

The criminal justice system remains the primary, and, for many people, the only imaginable, framework for socially validating the harm of sexual violence and the speech of survivors. As Susan Heinzelman (1990) argues, in a society where survivor speech continues to be denied, diminished and disbelieved, to abandon the law and the criminal justice system as a tool for asserting and acquiring authority for women's speech is to surrender one of the few avenues that women have. If Emily Doe's statement was heard and recognised around the world, and if she was able to act as a 'lighthouse' for other girls and women, this was, to a significant extent, enabled by the recognition and authorisation given to her speech by the criminal justice system. In the same way, as testified to in this chapter, legal validation of women's stories and punishment of the men who rape them are important sources of empowerment to many survivors. For this reason, continued strategic engagement with the law and legal reform may be particularly important for survivors who lack social or discursive resources to authorise or legitimate their stories in other ways.

On the other hand, the primary consequence of the history of feminist attempts to use the law to respond to the social problem of gendered violence has been, as Carol Smart (1998, p. 22) famously argued, to 'extend the imperial reach' of the law itself. In other words, taking for granted the law's status as the primary and most appropriate forum to speak and adjudicate the harms of rape entrenches this status, despite the fact that decades of law reform efforts have not delivered significant improvements for women who speak in the courts, unless they are able, as I described above, to manipulate the narrative frameworks offered by the law. Entrenching the law's status as a location for women's speech further marginalises the voices of those who do not or cannot mobilise the grammar of the criminal justice system to be heard. It entrenches a situation in which being heard relies on dominant narratives of race and class rather than an acceptance of women's right to be free of sexual violence and to be heard when they speak of it. As long as criminal justice sanctions are imagined and understood as the only way of 'taking seriously' or responding to narratives of sexual violence, then feminists will find themselves protesting short sentences and supporting lengthy ones. Even when these logics are attempted to be used against a Brock Turner, the effects of new mandatory minimum sentences and enhanced use of measures such as sex offender registers will be enacted upon the bodies of poor, black and brown men, and increase the narrative logic that says if a rapist is a criminal then only men who are seen as criminals can be rapists (Hoppe 2016). The punishment of someone like Turner as an 'exception' does not invalidate or challenge the class and racial logics which inform legal judgements.

As I note above, this does not mean invalidating or denying the experiences of women who are able to be heard and recognised by the law. Nor can it mean, as Heinzelman argues, expecting survivors to abandon one of the only spaces open to them and their stories. But it does mean taking seriously the other part of the feminist project of speaking out, which was to decentre the law by providing other ways of speaking and other sites of speech, and thinking seriously about the potential and limitations of that project. This is one of the driving forces behind the scholarship in this book. It has also been a part of the story of online feminist speech and hashtag activism, which in recent years has seemed to offer the promise of providing a more open forum for women to speak and be heard. In the following chapter, I consider the phenomenon of collective speech online, asking, in part, whether it offers new possibilities for women to speak without the suspicion, doubt and rewriting that their stories are subject to in the legal domain.

5

#YesAllWomen and Heroic 'Silence Breakers': Online Speech, Collective Stories and the Politics of Belief

In December 2017, *Time* magazine named the 'Silence Breakers' its 'Person of the Year' in an article subtitled, 'the voices that launched a movement' (Zacharek et al. 2017). This was only the second time that *Time* had given its prestigious cover to a group. As discussed in the Introduction, the first group in 1975 was a collection of 12 women who represented the 'American Woman' who included Susan Brownmiller, author of *Against Our Will*. In 1975, Brownmiller's (1976, p. 15) epic political tract on rape was a small part of *Time's* homage to feminism. In contrast, 2017 saw 'speaking out' about violence honoured as a cultural and political phenomenon largely independent of its feminist origins. Feminism is only mentioned twice in the *Time* cover story, with both emphasising the difference and distance between the 'silence breakers' and feminism as classically understood. The article notes that in the 1990s, feminists placed loyalty to the Democrats above belief in the women who accused the then-US president Bill Clinton of sexual violence, an argument I return to in the conclusion. The second reference declares that this new movement, built through social media, is based on the mass stories of ordinary women, and smaller numbers of men, many of whom 'would never call themselves feminists' (Zacharek et al. 2017). Social media, it might seem from the *Time* editorial, represents the culmination of the

© The Author(s) 2018
T. Serisier, *Speaking Out*, https://doi.org/10.1007/978-3-319-98669-2_5

political and cultural potential of speaking out. In this chapter, I assess some of the impacts of social media on speaking out before moving on to a more detailed discussion of feminist debates about the politics of speaking out in the second half of the book.

The origin of *Time*'s cover story was the birth of the 'Me Too' moment or movement two months earlier. On October 5, the *New York Times* published an exposé of Hollywood Producer Harvey Weinstein's long-time history of workplace sexual harassment and assault, while the *New Yorker* magazine was known to be preparing its own story on Weinstein, released on October 23 (Kantor and Twohey 2017; R. Farrow 2017). The actor Alyssa Milano tweeted a response to this story on October 15. In it, she suggested that if 'all the women who have been sexually harassed or assaulted wrote "Me too" as a status, we might give people a sense of the magnitude of the problem'. Her tweet ended with a request: 'If you've been sexually harassed or assaulted write "me too" as a reply to this tweet'. Approximately 500,000 tweets and 12 million Facebook posts featuring the hashtag were written or shared in the following 24 hours (Santiago and Criss 2017). By the time 'The Silence Breakers' was published, several prominent men, primarily in the entertainment industry, faced professional sanctions, including job loss, due to revelations of sexual harassment and assault. As the *Time* piece put it, this 'reckoning' appeared 'to have sprung up overnight' but had actually 'been simmering for years, decades, centuries' (Zacharek et al. 2017). The events and speech traced in the preceding chapters of this book provide an important part of the historical context that enabled the #MeToo 'reckoning', but it was also preceded by a number of other prominent hashtag campaigns around violence against women, such as #YesAllWomen, #BeenRapedNeverReported and #NotOkay. Like #MeToo, these hashtags began in response to specific events: the 2014 Isla Vista shootings by self-described 'beta male' Elliot Rodger (M. 2015), victim-blaming in 2014 media coverage of the Jian Ghomeshi trial (Mazza 2014), and the leaked video of Trump bragging about sexually assaulting women in 2016, respectively (Domonoske 2016). As a number of African-American women on Twitter quickly pointed out, Milano's hashtag phrase was directly taken from the community organiser and activist Tarana Burke, who had coined the phrase 'Me Too' a decade earlier in her work with 'mostly black and brown girls to let them know "you're not alone"' (Hill 2017; Burke 2017).

The first drafts of this chapter were begun when Harvey Weinstein was still a powerful Hollywood producer and stalwart ally of the Democratic establishment. The rapid pace of cultural change online, and an associated growth of public interest in the problem of sexual violence, has necessitated numerous redraftings of this chapter. These redraftings are symbolic of the fact that the consequences and meaning of events like #MeToo, and the phenomenon of hashtag feminism more broadly, remain undetermined, to be decided by processes of discursive activism, backlash and political contestation that is on-going at the time of writing. Instead of offering a definitive account of the meaning of social media for speaking out, this chapter contributes to an expanding pool of feminist analyses that seek to understand various aspects of online speech about sexual violence (see, for instance, contributions in Portwood-Stacer and Berridge 2014, 2015; Berridge and Portwood-Stacer 2015). The account provided here, like those of many other scholars, is far more cautious about the effects of social media than much media commentary. A profile of 35 of the then 46 women accusing Bill Cosby of sexual assault in *New York* magazine, for instance, began with the assertion that more 'has changed in the past few years for women who allege rape than in all the decades since the women's movement began'. It continued by suggesting that the 'megaphone' of social media has convinced many young women that 'speaking up is the only thing to do' in response to experiences of sexual violence (Malone 2015). Here I attempt to provide a more complicated and nuanced picture, exploring the positive and negative effects of social media on women's efforts to speak and be heard about sexual violence. I argue that, in significant ways, social media continues long-standing processes of judging women's narratives discussed in the previous chapter.

The first section of the chapter considers the implications of collective storytelling through 'hashtag activism' (Yang 2016). While hashtag activism is not the only form of discursive activism or political speech online, it is a prominent and distinctive element of online speech (Mendes et al. 2018). I am interested in the potential hashtags provide for a genre of individual stories to form a single collective story in ways that mirror earlier feminist traditions of using consciousness-raising and speak-outs to build a collective feminist story of sexual violence. I discuss both the story of, and the story told by, two important feminist hashtag campaigns around violence, #YesAllWomen and #MeToo. I draw primarily on accounts offered by their founders, Kaye M., and Tarana Burke and Alyssa Milano, respectively. These narratives draw attention to the power of collective storytelling and also to the processes of marginalisation and homogenisation along axes of race and class that can limit women's ability to participate within and shape these stories. The second half of the chapter returns more directly to questions raised at the end of the previous chapter around the influence of women's speech online, and the ways in which this speech is judged, doubted and denied. Here I examine changing public responses to Dylan Farrow's story of childhood sexual abuse by Woody Allen to explore these questions. I argue that online speech does offer new benefits for women, but that these sit alongside new ways of doubting and disbelieving women's stories, alongside older modes of judgement. As in the first part, I suggest that the concept of genre helps to articulate these processes. Narratives which are seen to have collective validation are believed, while those that don't belong in genres such as #MeToo continue to be met with disbelief and doubt. In the final section, I return to the assertion that 'speaking up is the only thing to do' when it comes to sexual violence and suggest that an increased belief in the necessity and power of speaking out may be one of the largest effects of social media. I ask what this belief can tell us about the politics of speaking out more broadly.

Hashtags and the Production of Collective Stories

The construction of hashtag stories on social media is a complex interaction between individual stories, genre formation and the production of collective stories of speaking out. At one level, hashtag campaigns such as #YesAllWomen and #MeToo are a collection of individual narratives, or narrative fragments, of personal recounting of experience (Yang 2016; Hearn 2018). These stories come together in a genre, marked and bounded by a hashtag, and with structures, limits and rules for participation.

The structure of Twitter allows these stories to be juxtaposed so that they construct a collective story which changes the meaning of the elements within it (Karlsson 2018). This story is produced within Twitter through searching or following a hashtag, and also by media summaries and selective reproductions of contributions, which themselves are frequently widely shared by participants in the hashtag (Yang 2016). Another layer of meaning is given by the story of the hashtag itself: how it was started, who participated and how and why they did, what the hashtag came to mean, and the effects that it had. In this section, I begin by considering the stories of #YesAllWomen and #MeToo, as told by their founders, in order to unpack the complexity of these multi-level stories that are simultaneously collections of personal narratives, and a collective story that attributes a social meaning to the conglomeration of individual contributions.

In May 2014, Elliot Rodger, a self-described 'beta male' and 'incel' (involuntary celibate), killed six people and injured several more before shooting himself in the town of Isla Vista, in California, USA. He left behind a manifesto full of racism and misogynist rage at women who he believed had unjustly rejected him romantically and sexually. In response to discussions online and elsewhere about the connections between the shooting and structural gendered violence, the hashtag #NotAllMen began trending on Twitter shortly afterwards. In response, Kaye M., a Muslim feminist activist, launched the hashtag #YesAllWomen in an attempt to recentre the problems of gendered and racial violence. #YesAllWomen quickly eclipsed #NotAllMen. It was tweeted and shared over 1.2 million times within two days, and garnered extensive mainstream media coverage. Kaye M., however, had left the hashtag after the first 24 hours, temporarily withdrawing from social media, tweeting that the 'hashtag I created has not been a safe place for my voice since the first twenty-four hours since I tossed it out'. As she described it in a retrospective account published a year later, that night she 'curled up in bed and waited to die':

> My Twitter mentions were bursting with reasons why I should. I was a man-hater. I was a rabid feminist. I was capitalizing on a tragedy. I was a terrorist in sheep's clothing. I was a hypocrite. There were many that had creatively utilized a 140-character limit to fantasize about particularly creative ends for me. (M. 2015)

The existence of extreme misogyny and violence directed against women online, and especially against women of colour, feminists and those who speak about sexual violence, has been well-documented (Jane 2014; Mantilla 2015). But this was not the sole cause of her leaving the hashtag. As the hashtag gained prominence, online and off, contributions by Kaye M. or other women that sought to discuss intersectional issues were 'suppressed, marginalised and trampled': ignored by media coverage of the hashtag and silenced by the increasingly dominant voices of white women on Twitter who claimed that these contributions were 'distractions' or 'divisive'. Alongside others, Kaye M. initiated the hashtag #YesAllWhiteWomen to draw attention to intersectional issues, and to racism within feminism. It was a space which enabled stories that were marginalised in the original hashtag, but it never achieved the same prominence or recognition.

Tarana Burke initiated the 'Me Too Movement' in 2006 while working as a youth worker. It arose from her response to a young woman, Heaven, who tried to talk to Burke about being sexually abused by her mother's boyfriend. In the moment, Burke writes:

> I could not find the courage that she had found... I could not find the strength to say out loud the words that were ringing in my head over and over again as she tried to tell me what she had endured... I watched her put her mask back on and go back into the world like she was all alone and I couldn't even bring myself to whisper...me too. (Burke 2013)

Before it was a hashtag, the 'Me Too Movement' of 'empowerment through empathy' originated as an apology to Heaven, and a commitment to ensuring other young women of colour would not be left alone. Burke has admitted to ambivalent feelings on discovering that her grassroots movement focused on young women of colour had become a global hashtag in response to an exposé of sexual harassment in Hollywood. She told an interviewer, 'I felt a sense of dread, because something that was part of my life's work was going to be co-opted and taken from me and used for a purpose that I hadn't originally intended' (Garcia 2017). The beginning of the hashtag seemed like an echo of Kaye M.'s story. A moment of women's empowerment was produced through a lack of recognition of the work of women of colour, so that 'sisters still managed to get diminished or erased'. But, as Burke notes, 'slew of people raised their voices so that didn't happen', and Burke's story, with its double dynamic of marginalisation and recognition, has been a major part of the narrative of #MeToo and debates about the meaning of its story (Hill 2017).

Both Kaye M. and Burke are clear about the political potential of the collective speech enabled by hashtags. Kaye M. (2015) writes that she remains proud of having started a hashtag which 'gave women a place to speak and be heard and acknowledged on a worldwide scale'. Feminist analysts have argued that hashtags can operate simultaneously as sites of consciousness-raising and as locations for producing public speech in the tradition of rallies and speak-outs (Rentschler 2014). As in Susan Brownmiller's 'West Village I' consciousness-raising group, participants use each other's stories to engage in 'joint learning' and 'knowledge-building' and the construction of a collective political meaning out of these shared experiences (Karlsson 2018, p. 11). The collective narrative helps to authorise the individual stories and give them broader significance, meaning that through participating in the hashtag, individual stories cannot be ignored (Yang 2016). The feminist commentator, Rebecca Solnit (2014), describes how this process worked in the production of a story of male 'sexual entitlement' out of the narratives collected into a single story in #YesAllWomen. After the hashtag went viral, she writes, the term was suddenly 'everywhere'. First, feminist 'blogs and commentary and conversations began to address it with brilliance and fury' through talking to and learning from each other. This public process of online consciousness-raising quickly brought the 'phrase into everyday speech', forcing it to the attention of increasing numbers of people, and allowing them to 'identify and discredit manifestations of this phenomenon'.

Where the memoirs I discussed in Chap. 3 prioritise the literary force of storytelling for their effectiveness, hashtag campaigns rely far more heavily on the impact of repetition and genre. Milano's tweet, quoted at the start of the chapter, articulates the conviction that multiple and repeated narratives, or narrative fragments, can work to represent the magnitude of gendered and sexual violence and force a recognition of the political urgency of the problem. Similar beliefs are expressed by the founders of other hashtags. Kelly Oxford (@kellyoxford), for example, asked women to tweet their first assaults after seeing the *Access Hollywood* video of Donald Trump bragging about sexual assault on October 8, 2016. Later that day she posted: 'women have tweeted me sexual assault stories for 14 hours straight. Minimum 50 per minute. harrowing. do not ignore. #notokay'. The magnitude of this repetition bolsters the authority of individual stories and makes them simultaneously tell a political and social truth. The hashtag is used to imply that the stories, whatever their particularities, share a sameness of content and meaning. The replacement of narrative specificity with a claim to generic commonality, at its best, prioritises a politics of solidarity that enables shared meanings to be constructed out of distinct experiences that may be understood in distinct ways by those who share them. This effect is achieved through the hashtag functioning as what Derrida labels a 're-mark' of participation in a genre. The re-mark is not so much part of the story, but signals belonging to the genre while also drawing attention to the constructed nature of generic commonalities. In the words of Derrida (1992, p. 230): 'Making genre its mark, a text demarcates itself'. So, a hashtag marks the social media post as taking part in the genre of individual narratives of experience. But it isn't itself part of this personal narrative. Instead, it is a signal that the author wishes to participate in the genre and, therefore, it provides a guide to reading and understanding the message of the tweet.

Hashtags, Akyel (2014, p. 1102) argues, are a 'rhizomatic form that connects diverse texts, images, and videos', constructing a shared narrative through inference and reader understandings of what it is that the hashtag signals. Hashtags can act as substitutions for parts of the narrative or even provide its central meaning or act as a synecdoche for the story the author wishes to tell, as when someone simply posts '#MeToo'. No story is told. Instead, an individual story is inferred from the re-mark, indicating that the author is participating in the genre and in the construction of the collective story it tells. This can function in different ways in different hashtags. For instance, the hashtag #RapeHasNoUniform trended in March 2014 after the photographer Christine Fox (@steenfox) asked survivors to tweet what they were wearing when they were assaulted (Dockterman 2014). Adding the hashtag to a description of clothing turns what is often a list into a collective act of storytelling with a clear meaning or moral, in this case that clothing does not cause or provoke rape. As Tarana Burke commented in an interview, 'me too was just two … magic words that galvanised the world' (*Telegraph* 2018). The words are magical not because of their meaning but because of the number of people they inspired to participate in the construction of a collective story of gendered violence.

As Lena Karlsson (2018) notes, the meaning of the collective story is beyond the control of individual participants or even the founders of hashtags, and the force of repetition may in fact lead to dominant interpretations becoming hegemonic. While there is a widespread presumption that the meaning of #MeToo or #YesAllWomen is clear, the stories told by their founders reveal that this meaning is produced both through political contestation within the discursive space of the hashtag and the way the story of the hashtag is retold and represented externally. The question of meaning is intrinsically bound up with the boundaries, limits and exclusions that, for Derrida (1992, p. 224), constitute the 'law of genre'. This is an issue, as discussed in Chap. 3, of whose stories do and don't count as part of the overall meaning of the collective narrative. So, if #YesAllWomen is defined as speaking to a universal and essential experience of gender, then it will exclude stories that insist on discussing race, class and other axes of difference. The dominance of this definition, according to Kaye M. (2015), led to a story that centred and prioritised the experiences of white, middle-class women, but with the racial and class boundaries obscured by an appeal to universalism. It became a story and a space for 'only some women' who were 'privileged enough to hang in'. This process is bound up with power relations and, as I argued in Chap. 2, with the ability to tell stories that reflect and reinforce existing 'common sense' or taken-for-granted ideas, that there is a universal experience of 'womanhood' that is able to be narrated by white middle-class women. As Michael Salter (2013) observes, we should not be surprised that online feminist spaces and collectivities are marked by the same hierarchical relations of power, privilege and dominance as offline feminist spaces, and that the construction of communities and stories for 'all women' remains fraught and illusory in online spaces as well as offline spaces. As Kaye M. (2015) writes: 'Not everything about #YesAllWomen makes me proud. I am particularly bitter, and disappointed, that it did not live up to its name and its promise. As a marginalized woman, even I could not provide a safe space for more than a few hours for others like me'. But there is another story of possibility in the story of those few hours when the meaning of the hashtag had not yet reified, and it could be interpreted as a story of how 'all women' experience gendered violence in multiple ways, refracted through experiences of other vectors of power. Insisting on this meaning, as the hashtag #YesAllWhiteWomen and the related hashtag #EachEveryWoman did, created spaces where it was stories that refused to acknowledge the racial and class modalities of women's experiences that were excluded from the genre. Both stories were part of the narrative of #YesAllWomen at its inception, and as Kaye M. (2015) notes, 'for those few hours, I loved what it was and could be'.

In the case of #MeToo, Tarana Burke similarly questioned how the collective story would be told and who would be included in 'the discussion of what #MeToo is really about' (Burke 2017). In a series of tweets on February 22, 2018, she voiced her concerns about media framing of the movement and of her role: 'While it's true that I have been widely recognized as the 'founder' of the movement – there is virtually no mention of my leadership. Like I just discovered something 12 years ago and in 2017 it suddenly gained value'. She continued, 'watch carefully who are called "leaders" of the movement' (@TaranaBurke). In her comment that it is 'very possible to be acknowledged and erased', she supported Alcoff and Gray's (1993) argument about the way media can give voice to survivors and restrict their authority at the same time through limited recognition of their speech and its meaning. Burke's story, and that of #MeToo to date, has also been a story of critiquing and contesting those processes. Burke has noted frequently that other black women insisted that her leadership be recognised, and some of her critiques of media framing have been reported and discussed within mainstream media forums (e.g. Read 2018). Even if it is unrealistic to think that online spaces are free from social power dynamics, it is important to recognise that they can allow these dynamics to be contested (Clark 2016). Ultimately, as I noted above, the meaning of the collective narrative of #MeToo is still being contested and determined. And, as with #YesAllWomen, there are already moments where the story might be or become the shared property of 'each and every one of those people who shared it is an individual person who has a story and took a chance' (Burke 2017).

Online Stories and Generic Judgements

A key function of collective storytelling in the case of sexual violence is designed to counter the denial and disbelief that frequently greets individual women's stories, particularly in cases of 'simple' or acquaintance rape, or where the man is considered more 'respectable' than the woman telling the story of violence. If many women speak, and if their stories can be aligned and placed next to each other in a Twitter stream, social 'structures are made visible' and 'stories are automatically re-contextualised', forcing a shift in focus from the credibility of an individual account to recognition of structural gendered harm (Karlsson 2018, p. 13). As Deb Waterhouse-Watson (2013) demonstrates, the repetition and retelling of narratives or narrative details creates a 'semantic thickness' which makes stories seem more self-evidently 'true'. In the case of hashtags such as #MeToo or #YesAllWomen, individual stories that might struggle to obtain hearing of belief on their own are granted significance, credibility and validation as part of the collective story. The fact, as noted above, that core elements of the narrative often remain unspoken means that individual contributions are read through the validating lens of this semantic thickness. These processes of belief do not, however, transfer automatically to individual stories that lack this thickness and which may seem, by comparison, too isolated and flimsy to believe. In fact, individual stories may find themselves subject to new processes of judgement and doubt, because they fail to attain these measures of semantic thickness, or they are not seen to 'belong' to the genre of collective narrative authorised through hashtags. Belief, then, as I argue in relation to the changing public reception of Dylan Farrow's story of sexual abuse by Woody Allen, may hinge more on processes of generic belonging than on other traditional modes of judging the credibility of women's stories.

In February 2014, Dylan Farrow (2014) published an 'Open Letter' on the blog of *New York Times* journalist Nicholas Kristof, detailing her experience of childhood sexual abuse by her adopted father, Woody Allen. The story was not new, having been widely reported during a custody dispute between Allen and Mia Farrow, Dylan's adopted mother. It was, however, the first time that Dylan Farrow had spoken publicly about her story. The letter began and ended with the question, 'what's your favourite Woody Allen movie?' It then told readers that 'there is something you should know' before answering. As with other narratives discussed here, Farrow described how the harms of sexual violence were extended by social responses:

> Each time I saw my abuser's face – on a poster, on a t-shirt, on television – I could only hide my panic until I found a place to be alone and fall apart… It felt like a personal rebuke, like the awards and accolades were a way to tell me to shut up and go away.

In addition to demanding of general readers that they imagine their 'seven-year-old daughter being led into an attic by Woody Allen' and then to 'imagine a world that celebrates her tormenter', Farrow addresses specific questions to celebrities who have worked with Allen: 'What if it had been your child…? What if it had been you…? Have you forgotten me?' In the letter, Farrow (2014) firmly asserts that to honour Allen without reference to her and her story is equivalent to disbelieving her or saying that her story doesn't matter. After years of silence, she writes, it is other survivors of sexual abuse who 'have given me a reason to not be silent, if only so others know that they don't have to be silent either', clearly placing her story within the genre of speaking out narratives.

In the aftermath of her 2014 *New York Times* piece, Farrow's story was subject to the kind of strategic narrative contests that characterise criminal trials, as discussed in the previous chapter. Farrow's interpretation of events is supported by her mother, Mia, and brother, Ronan, also the journalist on the *New Yorker* story about Harvey Weinstein. It is contested by Allen and another sibling, Moses (R. Farrow 2016; M. Farrow 2018; Allen 2014). While each of these family members has intervened in the narrative, the primary proponent of the opposing narrative to Dylan's is Robert B. Weide, the director of a biopic of Allen and the author of three online articles, each of which are direct rebuttals of articles by Dylan or her brother Ronan (Weide 2014, 2016, 2017). Weide's articles are a useful case study in the methods used to discredit women's narratives in the social media era. He is aware of 'opening myself up to accusations of "blaming the victim"' and is thus careful to assert that it is 'possible to believe Allen without calling Dylan Farrow a liar' (Weide 2014, 2017). Weide goes to great efforts to invoke tropes of reasonableness and even-handedness, giving his interventions titles like 'The Woody Allen Allegations: Not So Fast' and 'A Q&A with Dylan Farrow', which she is of course not directly involved in. He writes that 'we can each believe what we want', and that he is merely 'presenting facts' or 'floating scenarios' (Weide 2014). In contrast with Dylan's insistence that her story be believed and acted upon, Weide seems to simply ask that the reader pay attention to both stories, a request that is framed as perfectly reasonable.

Weide's speech demonstrates the persistence of what Leigh Gilmore (2017, p. 17) describes as long-standing ways of doubting 'what women say about their lives', which persist in the age of social media. Faced with women's testimony, and particularly with the kind of disputing of that testimony offered by Weide, there are two common tropes that are used: 'he said, she said', which implies that when there are two different narratives it is futile to choose between them, and 'nobody really knows what happened', a reference to the private and unknowable status of rape. While these tropes enact a veneer of impartiality, it is only, argues Leigh Gilmore (2017, p. 17), in cases of sexual violence that 'people feel virtuous, objective and fair' when they claim that the conditions that generally initiate investigations render them moot from the outset, thus placing women's stories outside the domain of justice. Weide's use of statements such as 'we can each believe what we want' not only invokes these tropes but shows their deployment within an overall erasure of Farrow's story because the truth is simply unknowable. Weide does not, however, use these tropes to render investigation moot. Instead, in a narrative development that is enabled by social media, Weide undertakes his own investigation and encourages the reader to follow his example. He encourages readers to follow links to court records and reports. But while these documents are interpreted as objective, they are framed, explained and provided with a 'narrative glue' by Weide so that the reader is exhorted to conclude that Farrow's story is untrue or, at the very least, that nobody can really know for sure what happened (Brooks 2008).

Weide's narrative glue prioritises certain pieces of evidence over others. This is most clear in his relation to the credibility of the major characters in the story. Allen is presented as inherently credible so that, for instance, an unsupported claim by Allen that Mia Farrow threatened to 'do worse' than shoot him in a late-night telephone call is taken as factual 'evidence' of Mia's instability and vengefulness (Weide 2017). Mia is characterised as inherently untrustworthy, while Dylan Farrow is portrayed as 'hysterical and bitter' (Brigley Thompson 2017, p. 67). Any statements that Dylan Farrow or her family make about Allen that do not have external verification are therefore disputed or dismissed. Documentary evidence undergoes a similar process. Weide cites a Yale psychiatric evaluation that found 'no evidence' of child abuse as authoritative without mentioning it has been severely criticised by other experts who point out that the 'inconsistencies' in Farrow's testimony which form the basis of its conclusions are common in children who have experienced abuse (Orth 2014; Weide 2014, 2017). On the contrary, he finds a prosecutorial statement that the decision not to charge Allen was taken on the basis of Farrow's mental health rather than a lack of confidence in the evidence to be 'incredible', without acknowledging that the reluctance of victims and their families to go to trial is a common reason for not pursuing these sorts of allegations (Madigan and Gamble 1991; Weide 2017).

As in the courts, it is not evidence that primarily provides meaning to Weide's investigation of the facts. Rather, he relies on long-standing tropes and 'stock characters' of women who speak about sexual violence as lying, deceitful and vengeful, and men as the victims of their irresponsible speech. Even as Weide insists he is not calling Farrow a liar, his story relies on undermining her credibility so that even if she is not 'lying', she is not to be believed. In other words, in a distinction I elaborate in more detail in Chap. 7, Farrow might be sincere, but her story is not true. She believes what she is saying because she has been manipulated by her mother. Or, as Dylan herself writes, 'Allen's savvy affiliates know that it's unseemly to direct attacks at me, an alleged victim, and so the invective is directed at my mother again and again'. Mia Farrow, in Weide's account, is a 'scorned woman' who manufactured an allegation of child sexual assault against Allen as revenge for his leaving her for her adopted daughter. Weide asserts that 'there are many, many people who believe this whole case boils down to Mia Farrow's (understandable) rage at Woody Allen for falling in love with her adopted daughter, Soon-Yi Previn' (Weide 2017). Despite another performance of reasonableness, the only way that this narrative is 'understandable' is if the central characterisations of Mia as so obsessed with revenge on Allen that she would brainwash her daughter into telling a lie for two decades, and Dylan as so devoid of agency that she would believe and repeat that lie her entire life. The reliance of the story on these characters is attested to in Weide's frequent references to other parts of Mia's life, specifically her 'hypocrisy' in maintaining a friendship with the director Roman Polanski and her 'immorality', evidenced in Weide's belief that she cheated on Allen with Frank Sinatra (Weide 2014, 2016, 2017). Rather than being factually irrelevant to the story, these are important elements in Weide's writing of Mia as a lying woman out for revenge and, by extension, Dylan as the 'mad' woman whose speech cannot be believed.

Prior to December 2017, Weide's narrative intervention was largely successful in positioning the 'real' story of what happened as unknowable and depriving Farrow's account of the ability to compel belief or action. The existence of two versions of the story kept it within the seemingly just and reasonable domain of 'he said, she said', and Weide's self-presentation as a disinterested yet authoritative source was accepted by many journalists writing about the case (e.g. Winter 2014). The actors called on by Farrow also largely accepted this framework, and the accompanying one of 'nobody really knows'. Kate Winslet, for instance, declared in an interview, 'I don't know anything, really, and whether any of it is true or false' (D. Farrow 2017). In a common pattern, while Allen's actions could not be judged, the same was not true of Dylan's speech. Scarlet Johansson, for instance, described Farrow's letter to an interviewer as 'irresponsible' because it took 'a bunch of actors' and threw 'their name into a situation that none of us could possibly knowingly comment on' (Cadwalladr 2014). Within the framing of 'he said, she said' and 'nobody knows', Farrow's ethical demands registered as unreasonable and blameworthy in themselves. While Farrow required explicit belief and consequent action as a response to her speech, Weide only had to have the possibility that either narrative could be true and accepted in order for the 'he said, she said' logic to take its course. Despite isolated instances of public figures declaring their support for Farrow, in the aftermath of her open letter it seemed that little would change for Allen.

This response to Farrow's speech demonstrated that even in the era of social media, women's speech is not necessarily or automatically believed, and it can assist in looking again at the role of speaking out in celebrated cases such as Bill Cosby and Weinstein. These are important because, as I discuss below, they would become comparisons used to attempt to discredit Farrow's speech. As with Farrow's story, the allegations against Weinstein and Cosby were not new when they became news on social media. The allegations against Weinstein were an 'open secret' reported anonymously on Hollywood gossip sites, and the stories about Cosby had been known since he settled a 2006 civil case brought by one woman but in which a number of other women supplied depositions (Kantor and Twohey 2017). Some of these women were even interviewed on television at the time (Bowman 2014). In both cases, however, it took external verification for the women's stories to be heard and believed. Weinstein was exposed by the two exposés already mentioned and Cosby, bizarrely, became a figure of public outrage after a clip of a male comedian calling Cosby a rapist was uploaded online (McQuade 2014). As Barbara Bowman (2014), one of the women who had been speaking publicly about Cosby for decades, notes, society's willingness to ignore her and other women, but rush to believe a male comedian with no direct knowledge of the cases, is hardly a sign of increased willingness to believe women who speak about sexual violence. The stories about Cosby and Weinstein, when they did become publicly acknowledged, involved large numbers of women. The question of what would have happened in either case if there were only a single narrative is impossible to say but easy enough to imagine. In these cases, the stories told benefited from a 'semantic thickness' of repeated narratives with common elements. They operated, in some ways, like the much broader hashtag movement of #MeToo, which created a widespread story of the ubiquity of sexual violence and abuse.

Following the beginning of the #MeToo movement, Dylan Farrow (2017) made a second major intervention in an opinion piece for the *Los Angeles Times* asking: 'Why Has the #MeToo Movement Spared Woody Allen?' In this piece, she did not so much revisit the evidence or credibility of her story that had been disputed by Weide. Instead, she based her claim to belief on the assertion that her story generically belonged within the collective story of #MeToo and that it therefore warranted the same response. Just as I noted in the previous chapter that women can make use of the resources provided by the courts, Farrow made use of the newly available 'semantic thickness' of #MeToo to demand a new hearing. She emphasised the 'sameness' of her story with the other stories included within the collective narrative of #MeToo, arguing that the system of silence and denial that 'worked for Harvey Weinstein for decades... works for Woody Allen still'. She even implicitly used this contrast to make a similar point to Gilmore: 'It is also our collective choice to see simple situations as complicated and obvious conclusions as a matter of "who can say"?' She again named celebrities, but this time focused on their divergent responses to the allegations against Weinstein and Allen, using her assertion of her own generic belonging to frame them as incoherent or even hypocritical. For instance, she quoted the actor Blake Lively as saying in relation to #MeToo that it is 'important that women are furious right now... It's important that we don't ... focus on one or two or three or four stories, it's important that we focus on humanity in general and say, "This is unacceptable"'. In contrast, Farrow quoted her as saying in relation to Allen: 'It's very dangerous to factor in things you don't know anything about. I could [only] know my experience'. Placing herself within the collective #MeToo narrative achieved what simply telling her story could not. At the time of writing, numerous actors have announced that they will no longer work with Allen and his career appears to be in serious jeopardy. The changing fortunes of Farrow's story demonstrate the power of collective narratives to compel belief and the fact that this power does not extend to individual narratives that seek to compel belief and action on the basis of their authority alone.

Farrow's success in moving the debate to the realm of generic belonging created a shift in the responses of Weide and the terms of public 'debate'. Instead of disputing the credibility of her story, Weide's goal was now to show that it belonged outside of the #MeToo genre. In large part, this attempt rested on the logic that an individual woman's story, without external or legal validation, does not belong in the same genre as stories that have these external sources of validation or the validation of a collective narrative. This, for Weide (2017), is the essential truth of #MeToo:

> Clearly, one thing shared in common by Cosby, Weinstein, Kevin Spacey, James Toback, Donald Trump, and several others, are the multiple accusations

made against all these men, and for each of them, respectively, the claims are all strikingly similar. Woody Allen faces a single accusation of a single alleged incident made by one understandably furious ex-lover in the middle of custody negotiations, after warning him of her intentions.

Weide claims, in italics, that in researching Allen's career '*I have yet to find one single actor or actress who claims they were mistreated by the director in any way*'. Leaving aside the fact that widely reported stories by Mariel Hemingway about her discomfort with Allen's sexual advances towards her do not appear in any of Weide's articles, the inference is that only stories that are one of many should be told within the logic of #MeToo (Orth 2014). Weide enacts a second and more absolute generic distinction which builds on his earlier claims. This story does not belong in the genre of #MeToo because it is not a survivor or victim's story of harm but an 'ex-lover' enacting a revenge narrative of romance gone wrong.

Weide's insistence that Farrow's story is marked by its generic difference from #MeToo has been repeated by several journalists and commentators. Much of the continued distrust of Farrow's narrative points to ways that the stories told of Weinstein and Cosby have inadvertently reproduced and strengthened the social myth of the 'sex offender' as a pathological monster with uncontrollable compulsions, quite distinct from ordinary men (Bumiller 2008). Although this myth is contradicted by the statistical realities of sexual offending which has lower rates of recidivism than many other categories of crime, widespread belief in this myth supported a generic boundary used to render Farrow's story illegitimate. For instance, a *Guardian* columnist wrote that it is 'wrong, lazy and dangerous' to compare Allen to serial predators such as Weinstein and Cosby. The journalist acknowledges that even a single allegation, 'if true', is clearly a terrible thing, but goes on to argue that the fact that Allen does not appear to have committed other sexual assaults on children means that he cannot be placed within the story of the monstrous sexual predator that is now told about Weinstein and Cosby (Shoard 2018). The absence of other similar stories, in an environment where collective stories seem to abound, works here as evidence that Farrow's story is not and cannot be true. This is another way in which the meaning of the collective story of #MeToo remains contested. It can be told as a narrative of the 'normality' of sexual violence in workplaces and families or it can be a story that reasserts boundaries around 'real' sexual assaults committed by 'real' predators. In one reading Farrow's single story of sexual violence in a domestic setting is part of the story, and in the other it is not.

The intersection of issues of belief and generic belonging was also demonstrated in debates around *Babe.net*'s publication of a story about a date between Aziz Ansari and a woman known only by the pseudonym Grace, who described the night as the 'worst' of her life (Way 2018). Through the journalist, Katie Way, who tells her story, Grace describes how, after dinner, she and Ansari returned to Ansari's home. She recounts a sexual encounter which may have begun consensually but where Ansari 'ignored clear non-verbal cues' and that even after she asked him to slow down and 'chill', 'nothing changed'. On one level, the article is a contemporary case study in the way that sensationalist media framing can recuperate or contain the transgressive potential of women's speech, as it contextualises the story through the tropes of gossip reporting, commenting on Grace's outfit and including Instagram pictures of food (Alcoff and Gray 1993). However, it also reveals the political stakes of generic belonging, and here I want simply to note that responses to the story took the form of a debate about generic boundaries and inclusion.

The article signalled its generic participation in #MeToo through explaining that Grace decided to speak publicly after she saw Ansari wearing a 'Time's Up' badge at the Golden Globes award ceremony which doubled as the launch of the anti-sexual harassment campaign (Way 2018). In the following days and weeks, her story and her assertion of generic belonging were contested through a public assertion and attempt at enforcement of generic boundaries around #MeToo. The most influential performance of this boundary policing was undertaken by the CNN journalist Ashleigh Banfield, the same journalist who had previously read Emily Doe's statement live on air (Pallotta 2016; CNN 2018). In this case, Banfield read out her own open letter in which she described Grace's speech about Ansari as 'appalling' and generically inappropriate. For Banfield, Grace's story does not belong in a genre focused on gendered injustice and sexual harassment. As she repeats at several points: 'By your own admission, this was a bad date' (CNN 2018). She defines the boundaries of acceptable speech through the legal criteria of sexual assault and harassment, specifying that if, and only if, Grace's speech meets either of these, then she has the right to place her story within the genre of #MeToo. But, in illegitimately asserting her belonging, she has, according to Banfield, damaged the very foundations of the genre: 'You have chiselled away at a movement that I, along with all of my sisters in the workplace, have been dreaming of for decades, a movement that has finally changed an oversexed professional environment that I, too, have struggled through at times over the last 30 years' (CNN 2018). If Kaye M. (2015) described attempts to limit stories told through the genre of #YesAllWomen to stories that emphasise the sameness of 'all women's' experiences, the boundaries that were asserted in response to Farrow and Grace's stories have to do with external validation, either through collective narratives or the legal system.

These generic restrictions on what stories do and don't belong in the genre are simultaneously debates about the stories it can and can't tell. It precludes a vision of #MeToo as telling stories that challenge or problematise normal or accepted behaviours of heterosexuality or the patriarchal family and accepts distinction between public speech and the private domain of romance. This is made explicit by Banfield when she suggests appropriate genres within which Grace might speak and actions that she might take. She advises Grace not to 'go on a second date' with a man like Ansari and definitely not to 'marry' him, and even accepts that she should 'warn your friends' about him and his behaviour (CNN 2018). What she should not do, however, is speak within a public or political register, demand a public or ethical response, or place her story within the generic boundaries of #MeToo.

A different response was offered by Tarana Burke in media interviews when she was asked whether Grace has 'the right to attach to #MeToo to her story'. Understanding the question through Derrida, this can be read as asking about her right to make use of a generic re-mark and claim participation in the genre. Burke refused to define limits or boundaries in response to the question, stating: 'I won't tell anybody that they don't have that right' (Walden 2018). She insisted that what unites the stories of #MeToo is their grounding in a subjective experience or interpretation rather than external validation or meeting legal definitions of assault and harassment. For her, debates about generic boundaries and the legitimacy or illegitimacy of women's speech, miss the opportunity presented by #MeToo: 'We've got to shift from that. Narrative change in this movement is so important because if we keep on talking about this in the ways that we're talking about it, we're going to lose an opportunity' (Burke, in Wagmeister 2018). As I discuss in the final section, the nature of that opportunity, like the generic boundaries of the speech included in the #MeToo hashtag, is far from determined. The changing response to Farrow's story particularly demonstrates that those boundaries are not set, and that the collective story of #MeToo has opened possibilities for women to demand that their stories be heard even if, as I argue here, it has not removed the doubt and suspicion that individual women's stories continue to face. As Derrida (1992) makes clear, genres of speech and story always enact generic boundaries. The question of where and how these are set is what is at stake in the construction of collective stories and the judgement of whose narratives can be heard within them. At the same time, contestations over what belongs in the genre of stories that make up a hashtag is another way of determining what the collective story of the hashtag is about, and what kinds of politics it might produce (Karlsson 2018). This is the question I turn to in the final section.

Keep Telling People? Online Speech and 'the Work' of Combating Sexual Violence

The legacy and meaning of #MeToo remains, as I have argued, undetermined. They will be decided by the force of the collective story it has unleashed and the cultural contestations over what that story means. This is not simply a contest between those who are for and against women's speech, but a political debate between and among women who tell their stories and those who seek to support and amplify them. I conclude this chapter by considering the different visions of the meaning, potential and limitations of #MeToo as a form of collective speech that has been put forward in the statements and work of the two women who can claim to be the founders of the hashtag. These women, Alyssa Milano, the actor who asked others to respond by tweeting #MeToo, and Tarana Burke, the community organiser who founded her movement of 'empowerment through empathy' a decade earlier, have offered very different conceptions of what it means and what it might become.

In December 2017, Milano, working with other professionals under the banner of the 'Creative Coalition', launched a website and 'PSA' or Public Service Announcement video. The website and video, sponsored by *USA Today*, operate under the exhortative hashtag, #KeepTellingPeople. According to the website:

> With every new voice that speaks up, another person is empowered to tell their story. Another person calls out harassment. Another person becomes an ally in the fight against assault. (Creative Coalition 2017)

Change is conceptualised here as a continuing commitment to speech and to speaking, a circular logic that is more fully expressed in the PSA video. In what has itself become a recognisable generic format, the PSA video features numerous celebrities speaking and holding signs. It begins with the statement that 'everybody knows what's been going on'. The phrase 'everybody knows' is repeated throughout, and by the end of the video its meaning has shifted. At this point, the audience is encouraged to tell people about unwanted sexual behaviour in their workplace or elsewhere, and to officially report it. We need to do this, the video suggests, so that 'everybody knows' what is happening (Creative Coalition 2017).

The end of the video returns us then to the beginning where 'everybody knows what's been going on', producing a closed circle of speech and knowledge. This could be taken as an implicit recognition that speech, once heard, can be easily forgotten, an issue I discuss in Chap. 8. But it offers no movement beyond or outside of this cycle. An analogy offered by Tarana Burke in an interview makes clear the limits of this approach. Referring to the sheer scale of #MeToo, she notes 'the difference in how people think about the disease of sexual violence' as compared to other social problems: 'If, in this country, we had an outbreak of some communicable disease that 12 million people got in a 24-hour time period, we would be focused solely on the cure' (Wagmeister 2018). The problem is not, post #MeToo, or even before it, that people 'don't know' about epidemic levels of sexual violence, just as they didn't not know about allegations against Cosby or Weinstein. It is that this knowledge doesn't produce action and is allowed and enabled to be forgotten or accepted as simply the way things are, so that everyone does indeed know what's been going on, but this knowledge produces no response. It is as if, to return to Lyotard (1988, p. 8), there is 'no referent'. And there is no sense that knowledge might produce a collective social or cultural response. In its focus on enabling speech, the video offers no possibility that the conditions that necessitate this speech might ultimately be changed by the speech that seeks to contest them. What 'everybody knows' becomes, through a seemingly common-sense formulation, an eternal truth rather than a contestable reality.

The #KeepTellingPeople video demonstrates the cultural authority and even hegemony of speaking out as a political response to sexual violence, even as it opens questions about the meaning and limitations of this narrative politics. In a very real sense, the 'after' or legacy of #MeToo is imagined as a maintenance of the #MeToo moment. Even as the video declares that 'things need to change', it offers a vision of on-going sameness (Creative Coalition 2017). Discussing the 'unprecedented capacity' of online activism as a political tool, Clark highlights 'hashtag activism's ability to circulate revised normative interpretations of social phenomena… that validates, rather than denies, victims' (2016, p. 800). But these validating interpretations may themselves be revised and contained in ways that buttress rather than unsettle the established generic boundaries around women's speech, as discussed in the previous section. In constructing a vision of the 'meaning' of #MeToo that is restricted to the need to continue speaking, #KeepTellingPeople makes visible the limitations of a politics of speaking out detached from a wider political discursive framework. Rather than enacting or looking towards political transformation, such a vision instead produces a vision of the future that is not recognisably distinct from the present.

Tarana Burke's media statements in the aftermath of #MeToo have operated according to a completely different political logic. Far from a call to 'keep telling people', within weeks of the birth of the hashtag phenomenon, she was arguing that 'amplification has happened' and that we 'have to be in a moment of strategy' where 'organising has to happen'.

Questioned specifically about the launch of a new hashtag campaign Burke replied, 'we don't need another "thing". If we keep on "making statements" and not really doing the work, we are going to be in trouble' (Walden 2018). In Burke's language, 'the work' stands in for the concrete activism and change that #MeToo potentially enables but does not guarantee. She calls on others to participate in this work but does not limit or privilege 'speaking out' as a form of participation. As she said in an interview, 'the work is the work' (Brockes 2018). Burke refers to #MeToo as something that opens the space for that work rather than as a core component of it. She has, in interviews, variously described this work as 'radical healing' for survivors and real recognition of the harm of sexual violence alongside what she refers to as a 'spectrum' of accountability for perpetrators (Hill 2017; Brockes 2018). For Burke, the 'naming' of #MeToo 'is just the beginning of the journey' and the 'work' is 'what happens after you said "me too"' (Burke 2017; Walden 2018). Even Burke's public statements, however, leave this work largely undefined or only gestured towards. The question, again, of what kind of a politics speaking out might produce that goes beyond more speech seems difficult or even impossible to answer within a political frame in which the act of speech is so dominant. The work of building a politics out of narrative, debates about how this is to be done, and the relationship of feminism as a political practice to the genre of stories that have arisen out of it, are the subject of the second half of this book. The following chapter begins this conversation with a consideration of the political relationship between survivors, their stories and feminist experts who speak on their behalf.

Part II

The Politics of Speaking Out

6

Whose Business Is Speaking Out? The Bell Debate, Indigenous Stories and the Construction of White Feminist Expertise

In 1989, the article 'Speaking About Rape Is Everyone's Business' appeared in the feminist journal, *Women's Studies International Forum* (*WSIF*), with joint authorship attributed to Diane Bell, a white American anthropologist and prominent radical feminist, and Topsy Napurrula Nelson, an Elder of the Central Australian Indigenous community within which Bell had worked for a prolonged period (Bell and Nelson 1989). In keeping with the title, the article, like many of the texts discussed in this book, is less concerned with rape than with the importance of speaking about intra-racial sexual violence in Indigenous communities or, in Nelson's words in the article, the conviction that '*it's important to show this story*' (p. 404). The article asserted that white feminists are obligated to speak about the violence in Indigenous communities and that not to do so is to become complicit in the perpetuation of this violence. Over the next two years, this article would sit at the centre of a debate in Australian feminism and anthropology about speech, power and knowledge production between women and across divides of race and colonisation. It would enflame long-standing arguments about the possibility and limits of solidarity, and the dangers of neocolonialism, in relations between white feminists and Aboriginal women (e.g. O'Shane 1976; Moreton-Robinson 2000). While it was not always necessarily immediately present in contributions to the debate, the provocative assertion in the article's title provided the impetus for one of post-second wave Australian feminism's most controversial chapters. The debate revisited this question, asking whose business is speaking about rape in remote Aboriginal communities and what are the implications of white academic feminists speaking about sexual violence on behalf of Indigenous women?

Twelve Aboriginal women, led by the historian Jackie Huggins (Huggins et al. 1991, p. 506), wrote to *WSIF* following the article's publication to 'dispute the central proposition that rape is "everyone's business"'. They contended that Bell's determination to speak about rape in Indigenous communities was an example of 'white imperialism of others' cultures which are theirs to appropriate, criticise and castigate'. They contended that crediting Nelson as 'co-author' rather than 'chief informant' was 'unethical' and functioned primarily to forestall criticism of Bell's position and her right to speak about Indigenous politics. Insisting that 'our country was colonised on both a racially and sexually imperialistic base', they concluded their letter with the assertion: 'Sexism does not and will never prevail over racial domination in this country' (p. 507). Initially, *WSIF* declined to publish the contribution. The piece, editor Robyn Rowland (1991–1992, p. 430) later declared, failed to engage with the substantive content of Bell and Nelson's article, was 'not a coherent argument, and contained points that would be unclear to an international readership'. Following Huggins et al.'s public distribution of their correspondence with *WSIF*, another journal, *Anthropological Forum*, published an article by Jan Larbalestier (1990) which was supportive of Huggins et al. alongside a reply from Bell (1990), with a letter from Rowland explaining *WSIF*'s position included in the following issue. The matter was widely discussed and even featured on a 'women's programme' on Australia's main public radio station, Radio National (Yeatman 1993). The following year, *WSIF* published Huggins et al.'s contribution as a 'letter to the editor' alongside a brief response from Nelson (1991), and a letter and article from Bell (1991a, b). In their accompanying editorial, which was highly sympathetic to Bell, they wrote that it was 'deplorable that speaking out about rape still means paying a price – even in feminist circles' (Klein 1991, pp. 505–506).

In a retrospective piece on the debate, Bell (1996, p. 247) claimed to be bemused by the furore: 'Speaking out, speaking of, speaking with, speaking about, speaking for... What did I say to bring the furies down on my feminist head? At the time, it was really very simple'. While Bell infers that, in the end, there was little at stake in the debate, I argue here that it demonstrated that distinctions between these forms of speech are in fact of crucial importance, and that this was implicitly recognised by all participants, including Bell. Following Sara Ahmed (2000, p. 51), I insist that there remains a lot more to be said about the 'relationship between white Australian feminism, the processes of racialisation through knowledge, and forms of racism' that the debate revealed. The 'emergent politic of voice and representation' and contestation of the 'historically established dominance of white settler women in Australian feminism' is of key significance for a feminist politics of sexual violence built on a faith in the political effects of speech and narrative (Yeatman 1993, p. 239). This chapter opens a series of analyses of the political and ethical complexity of relationships between feminists, survivors and their stories through a discussion of the political problems that arise when feminists claim to tell the story of other women, especially when they do so across racial divisions and lines of power.

My primary interest is in Bell's position as a figure of feminist authority and expertise. I begin with a discussion of Huggins et al.'s two major criticisms of the article: the question of co-authorship and its central claim that speaking about rape in Indigenous communities is 'everybody's business'. I use these questions to open up a discussion about the relationship between speaking for and speaking about or on behalf of marginal voices through an analysis of the claims made in the debate about Nelson and her speech, but also a discussion of the silent and unnamed Aboriginal women whose stories are told by Bell and who were often ignored within the debate itself (Moreton-Robinson 2000). The second section is concerned with what Bell (1991b, p. 513) at one point described as the 'special voice' of feminism within discussions of sexual violence. I trace Bell's movement between different forms of expertise: shared feminine experience, feminist political insight and scholarly authority. I argue that, as Huggins et al. suggest, Bell relies far more on the latter than she is willing to acknowledge. In the concluding section, I consider what is at stake in these debates about speech and discourse. As Huggins et al. assert, speech about sexual violence in Indigenous and other racially marginalised communities does have real effects, but so too, as Nelson insists in her contributions, does a refusal to speak. The former runs the real risk of entrenching racist beliefs and repressive governmental measures, while the latter fails to contest violence inflicted on women. In the quarter of a century following the Bell debate, sexual violence continues to be an endemic problem within Indigenous Australian communities, and the failure to develop a politics of speech and listening that can witness sexual violence against Indigenous women without reproducing 'white stereotypes' and colonial domination of Indigenous communities is on-going (Huggins et al. 1991, p. 507).

The backdrop to this story is one of long-term social and governmental neglect punctuated by precisely the kind of measures that Huggins et al. warn against. The *Emergency Northern Territory Response*, commonly referred to in Australia as 'the Intervention', was instigated by the conservative Howard Government in 2007 as a direct response to a report, '*Ampe Akelyernemane Meke Mekarle*: Little Children Are Sacred', produced for the Territory Government on sexual abuse in Indigenous communities (Anderson and Wild 2007). The response, which has been continued in adapted form by subsequent Australian governments, did not adopt the majority of recommendations from the report, but instead introduced a range of highly repressive governmental measures, from direct military policing and forced closure of Indigenous communities to income management and the control of sales of alcohol and pornography (Behrendt 2007). Bell's (1991b, p. 513) letter to the editors of *WSIF* concludes: 'who speaks of the anguish, shame and risk for Aboriginal women? The question is still floating out there'. I argue that Bell's question is indeed still floating out there. This chapter attempts to provide an elaboration of some of the reasons the question remains unanswerable within the political framework provided by Bell and the feminist politics she represents.

Speaking Out, Speaking with or Speaking For?

In her contribution to the debate, Jan Larbalestier (1990, p. 146) notes that 'for feminists of whatever variety, what was problematic was the shaping of the speech, rather than what was spoken'. From the original article onwards, the meaning of what was said was secondary to, and, indeed, largely determined by, the practice of speech, its framing and the position of the speaker. The claim to joint authorship made by Bell and Nelson (1989), for instance, enacts the shared responsibility for speaking about rape that is declared in the article's title and argued for in its content. The shaping of the speech within the article, however, complicates this enactment. Nelson's contributions, which I return to below, are limited to four short, italicised excerpts between one to three paragraphs long. Bell's writing, which constitutes almost the entire article, barely refers to Nelson's contributions, although she states that her aim is to 'create a space in which stories, like that told by Topsy, will reach a wider audience' (p. 404). In her introduction, she explains that it was not actually Nelson's stories that motivated her to write the article but 'two recent cases' that 'have convinced me that my continuing silence is complicity' (p. 404). As I discuss below, these two cases appear to bear no relationship to Nelson's speech and they are only 'like' the stories told by her in the sense that they are stories of violence and Aboriginal women. In this section, I explore the relationship between the speech of Bell and other participants in the debate and these multiple stories of violence and rural Indigenous women. While Nelson and the women involved in the 'two recent cases' occupy different positions within the debate, both illuminate significant problems in the shaping of feminist speech about and on behalf of victims of sexual violence.

The most directly contested elements in the debate were the title and co-authorship of the original article. For Huggins et al. (1991, p. 506), they act together to mask Bell's appropriation of Nelson's 'authentic' speaking position to authorise her own speech. They draw attention to the fact that Bell's speech is written in the first person singular, with little reference to Nelson's contributions. Nelson's passages on the other hand, they claim, have 'little relevance to the chapter' and 'nothing to do with rape'. Bell (1991b, p. 509) responded to this criticism by asserting that although Nelson's 'narrative contributions, which are italicised in our article, do not constitute 50% of the total wordage, her imprint is firmly on the ideas and structure of the piece'. To refer to her as an informant would therefore 'demean' her contribution (Bell 1990, p. 162). Further, she and her supporters accused Huggins et al., and those who supported them, of effectively denying Nelson's agency and, by extension, that of rural Indigenous women generally. As Robyn Rowland (1991–1992, p. 432) wrote in her contribution, 'I am appalled at the way Topsy Napurrula Nelson has been discussed as an object rather than a person and an active participant in the published article'. Sara Ahmed (2000, p. 55) notes, however, that the difference between naming someone a co-author or informant does not substantively alter the conditions under which knowledge is produced and authorised. In other words, to simply assert Nelson's 'authorship' 'rather misses the point'. The issue is 'not whether or not Nelson has a voice, but whether or not her voice can be heard *within* the article itself' and, I would add, within the subsequent debate.

While Huggins et al. are right that Nelson's contributions have little relationship to Bell's speech within the article, it is not true that they are irrelevant to the stated subject of speaking about rape, or to the topic of sexual violence. Her speech is spaced throughout the article, first appearing immediately following a set of 'facts' and 'questions' about Aboriginal women and sexual violence which open the chapter. She discusses the harms of rape, beginning with the special status of women's bodies: '*Woman's body is important because it's mother*'. She goes on to assert her concern about the loss of community traditions and its connection to violence and women's bodily autonomy: '*If that girl likes that man, all right, but he just can't force it, can't push himself. She be scared. She has to have feeling. No-one can take your body; that's her own thing*'. She concludes the passage with what Bell describes as her 'instructions' that it's '*important to show this story, not just for you and me, everyone got to know that one*' (Bell and Nelson 1989, p. 404). The second passage is four lines and forms part of a lengthy description by Bell of their relationship, titled 'Speaking To Each Other'. Where Bell describes their relationship as intimate, close and based on the solidarity of gender, Nelson's contribution seems to speak to the incommensurability of their experience. In the passage, she points out that Bell and other Indigenous people can leave, but '*in our land, people don't move*' and '*we've only got one history, here*' (p. 405). In the following section, 'Aboriginal Women's Perspectives', Bell gives an account of Aboriginal women's lack of understanding of feminism due to 'the influence of the socialist left on Aboriginal activists' (p. 410). This means that Aboriginal activists are unable to respond adequately to rape. Referencing her own anthropological work, Bell suggests that the 'most tragic' element of this situation is that contemporary feminist efforts to provide 'safe spaces to which women might retreat... have a traditional analogue in the *jilmi*', a women's area separated from the main camp. The practices and customs associated with this area are being lost and Nelson describes the impact of this. In the old days, she says, men '*never look straight at woman... that way you can't have trouble*'. Now, in contrast, children can watch women and men having sex, and a man '*might get woman before she gets ngapurlu [breasts]. They should wait for women's body but they don't and parents don't care*' (p. 411). Nelson's final passage is positioned as evidence for Bell's hope that a cross-racial alliance may form in opposition to a strip club in Tennant Creek. She quotes Nelson's contribution to a town meeting even though it doesn't actually oppose the club, which is a source of employment, but calls for the club to provide childcare to avoid the children simply going and watching the strip shows (p. 413).

The issue is not the 'relevance' of Nelson's speech, which maintains a closer focus on the theme of sexual violence than Bell's wide-ranging discussion of the problems of contemporary Aboriginal politics. The problem is, as Ahmed suggests, that the article is structured in a way that precludes her speech from registering or making meaning, despite Bell's insistence that Nelson's contribution is central. Bell's pattern of limited and selective engagement continues throughout the debate in ways that validate Huggins et al.'s criticisms. In her subsequent contributions, for instance, Bell frequently references her own writing in the original article but only makes a single reference to Nelson's contributions. In her article-length response to Huggins et al., she includes Nelson's quote about the strip club in a list of references to feminist authors such as Andrea Dworkin and Catharine MacKinnon, asserting that pornography has a direct causative relationship to rape (Bell 1991a). This is not, however, as I have already indicated, the argument made in Nelson's quote, which is literally 'ventriloquised' by Bell into a radical feminist perspective that there is no evidence that Nelson endorses or shares (Phipps 2016).

While Nelson does discuss sexual violence, it is true that she has nothing to say about the 'two recent cases' of rape that compelled Bell to write her article and break her silence about intra-racial rape in Aboriginal communities. Bell gives these far more space and attention within the article than she does Nelson's speech, even as her direct relationship with Nelson is not replicated in relation to the women whose stories she tells. Of these cases,

> one involves the prosecution of an Aboriginal male in a rape case where the defence relies on "customary considerations." The other, not yet reported, and most unlikely to ever come to court, involves the pack rape by Aboriginal youths of Aboriginal girls who were "surprised" in the act of house breaking. (Bell and Nelson 1989, p. 404)

Bell's sole source of information in the first case appears to be the transcript of a Supreme Court case, *R. v. Dennis Narjic*. The defendant was prosecuted for a rape committed in Port Keats, a town over 1000 kilometres from Tennant Creek where Bell and Nelson live. Narjic submitted a guilty plea and so the transcript is of a discussion around sentencing between the judge and the lawyers. Bell focuses her discussion on the defence's attempt to obtain a reduced sentence by claiming that, in Narjic's community, it is 'customary to beat women'. She approvingly cites the judge's question as to the women's perspective on this custom and his comment that 'no one ever asks them'. She writes:

> In most cases involving claims to customary law, a little intelligent anthropological research in the community can clarify that which is "tradition" and that which is local politics. I would put the statement that in Port Keats it is "customary to beat women" in the latter category. (p. 414)

Bell is echoing a criticism made by Sharon Payne (1990) that Aboriginal women are subject to 'white man's law, traditional law, and bullshit law', with the latter precisely the kind of attempt made here by white lawyers to excuse gendered violence on the grounds that it is 'customary'. These attempts have been strongly critiqued by Payne and other Indigenous women (e.g. Moreton-Robinson 2000, p. 170). What is notable, however, is despite her approval of the judge's comment about asking women and her reference to 'anthropological research', there is no evidence that either Bell or the judge have attempted to speak to women in the community. Instead, they rely on and reinforce the presumption that the law and anthropology already know what Aboriginal women would say, and that these disciplines are perfectly able to determine the truth of sexual violence without speaking to women in the community.

This presumption is also evident in the second case, even as Bell admits that 'what happened is not clear' (Bell and Nelson 1989, p. 411). According to Bell, a 'woman tenant' living temporarily in the Northern Territory while conducting research arrived home one day 'to find her place had been turned over, that food and clothes were missing but that her books were untouched' (p. 412). The tenant sought 'information from local Aboriginal women' who informed her that her flat had been broken into by a group of Indigenous girls, who were then 'surprised' by a group of male youths. The 'extent of the violence which then ensued is not fully known', although explanations range 'from simple theft explained by "if you work with blacks you invite theft," through dismissing the blood stains as menstrual, to a brutal pack rape'. 'If the latter is true', asks Bell, 'why has the assault not been reported?' She explains that 'one story' suggests the girls have been intimidated, while another suggests that in this town 'black women ... and even white women' 'are expected' to tolerate violence from black men, although there are no sources given for any of these explanations. Reading the narrative as Bell presents it, it is impossible to tell where the 'allegations' of a pack rape come from, and who, besides Bell, believes this is what happened. While Bell does not make this clear, her entire knowledge of the case appears to come from the woman tenant who is presumably, like Bell, a white anthropologist, although this is never made clear. The fact, however, that the tenant is racially unmarked while the locals are all described as 'black' or 'Aboriginal' is itself illuminating. This tenant seems to have acquired very little information from the 'local Aboriginal women'. When Bell says that the violence is not 'fully known', she is engaging in a politics of knowledge that locates herself and the tenant as 'knowers' who do 'not know' while dismissing the knowledge of the women themselves who obviously do know what happened but who do not count as 'knowers'. Like the woman or women who were victims in the legal case, there is no suggestion that they have a role to play in telling the story of the violence enacted against them.

These women whose stories are told at a distance by Bell function as an absent centre to the article, and to the debate around it. As Aileen Moreton-Robinson (2000) suggests, if Bell's primary aim in the article is, as she says, to tell these stories, it is almost impossible to escape the conclusion that Nelson functions as a substitute for them, and that Bell's relationship to her is used to authorise her telling their stories. This type of representational politics is famously described by Gayatri Spivak (1988) in her essay, 'Can the Subaltern Speak?' Spivak's essay is concerned with the possibility of dialogue between Third World women and those, such as 'western intellectuals', who seek to represent them. She argues that subalternity has no positive definition. Instead, it is marked by an inability to be 'heard or read' directly. The subaltern can only enter discourse through the representation of others and is only constituted within it as a figure of their representations. In other words, the subaltern is only present in narratives as a character in stories told by others. She has no capacity to tell her story or determine its meaning. Her figuration within the stories told by others, and particularly western intellectuals, works to enhance their authority through their ability to present and represent her as an object of their knowledge. Returning to the distinction drawn above, which I elaborate in the following section, she cannot be a knower but can only be known.

This pattern echoes that described by Lynn Higgins and Brenda Silver (1991, p. 1) in the history of Western representations of raped women. They argue that there is a simultaneous 'obsessive erasure' of the possibility of women speaking for themselves alongside an 'obsessive inscription' of their stories. These are used for a variety of symbolic purposes which have nothing to do with the desires or subjectivity of the raped women themselves. Instead, the raped woman becomes evidence of the 'real', a figure used to declare the speaker's position because she speaks for the 'reality' of women's suffering and on behalf of marginal women who 'really' suffer but who cannot speak (Hesford and Kozol 2001). Rather than subjects who are able to demand or receive recognition, the Third World woman and the raped woman merge in these discourses into a 'spectacle of distant suffering', used to mobilise and authorise positions in debates among Western feminists that they are excluded from participation in (Hesford 2004). In Bell's article and in the debate generally, the figure of the raped

Indigenous woman is made generic and instrumental, her individual voice, experience and agency replaced by her function as a representative figure of violability.

While Nelson does speak, her speech is largely over-written by her symbolic function of evidencing the need for stories 'like those told by Topsy' and authorise Bell's right to tell them. As Aileen Moreton-Robinson (2000) argues, if we listen to Nelson's speech rather than Bell's representation of it, she does not in fact provide Bell with the authorisation that Bell claims for herself. In her letter in response to Huggins et al.'s criticism, Nelson (1991, p. 507) affirms her long-standing and close relationship to Bell, as well as her lack of other options for communicating her story: 'I had no Aborigine to write this. Diane is like a sister; best friend. She wrote this all down for me. That's OK – women to women; it doesn't matter black or white'. Moreton-Robinson (2000) points out that within the clear protocols of storytelling and custodianship of stories that exist in Australian Aboriginal communities, the authorisation provided by Nelson is strictly curtailed: 'I want these things written down, for people to hand down and read again later. I was telling Diane to write this story for me' (Nelson 1991, p. 507). Nelson makes clear that she remains the custodian of the stories and how they should be told. She has not entrusted Bell with ownership of her stories and she does not claim the right to tell other women's stories. In fact, she never refers to these other stories which have occurred far from where she lives and, presumably, involve people she does not know. Nelson's letter specifies what is inferred in the narrative distance between Bell and the other stories that she tells. Nelson is Bell's only Indigenous informant or collaborator, and their relationship, however genuine, does not give Bell significant access to additional members of the community or the right to tell their stories. Nor does it grant Bell the authority to rewrite Nelson's *specific* authorisation as a *general* authorisation to tell the definitive story of sexual violence in Aboriginal Australia or the stories of other individual Aboriginal women. In this way, she erases the women at the centre of her stories and performs a ventriloqual appropriation of Nelson's voice. The two acts rely on and allow each other.

Bell constructs Nelson as an 'average Third World woman', a figure that Chandra Mohanty (1997, p. 258) claims simultaneously produces actual

Third World women as an interchangeable mass of suffering victims and represents the Western feminist as their heroic, enlightened and liberated champion. Through this logic, Nelson's individual identity and the specific and local stories she tells are over-written so that she becomes a cipher able to substitute for other Indigenous women, and to be represented differently depending on her position in the argument at the time (Moreton-Robinson 2000). In the original article, Bell (1990, p. 162) introduces Nelson through a 'distillation' of Nelson's self-description at a conference. She describes her as a leading figure in her community with responsibility 'for the maintenance of the mythology, songs, paintings, dances and ceremonies which commemorate these places', and an intermediary between her community and the wider world (Bell and Nelson 1989, p. 405). A year later, in defence of her position as Nelson's interlocutor, Bell (1990, p. 163) suggests that it is 'extremely problematic' to infer that Nelson would have any avenue for voicing her views beyond her community without Bell's assistance and amplification. Responding directly to Huggins et al.'s criticism of the power imbalance between the two women in 1991, Bell (1991b, p. 510) returns to and even extends her original characterisation:

> Napurrula has authority in her community, continuity with her land, extensive ceremonial knowledge, and standing in the wider community. Topsy Napurrula Nelson is one of the few women members of the Central Land Council and is often cited in Aboriginal publications… She has given critical expert evidence in land claim hearings and now speaks at international conferences.

On this basis, she asserts that Huggins et al.'s representation of Nelson is 'deeply offensive and smacking of exactly the racism that many protagonists in this dispute would root out and expose' (p. 510). In this context as well, Nelson's 'traditional authority' is contrasted by Bell to the position of the 'urban' women with whom she is in debate, who not only lack that authority but, unlike Bell, allegedly view it through the prism of racist stereotypes. I return to this point below.

The debate is in fact characterised by reciprocal allegations of racism in representations of Nelson exchanged between participants but not with

Nelson herself. It is this that makes Nelson, like the unnamed raped Indigenous women who provide the absent centre to the debate, a subaltern figure. Spivak is clear that subaltern status is not directly ascribed by racial identity, racial authenticity or racialised suffering, and so the position of Nelson, the unnamed women and Huggins et al. are all distinct, despite a shared experience of racial suffering and oppression. Subalternity is not an identity but a function of relations of power within a given discursive or political setting. So, it is possible for Nelson to, at different points, speak at international conferences, and be reduced to subaltern status within a debate about Indigenous women and sexual violence that occurs primarily within and through the medium of academic publications. The raped women in this debate are subaltern as they exist only as evidence for the truth Bell wishes to tell, and Nelson can be read as subaltern to the extent that her contributions do not figure in terms of meaning making or interpretation. As Spivak (1988, p. 288) argues, the 'subject of exploitation cannot know and speak the text of female exploitation'. The woman and her experience become the text of exploitation while the text is spoken and interpreted by the feminist interlocutor, and this relation is the subject of the following section.

Accounting for the 'Special Voice' of Feminists

Sara Ahmed (2000, p. 57) suggests that the significance of the Bell debate is best understood by moving beyond the question of 'who speaks'. To draw attention to 'the institutional conditions in which speech acts are made or not made', we need to also ask, 'who knows'. In this section, I argue that this question should be accompanied by an interrogation of the kinds of knowledge that are produced and the ways of knowing that are activated and exercised (Naples 2003). The Bell debate can be rethought through these questions. As discussed above, Nelson sees herself as a knower with authority over her story and the stories of her local community. She sees Bell as assisting her in communicating that knowledge. Huggins et al. (1991, p. 506) observe that Bell, 'like so many anthropologists', uses her relationship with Nelson to become an expert, 'documenting and transposing an alien culture into western patriarchal and feminist interpretations'. Bell's self-description is much more ambiguous and changeable. It speaks to the complexity of the position of feminist interlocutor of other women's experience. In perhaps her clearest summary, she directly refutes both Nelson and Huggins et al.'s characterisations of her role: 'I did not speak *for*, nor did I merely *report*'. Rather, she says, 'my task was to locate issues of gender and race within a wider perspective, one outside the experience of any individual' (Bell and Nelson 1989, p. 451, emphasis in original). Bell's self-appointed task, and the way in which she undertook it, is the focus of this section.

For Bell (1991b, p. 513), the key to her role in relation to sexual violence is what she describes as the 'special voice' of feminists. This voice enabled her to 'provide an analysis of social change' and 'formulate a critique for the wider society' which Nelson's narrower perspective, framed within individual experience, was unequipped to do (Bell and Nelson 1989, p. 451). She explained the special voice of feminism in the following way:

> [I]t was after all the feminist strategy of according women's experiences and narratives a centrality in social analysis that brought into the open the high level of rape, sexual abuse and incest in our society; that named the phenomenon of marital rape; that offered a critique of the blaming of the victim; and that argued for services for abused women. (Bell 1991b, p. 513)

The quote articulates a tension which I raised in the Introduction in relation to Susan Brownmiller's rewriting of the experiences of her consciousness-raising group. Women's narratives might be central to and necessary for feminist speech, but it is feminists who have made these stories political, through strategically leveraging them analytically and politically and, crucially, constructing themselves as experts at the same time.

In contrast to my approach here, considerations of feminist ways of knowing have generally focused on the ontological priority given to raped women's 'experience', and its adequacy as a source of 'truth'. Consequently, feminist 'experts' often remain, in the words of Joan W. Scott (1992, p. 32), removed 'from critical scrutiny as active producers of knowledge'. One feature of this lack of scrutiny is that the distinction between the positions of female experience and feminist expertise is collapsed, as in the famous formulation of the radical feminist legal theorist, Catharine MacKinnon (1989, p. 83) that feminism is the 'first theory to emerge from those whose interests it affirms'. In this construction, the 'special voice' of feminism is a kind of distilled or particularly insightful version of a more general female experience. It is, one might say, the 'raised consciousness' of female experience. Drawing on this characterisation, Bell (1991a, p. 386) asserts that:

> [W]riting as a woman carries certain baggage for when I speak of an issue as visceral as rape, I do not do so in the abstract; it has real substance for me as a woman, not for me as a gender-neutral person, or me as white woman, or me as an academic. It is me as a woman who is vulnerable, and while the qualifiers may assist me in reducing the risk I run of becoming a statistic, women are raped because they are women. Rape is indigenous to women, not just to the experience of indigenous women.

Key to this process is the same logic that I discussed in Chap. 2, where the epistemological primacy of gender is validated by the 'visceral' universality of rape, where race is no more essential to one's identity than professional status. The 'special voice' of feminism, understood as distilled gender experience allows Bell to make authoritative statements about rape and to dismiss Huggins et al.'s (1991, p. 506) claim that within Australia, 'white women have always been a part' of colonialism, undermining appeals to a shared identity based solely on gender.

An important element of the radicality of the feminist project was to insist on women's status as knowledge producers and on their ability to construct knowledge from experience. This project challenged ways of knowing and what counted as bases of knowledge. As Bell (1991b, p. 509) understands it, the original article needed to be 'experimental' because it needs to find 'ways of presenting in a written text for a scholarly journal, the oral narratives of Topsy Napurrula and an explicitly feminist analysis'. Within this framing, the scholarly text is built from the experiential knowledge of Nelson through Bell's feminist analysis. But, as this quote shows, rather than usurping traditional bases of authority, this 'experiment' produces feminist knowledge within and using the tools of traditional expertise and scholarship. In other words, Bell uses experience to produce feminist analysis but incorporates both experiential and feminist knowledge within the norms and structures of scholarly knowledge production. What she sees as experimental, Huggins et al. view as simply reproducing the power relations of the academy.

This debate is about what kind of knowledge was being produced and how it sits at the centre of the conflict between Bell and Huggins et al. At one level, the question is whether Bell and Nelson are co-producing political feminist knowledge through their joining of experience and analysis, or if Bell is producing academic knowledge with Nelson and the other Indigenous women as her objects of study. Unpacking this conflict is complicated by Bell's own movement between the three types of knowledge that she identifies above. In the same article in which she claims to be writing 'as a woman', she goes on to state that she 'speaks as an anthropologist', and, of course, she also refers repeatedly to the 'special voice' of feminism (Bell 1991a, p. 386). However, each of these positions entails different relations to Nelson and different processes and outcomes of knowledge production. The anthropologist relates to their informant across and through the hierarchies of education and professional status, and their authority to speak and to write rests on and reproduces the authority of the Western academy and sciences. Women relate to each other as 'sisters' with a common experience of femininity and violence, while a feminist augments this experience and converts it into social analysis and political knowledge. The apparent disparity between these identities and their bases of authority make the ease with which Bell shifts between them striking. This suggests that the 'special voice' of feminists relies on and mobilises the authority of shared experience and of academic expertise. It works to construct Bell as proficient in academic and feminist knowledge production, able to know Nelson and her experience, while Nelson is only able to narrate her story as 'raw experience' but must rely on Bell to give it an interpretation and meaning (Alcoff and Gray 1993).

As I noted in Chap. 3, even those who are most proficient in moving between discourses must occupy a specific discursive position in order to speak at any particular moment. They must partake in a certain genre and make use of a socially significant language to orient and authorise their speech (Bakhtin 1981). As Anna Yeatman (1993) argues, Bell's choice to 'speak out' in an academic journal, albeit a feminist one, was a choice to prioritise academic discourse and to base her claim to speak on her professional authority as a Western social scientist. In this context, regardless of the authority she has been given by Nelson to tell her stories, Bell is speaking in a context in which her version and interpretation of these stories cannot be contested and in which she and Nelson do not and cannot speak as equals. Or, as Huggins et al. (1991, p. 506) insist, neither Bell's status as a woman nor her identification as a feminist changes the fact that her relationship with Nelson was structured through anthropological fieldwork, and that this was the frame through which she interacted with Nelson and chose to represent their interaction. Perhaps even more tellingly, the more scrutiny was applied to Bell, the more her self-presentation involved 'the familiar claim of modern Western professional-scientific authority to speak about and on behalf of others without their voices being present to arbitrate, complicate and even contest this claim' (Yeatman 1993, p. 240). An example of this is her direct response to Huggins et al.'s criticism of the claim that 'speaking about rape is everyone's business'. She writes that the title, 'which Huggins et al find so offensive, draws on a Central Australian idiomatic formulation' and proceeds to provide several examples in the genre of traditional anthropological scholarship:

Question: "Who speaks for that one [person or thing]?"
Answer: "I'm [or a specified individual/group] boss for that." (Bell 1991b, p. 509)

Writing for a sympathetic feminist audience five years later in the anthology, *Radically Speaking*, which she co-edited with *WSIF* editor, Renate Klein, Bell gave a very different account, explaining that the title not only 'evoked Aboriginal notions of gendered etiquette on sensitive matters' but was also a 'defiant feminist statement about power and that silence about rape protects abusers of power' (Bell 1996, pp. 248–249).

Aileen Moreton-Robinson (2000) points out that both Bell's speech and her access to Nelson's knowledge and stories were dependent upon her institutional status as an academic. Nelson (1991, p. 507) states in her letter that she needed Bell to write her stories because she had nobody else: 'A lot of Aboriginal girls I asked to write down our stories; young people they didn't listen to us'. Moreton-Robinson (2000, p. 120) notes that although 'Nelson positions the Indigenous women as not interested, it has to be acknowledged that Bell is in the privileged position of having the resources, time, skills and knowledge to be able to undertake the task'. There could be, she continues, 'a number of reasons' why other Indigenous women did not 'participate in what could be perceived as a difficult exercise'. Limited education makes this a far more demanding task, while poverty may mean that young Indigenous women simply have other priorities. Bell, on the other hand, not only has a greater ability to undertake this task, but, as an anthropologist working in remote Indigenous communities, writing down and reproducing Indigenous women's stories is at the centre of Bell's work and necessary for her professional success. The act of transcribing someone's stories is undoubtedly far less burdensome for a highly educated academic who has received research funding to do precisely that.

None of this is to say that relationships between feminist academics and women whose stories they tell are necessarily exploitative or that academic work and feminist activism are mutually incompatible. But, it is to say that academic or institutional authority can be used to assert feminist authority, and that such claims should be open to scrutiny, particularly in cases where these relationships involve other vectors or dimensions of power, such as race and colonialism. As Yúdice (1991) argues, even in cases where a politically sympathetic collaborator works with a subaltern witness, they maintain their position of power as to how political concerns are understood, even if they come out of shared understandings and priorities. While it is undeniably true that both Nelson and Bell are concerned with problems of sexual violence in Indigenous communities, Bell's framing of them enacts a form of power to insist on her own interpretation over Nelson's, and even to render Nelson's opinions unknown and unknowable. More fundamentally, in the attempt to turn the subjective experiences of subaltern subjects into objective truth, there is a division between the person who knows and the known (Spivak 1988).

Bell reconstructs this division in relation to Huggins et al., whom she dismisses as 'well-educated urban Aboriginal women' (Bell 1996, p. 80).

This formulation is present even in Bell's original article, before Huggins et al.'s intervention, reflecting Bell's history of conflict with Indigenous women. As I noted above, Bell devotes a section of this article to those she dubs 'hostile urban Aboriginal and radical black women' (Bell and Nelson 1989, pp. 404–405). She describes them as unwilling or unable to face the problem of sexual violence in Aboriginal communities and portrays them as overly 'influenced' by the socialist left. More specifically, she calls her own relationship with them 'tense', and pronounces them unwilling to learn from the example that she and Nelson have to offer of the benefits of 'white women writing about black women' (p. 404). That these portrayals are, again, connected to her academic authority is made clear in her direct response to Huggins et al., who, she claims, are 'conflicted regarding the basis and authority from which they speak'. They cannot speak to remote Indigenous experience as she, as an anthropologist knows that there is a 'profound difference' between their experiences and those of Nelson. At the same time, they cannot contest Bell's academic authority, as none 'of the letter writers makes mention of any specific field work in the area, nor do they appear to think that such experience may be a relevant consideration'. She goes on to make the undoubtedly correct assertion that Aboriginal identity is 'a *political* identity' that 'does not entail sameness of situation or experience' without acknowledging that Huggins et al. have made a similar point about gender in a settler colonial society (Bell 1991b, p. 510, emphasis in original). Neither does she acknowledge that Huggins et al. (1991, p. 506) have not made a claim on the basis to sameness of experience, but on the fact that speech about Indigenous communities has 'individual, communal and societal consequences' for Indigenous people in general, due to the logics and practices of colonial power. Instead, she uses the authority she claims as a feminist and a social scientist to disallow their speech. While Bell's feminism allows her to mobilise multiple bases of authority, she casts their (insufficient) indigeneity as preventing them from accessing authentic experience, legitimate scientific knowledge or the 'special voice' of feminism.

Bell's response refuses the direct ethical demand made by Huggins et al. (1991, p. 507), a demand that is based on their particular position and location as 'urban' Indigenous women: 'You must listen to us also for we are Aboriginals who have felt the effects of colonisation far worse than our traditional sisters and brothers'. Anna Yeatman (1993, pp. 238–241) sees Huggins et al. as claiming the ethical and political position of 'minority intellectuals' who, unlike Nelson, have the discursive and institutional authority to contest Bell's arguments. For Yeatman, what is at stake ultimately for feminists is the ability of middle-class white academics such as Bell and herself to present themselves as the legitimate 'custodians of feminism'. This identity has allowed feminist academics and other feminist professionals to represent themselves as emancipatory voices in relation to mainstream politics while simultaneously drawing upon the governmental legitimacy of the 'universal civilizing mission of the middle class' to speak on behalf of all women. The point of Huggins et al.'s letter is to offer an ethical challenge to this self-representation. Sara Ahmed (2000, p. 64) suggests that such a challenge might be accepted as 'gift' by white feminist custodians such as Bell. It is a gift that would enable mainstream feminism to develop beyond the logic of white custodianship if white feminists were able to 'give those voices that refuse to be assimilated into its community of knowers a more just hearing'. Bell's response is the direct opposite of this. In addition to denying Huggins et al.'s authority to speak, she infers that those feminist custodians who do seek to give them a just hearing devalue themselves and feminism, writing scathingly of the 'unseemly scramble on behalf of certain academic women to position themselves as sympathetic to the position of Huggins et al' (Bell 1991b, p. 507).

For Bell to have given Huggins et al. a more just hearing would have required responding to their substantive objections and allowing that their points about the centrality of race and colonialism in understanding sexual violence might have merit. Bell's position on race can only be understood within the context of her understanding of the 'special voice' of feminism. It is premised on race being, at most, a qualifier to gender, rather than a substantial category of identity and difference. Bell acknowledges the importance of avoiding and countering overt racial stereotypes. However, the suggestion that race might have a more substantive place in feminist analysis is dismissed by her as a symptom of an 'anti-woman, male-affirming, race-prioritising syndrome' (Bell 1991a, p. 390). Ultimately, this leads her to enact a strange distinction between different types of sexual violence. As she notes, it is not quite true that 'radical black women' have not spoken of sexual violence: 'Aboriginal women have been telling us (other women, feminists, Australians) for some time that rape is part of the socio-political landscape, but it has been interracial not intraracial rape of which they spoke' (Bell 1991a, p. 386). Rather than valuing this speech, Bell seems to consider it, with its clear racial politics, to be something other and lesser than speaking out. It has, she writes, 'been acceptable to write of the rape of Aboriginal women by white men, in fact for some it was obligatory' (Bell and Nelson 1989, p. 408). Inter-racial rape is thus constructed as outside the realm of speaking out because it has been sufficiently spoken of, and because it can reinforce the 'race-prioritising syndrome' that Bell is seeking to counter. Anti-racist feminists and women of colour have consistently demonstrated the role that sexual violence, committed with impunity by white men against women of colour, has played in the politics of racism and colonialism (e.g. Davis 1983; Behrendt 1993; Razack 1994; McGuire 2010). For Bell, speech and knowledge around rape must be universal and cross-cultural to be meaningful (Larbalestier 1990). In the same way that the hashtag politics discussed in the previous chapter operated, speech that highlights the intersectional politics of rape is cast as divisive or distracting. This is a position that has been critiqued by many other feminist anthropologists and cultural theorists who insist that paying attention to the cultural differences between and among women's experience of rape is essential for understanding it, and for building a feminist politics against it (e.g. Sanday 1981; Ang 1995; Helliwell 2000).

As Chandra Mohanty (1992, p. 75) has written in another context, Bell's argument is 'based on the assumption that the categories of race and class have to be invisible for gender to be visible'. For Bell's version of feminist expertise to be valid, rape must be a universally shared experience, and, thus, fundamentally knowable to feminist experts such as Bell regardless of the cultural context within which it occurs, or the barriers of race, class or culture between her and the women whose experience she incorporates into her understanding. For Bell, 'cultural specificity' is only activated meaningfully as a marker of increased oppression and, therefore, increased need for Bell's self-assumed mantle of feminist advocate and protector. Nelson, and, through her Indigenous women generally, become symbols of the suffering and violence which unite all women as women. The idea of women, particularly women defined as absolutely victimised, dealing with rape without feminist interlocution is one that Bell cannot incorporate into her own narrative of sexual violence, a narrative that insists on the need for her, or somebody else, to use the 'special voice' of feminism to tell and interpret it.

Discoursing About Discourse?

This Australian debate about the relationship between feminism, Indigenous women and stories of sexual violence speaks to a set of underlying questions about the rights and responsibility of feminists to speak about sexual violence, and the complex relationships between feminists, survivors of sexual violence, and their stories. In my articulation of what was at stake in the debate, I would undoubtedly, like Bell's critics, face allegations from Bell and her supporters of avoiding the reality of sexual violence in Indigenous communities. As Bell (1990, p. 159) put it in her response to Jan Larbalestier's article in *Anthropological Forum*, 'Napurrula and I were trying to tell you (the reader) that Aboriginal girls and women were being raped'. She described Larbalestier and other critics as being more interested in 'discoursing about discourse' than the reality of sexual violence among Indigenous women. As this book is very much a project of 'discoursing about discourse', I finish with a consideration of this accusation. I reject the idea that the shaping of speech and the production of knowledge are a distraction from real issues and dispute Bell's contention that she, in contrast to her critics, was purely concerned with reality. As Larbalestier (1990, p. 146) argued, Bell's contributions to the debate were less focused on intra-racial rape than 'on the appropriateness of the theory and practice of "radical feminism" for Aboriginal women's struggles and the ability and moral responsibility of one White woman to discuss such issues'.

The *WSIF* editors similarly accused Bell's critics of focusing on discourse and refusing to face the reality of gendered violence in Indigenous communities:

> It is much easier to feel comfortable in the abstract language of "discourse", "subjectivities" and "positions" than to try to sort out the complex of issues

that cultural destruction, colonialism and patriarchal violence bring us when a young Aboriginal boy sees "rapist" as a career path and young Aboriginal girls are violated regularly. It hurts to hear about the real pain, the real violence, the real powerlessness of women relative to men. It is much easier for women, Black and White, to attack a White anthropologist and White academics than to grapple with the painful truth of violence towards women. (Rowland 1991–1992, p. 434)

As Sharon Marcus (1992, p. 385) contends, while 'rape and the raped woman's body' are frequently drawn on by feminists as 'symbols of the real', feminist 'emphasis on *recounting* rape suggests that in their view actions and experiences cannot be said to exist in politically real and useful ways until they are perceptible and representable' (p. 387, emphasis in original). As Larbalestier suggests, Bell's contributions reveal a deep belief in the very real effects of recounting rape. This is after all the foundational argument of the original article and its title, 'Speaking about Rape is Everyone's Business'.

This leaves Bell and her supporters in the apparently paradoxical position of arguing that speech is crucial to fighting rape, but that to analyse or discuss this speech is a distraction. The paradox is resolved by casting 'speaking out' as something quite different to ordinary speech. Speaking out is seen as inherently radical, and criticism as simply affirming that radicality. When Bell (1990, 164) concludes that she has 'indeed transgressed and said the unsayable', she is operating under a presumption that the unsayable is precisely what needs to be said. This further contextualises her dismissal of speech about inter-racial rape as 'acceptable' and even 'obligatory' and, thus, unable to partake in the practice of speaking out. To speak out about violence is to refuse to accept the denial and obfuscation of those who would silence women's experience and deny the reality of rape. Writing of speech about sex, Foucault calls this logic the 'speaker's benefit'. If rape is 'condemned to prohibition, nonexistence, and silence, then the mere fact that one is speaking about it has the appearance of a deliberate transgression. A person who holds forth in such language places himself to a certain extent outside the reach of power; he upsets established law; he somehow anticipates the coming freedom' (Foucault 1998, p. 6). This is a form of speech that is uniquely performative and uniquely political. In contrast, the speech of Huggins et al., Larbalestier and other critics is not simply a distraction but part of the cultural processes of silencing that feminists must confront. In a sense, then, even as Bell and the editors of *WSIF* rail against their critics, the existence of those who seek to stop them from speaking only proves the urgency of their project.

The only appropriate response to attacks such as those on Bell, therefore, is found in the conclusion to Renate Klein's (1991, p. 506) editorial which precedes Huggins et al.'s letter:

> We are deeply distressed about these happenings but more than ever determined to continue publishing radical analyses of the grim realities women continue to face globally. We urge our readers to send us papers on violence against women: we must continue to speak out in order to devise strategies to stop the abuse of women.

As speaking out blends into speaking about, speaking out and exhorting others to speak out, the boundaries between reality, representation and discoursing about discourse become more difficult to maintain. Klein's editorial is far more focused on 'papers on violence against women' than it is on the 'grim realities women continue to face globally'. It displaces the story of suffering and heroic speech about rape from the survivor who tells her own story to the feminist speaker who speaks, and resists, on her behalf, and who is silenced and attacked for doing so. As Robyn Rowland (1991–1992, p. 430) writes in *Anthropological Forum*: 'I have heard since this debate that a number of White feminist anthropologists are now loathe to write about violence against Aboriginal women for fear of being publicly abused. The power involved in that silencing process has yet to be discussed'. Experiences of resistance and victimisation are transferred from those who experience violence to the courageous but repressed feminist activist. As I noted above, there is a mirroring between the relationship of feminist speakers to raped women and white feminists to Aboriginal women as the position of heroic speaker and silent victim are increasingly reified. Bell and Klein's anthology, *Radically Speaking*, undertakes a similar transferral in relation to Bell's story. Her chapter, 'Speaking of Things That Shouldn't Be Written: Cross-cultural Excursions into the Land of Misrepresentations', not only tells the story of her heroic efforts to speak on behalf of Indigenous women, but does so within a section of the anthology titled 'Radical Feminists Under Attack' (Bell 1996).

As Alison Phipps (2016) has argued, this usurpation relies on a mobilisation of the politics of experience so that the experiences of those with the most access to avenues to articulate them are prioritised over the experiences of those without such access. This entrenches relations of power within feminism, particularly along racial lines, as the quote by Rowland suggests. Bell is even more explicit in her racial logic, writing ominously about 'white listing' and the playing of the 'race card'. This reifies the racialised logic of speech and knowledge production discussed in the previous section, erasing the possibility that Aboriginal women might either be agents of speech or heroic resisters acting on their own behalf. It also equates speaking about race with 'discoursing about discourse' and the silencing functions of power. Just as inter-racial rape does not deserve or need to be spoken about, the racial critiques raised by Huggins et al. simply silence the white women who wish to courageously speak about rape. Aboriginal women are therefore imagined as acting on the side of power, and the silencing of narratives by white women is equated as silencing any speech about rape. This ignores the possibility implicit in Huggins et al.'s letter, that Indigenous women could speak about and tell stories of rape on their own terms. As the letter makes clear, Huggins et al. (1991) do not object to speech about rape but rather to telling Indigenous stories of suffering from a 'privileged white, middle-class perspective'.

Huggins et al. share with Bell a conviction that speech about rape can produce real consequences, but it is the unintended racist and colonial consequences of this speech that concern them. They refer to 'stereotypes' and 'racists in the community' but are, of course, unable to envisage the connections that will be made in 2007 between speech about sexual violence and the enactment of a spectacular intervention in Indigenous communities in 2007, mentioned above. Responses to 'the Intervention' have been mixed in Indigenous communities, but there is little doubt that it was, in Larissa Behrendt's (1993) words, 'the Intervention that we had to have'. In other words, there was no way of responding to the existence of sexual violence in Aboriginal communities outside of and beyond the discourses, institutions and governmental operations of colonial power. My intention is not to draw a direct line between the Bell debate and the Intervention, but rather to contend that for feminists to insist on only viewing rape through a gendered lens is to dangerously ignore other axes of power, a point that has been made in previous chapters. For white feminists who speak about sexual violence within racially marginalised communities such as Aboriginal Australia to see race as only ever detracting from the gendered politics of violence opens feminist discourse to racist narratives that locate the source of violence in Indigenous 'culture' rather than gender relations and the solution to these problems as more invasive practices of colonialism.

Placing these arguments more firmly within the concerns of this chapter, the Bell debate demonstrates the importance of 'discoursing about discourse' or interrogating the processes of feminist knowledge production and the discursive bases of authority that are used to authorise that knowledge production. As I demonstrate in the following chapter, the role of feminist audience is a powerful one in relation to women who speak about rape, and the operations of that power can have damaging consequences. To say this is not to denounce or reject speaking out. Rather, it is to insist that it is a political practice, and that politics involves multiple vectors of power. In certain situations and relationships, feminists have significant power. This entails a responsibility to consider the political implications and effects of speech and the role that feminists play in producing, shaping and hearing stories of sexual violence.

7

Turning Rape into Fiction? Judgement, Genre and the Politics of Belief

Feminists have fought for women's right to be recognised as truth-tellers when it comes to rape. This struggle has complemented the project of bringing rape, and speech about rape, into the discursive orbit of feminism. Beginning with the speak-outs and consciousness-raising groups of the 1970s, the goal of producing a new genre was to create a space where women's stories were met with belief rather than suspicion and where the truth of their experience would be accepted, supported and amplified. When women told their stories in consciousness-raising groups or speak-outs, or later, in sympathetic media forums, they did not find themselves cast automatically as liars. Instead, they were given the generic tools and structures to tell a story that would compel belief based on a new understanding of the 'reality' of rape that opposed legal myths and reflected the commonalities of women's experiences.

In this chapter, I expand upon the argument that genre is simultaneously an enabling and constraining force to show that while feminists have expanded the conditions under which women's stories can be and are believed, the construction of a new genre has also instigated new modes of judging and disbelieving certain stories told in certain ways. Constructing spaces and audiences for speaking out about sexual violence has not erased processes of judging the truth of women's narratives but shifted the basis on which those judgements take place. This changes the experience of telling stories of rape, but still leaves the women in these stories in a vulnerable position, including and perhaps most of all, to their feminist audience. Where the previous chapter discussed the power dynamics of speaking on behalf of survivors, this chapter is concerned with the power of judgement and of granting or withholding belief. The construction of a genre involves the construction of generic expectations and conventions. These conventions and expectations shape ideas of believability and credibility in diverse ways. As I show, some narratives are cast outside of the genre of speaking out because of their failure to conform to readers' expectations, while others may be rendered suspect for conforming too closely to generic conventions, and thus appearing to be 'fictions' constructed through genre rather than authentic reflections of experience. In this chapter, I explore how the functions of these two types of disbelief operate as a limit on the ways in which women's stories may be told and on the ability of speaking out to compel belief.

Legal and feminist genres operate according to different truth criteria, or standards of 'believability'. In other words, they prioritise Bernard Williams' (2002) two main virtues of truth-telling differently. Williams shows that to be considered 'true' a story must meet the criteria of both veracity, or fidelity to external reality, and sincerity, a narrator's belief in what she is saying, although these may have different levels of importance within different genres of speech. Where the law holds women's sincerity to be suspect unless the veracity of their narratives can be externally verified, feminists have insisted that women's sincerity can and should compel belief in the veracity of their narratives. While there is no question that these new feminist truth criteria have expanded the conditions under which women's narratives are believed, sincerity is still a criterion for judgement, and one that can easily produce disbelief. As Andrew Taslitz (1999, p. 7) remarks in relation to rape, even feminists 'find that absent corroboration and given any hint of the "abnormal", they just do not believe the victim'. Verifiability, or legal truth criteria, can and do co-exist with feminist criteria, just as, as I argued in Chap. 2, criminal justice framings of rape as a crime can co-exist with feminist understandings of rape as gendered violence.

As I discuss in the first section, judgements of sincerity rely on generic conventions and audience expectations of the story and its teller. Narrators who do not fulfil audience expectations, and who are themselves considered suspect, are likely to find themselves met with suspicion and disbelief even by feminist audiences, and with demands to produce evidence to verify their narratives. These demands may, ultimately, end up not looking that different from the processes of judgement discussed in Chaps. 4 and 5. I explore the workings of feminist judgements through the disbelief that met the controversial radical feminist Andrea Dworkin (2000) when she told her story of being 'drug-raped' in a Paris hotel room in 1999. The narrative was widely disbelieved by feminists, including those who wished to support Dworkin. The combination of the mode of telling and the public status of Dworkin herself produced a narrative that was, at best, able to compel some belief in her sincerity but which entirely failed to compel belief in its veracity.

Generic judgements around credibility are, especially within feminism, linked to demands for authenticity. As Joan W. Scott (1992) has famously shown, experience is privileged in feminist discourse because it is seen to have a transparent relationship to 'what really happened', untainted by patriarchal ideology or masculinist discourse. Paradoxically, feminist practices such as consciousness-raising and speaking out demonstrate the profoundly ideological and discursive nature of experience. To understand feminism as producing new genres of speech is to see it as producing new narrative conventions which make new understandings, literally changing, in some cases, an experience from one of 'normal' sex to one of sexual violence. At the same time, feminists continue to argue that women's stories should be believed because they are authentic representations of experience. In the second section, I consider the allegation, made by the English literature graduate student and critic of 'rape-crisis' feminism, Katie Roiphe (1991), in the early 1990s that in their efforts to create a new genre of survivor speech, feminists were 'turning rape into fiction'. Rather than producing new avenues for women to speak the authentic truth of experience, claimed Roiphe, feminists were producing a new set of stock plots, drawn from sexist and Victorian archetypes of women as virginal victims, unable to cope with the dangers of sex. I suggest that Roiphe uses the very generic conventions that enabled women's speech to render women's narratives suspect and incapable of meeting her criteria of authenticity. The critique she offers of feminist politics relies on mobilising a generic standard of authenticity to doubt the stories produced by women about date and acquaintance rape particularly.

While Roiphe's critiques are often dismissed as simply anti-feminist backlash, she is not alone in accusing women's narratives of violence of being overly generic. The third section of the chapter discusses a more contemporary version of this critique, made by the feminist author and film critic, Laura Kipnis (2017), in her book, *Unwanted Advances*. Kipnis argues that campus feminism has been 'hijacked by melodrama', asserting, like Roiphe, that as a genre, it has become a producer of stock plots and fictions rather than an enabler of political truth. While Roiphe's critique remains at the level of the genre, Kipnis enacts a public doubting of the veracity, credibility and sincerity of specific narratives and, by extension, the genre that enables them. While Dworkin's doubters assert that she does not belong in a feminist genre of experiential narratives of violence, Kipnis uses some of the same criteria to critique the entire genre. In the concluding section, I ask what these processes of generic judgement reveal about the overall limitations of the politics of speaking out.

These examples are united by the process of generic judgement and the relationship between truth or reality and lies or fiction. This allegation is made most clearly by Katie Roiphe (1991), who wrote in the *New York Times* that while 'real women get battered, while real mothers need day care, certain feminists are busy turning rape into fiction' through the construction of a mythical genre of date rape stories out of real experiences of 'messy' or 'complicated' sex. But the allegation recurs throughout the chapter. Those doubting Dworkin accused her of producing, either deliberately or unintentionally, a fictional narrative of rape. Even those who believed she was telling the truth as she understood it did not believe that this truth matched what 'really' happened. Kipnis insists that the stories she discusses are fictions shaped by a generic tendency to melodrama that denies the nuance and complexity of women's experiences of real-life sex. All these examples show that even among feminists, women's narratives of rape may be subject to judgement and scrutiny. I focus on the demand that women's stories be authentic and that the women who tell them be considered credible, and the processes by which these criteria are judged.

How Can a Woman Who Is Raped Be Believed?

In June 2000, the radical feminist Andrea Dworkin (2000) published a description of her experience of 'drug rape' in a Paris hotel room in the *New Statesman* magazine. By the time of this account, Dworkin had long been almost inarguably the most controversial figure in modern feminism, a 'feminist icon', onto whom a 'disproportionate amount of loathing and adulation' was projected (Serisier 2013, p. 26). For supporters, she was a dedicated campaigner against gendered violence and 'the foremost feminist to insist that rape, incest, pornography and battery be at the centre of the feminist agenda' (Jenefsky 1998, p. 3). For opponents, she was an overall-clad militant feminist who believed that 'all sex is rape' and who was willing to bring down the coercive force of the state on feminists and queers engaged in sadomasochism or pornography and erotica in the name of protecting women from violence (Levy 2007, p. 12). As I discuss below, the reception of her account, and debates over its generic status, cannot be separated from who Dworkin was and how she was perceived.

Her story begins with her drinking in the hotel bar. She describes how she felt 'sickish' or 'weakish' after a second drink that 'didn't taste right'. She ordered room service before retreating to her room where she 'conked out', only awakening briefly when the waiter entered the room. Hours later, she awoke on the bed with the curtains still open and with pain 'deep inside' her vagina, vaginal bleeding and bruising and gashes on her breast and legs. She 'couldn't remember' what happened, but her injuries led her to conclude that she had been drugged and raped by the hotel waiter and bartender: 'I thought that the deep, bleeding scratches, right leg, and the big bruise, left breast, were the span of a man on top of me'. She contacted her gynaecologist and her partner, John Stoltenberg. The gynaecologist said, 'an exam wouldn't prove anything one way or the other and that the call from me convinced her that she should have an unlisted phone number', while Stoltenberg 'looked for any other explanation than the rape' for Dworkin's health problems and 'abandoned me emotionally'. Dworkin did not report the assault, but she attributed her subsequent health problems and depression to the experience. The account concluded: 'I'm ready to die'.

A week later, *Guardian* columnist and self-identified feminist Catherine Bennett (2000) published a column, 'Doubts About Dworkin', that expressed her disbelief in Dworkin's story. She outlined several inconsistencies within the text and questioned Dworkin's motivation in publishing it. This article prompted what Julia Gracen (2000) described as 'an accusatory pile-on … in the UK press and on the Web' as other feminists also expressed their doubts. The debate that followed scrutinised Dworkin's veracity, credibility and even her sanity, while almost nobody, even supporters of Dworkin's such as Gracen, accepted the narrative as factually true. Dworkin attributed the sceptical response to her story to on-going social tendencies to disbelieve and deny women's narratives of sexual violence: 'If the Holocaust can be denied even today, how can a woman who has been raped be believed?' (Gibbons 2000, p. 10). Approaching this question from a different angle, I explore the reasons that Dworkin's account failed to compel belief among feminists when other narratives do receive support and sympathy. The answer lies, I argue, in processes of generic judgement and Dworkin's inability to present either her narrative or herself as credible. The doubts that accompanied her story rose from both how she was perceived and the failure of her story to fulfil the generic expectations of her audience (Serisier 2015).

Bennett's article questioned the veracity and the sincerity of Dworkin's claim. If the project was to bring women's rape narratives out of the discursive orbit of the law and into the orbit of feminism, Bennett's article demonstrated that the success of this project is partial and incomplete. She claimed that Dworkin's 'rape claim, like any other, seems to deserve scrutiny', a clear reflection of the legal attitudes to women's narratives discussed in Chap. 4. Feminists have constructed a new genre with new truth standards, but where narratives do not clearly 'fit' or 'make sense' within this new framework, they continue to be judged by traditional legal standards. They may, as in the case of Dworkin, be found wanting in terms of feminist criteria of credibility and authenticity and in terms of external verifiability. For instance, Bennett complained that where 'most people would expect to find facts ... Dworkin supplies inconsistency, absence of evidence, lack of support'. Surely, she argued, if both the waiter and the bartender were absent from their post at the same time, somebody would have noticed, and if the curtains to the room were open somebody might have seen something. She queried why Dworkin had failed to report the rape to the police and why her doctor and partner reacted with such callousness to her plight.

For Dworkin and her supporters, Bennett's response simply confirmed that when speaking of rape, there 'is always a problem for women: being believed' (Dworkin 1997, p. 16). It indicated that feminist gains around rape were being eroded so that 'the default response to the charge has changed. Instead of a tendency towards belief and sympathy, there is now considerably more caution and doubt' (Gracen 2000). They implied that, in her insistence that a 'rape either occurred or it did not', with the implication that Dworkin would have to demonstrate that it did, Bennett (2000) was applying misogynist legal criteria of veracity and external verifiability that has been used historically to dismiss women's narratives. In opposition to this mode of judgement, Deborah Orr (2005) argued that whether 'Dworkin's construction of events is true or not, is pretty irrelevant'. She suggested that a feminist response should privilege Dworkin's sincerity and the ethical and political obligation of feminists to support women's narratives through belief over investigation of the veracity of the claim. The central 'fact' of the case, according to Orr, was that Dworkin 'really believed this awful violation had been made against her, and understood that she was widely disbelieved'. Dworkin, she wrote, 'spent her final years suffering an abuse women are familiar with the world over. From the law courts of Britain to the villages of Iran, women are used to their accusations of rape being greeted with disbelief'. Dworkin's was one of many narratives that feminists have sought to enable, and this genre is inherently deserving of belief, regardless of the veracity of verifiability of an individual narrative.

To cast a story outside of the genre of legitimate rape narratives is simultaneously to construct the woman who tells it as a liar, undeserving of sympathy. As the title of Bennett's narrative made clear, she was not merely expressing doubts about a story, but rather 'Doubts About Dworkin' herself. This can also be seen in the content of the article. In a column that is 17 paragraphs long, Bennett only begins to discuss the specifics of the story in the ninth paragraph. The eight paragraphs before that are devoted to Dworkin and what Bennett describes as her 'curious' relation to the truth. She draws attention to the existence of a 'Lie Detector' section on Dworkin's website 'devoted to establishing what, in fact, Andrea Dworkin has, and has not, said or done'. She narrates several incidents from Dworkin's self-narrated 'dramatic' personal history and 'diabolical' treatment by men, building her inferences through the observation that Dworkin has only been 'questioned' about her experience once, and that she refused to answer the question. The first half of an article that claims to be concerned with veracity is in fact exclusively focused on the question of who Dworkin is, suggesting that rather than her story deserving scrutiny, 'like any other', her story deserves scrutiny more than any other, for precisely this reason.

It is this movement between doubting a story and denigrating the woman who tells it that leads Orr to describe Bennett's disbelief as a form of abuse. She suggested that for critics like Bennett, 'Dworkin was simply too old, fat and ugly to receive any sexual attention at all' (Orr 2005). Gracen (2000) similarly argued that responses to Dworkin's story contained an 'ugly lesson':

> It says that if you aren't considered a reliable witness to begin with, or if you are already considered a social outrage, the proof that you offer to overcome that tendency toward doubt had better be utterly unassailable in every respect, or the real gangbanging will begin.

It seems clear that Orr and Gracen are correct in implying that many of Dworkin's long-time opponents saw her and her account as beyond the realm of belief and sympathy. The extent of this loathing, and its impact on readings of her story, was testified to by Suzie Bright (2000), a 'pro-sex' feminist and long-time political opponent of Dworkin's: 'Plenty of my peers would say that they are utterly cold to any misfortune that might befall her'. These peers, like Bennett, believed Dworkin completely capable of lying about rape, or exaggerating or inventing a story, and thus they met her account with scrutiny. Further, as Bright states, it cast Dworkin's experience outside of the genre of feminist speech in terms of the ethical demands that it placed upon them. Even if true, they were not prepared to grant its generic and political claim to belief or sympathy. Indeed, apart from Bright, it is difficult to locate any feminists who responded with sympathy to Dworkin's story beyond her political supporters in radical feminism.

Even these supporters, however, were not prepared to testify to the veracity of her account. Gracen (2000), for instance, wrote that 'there is no question that *something* happened to Dworkin last year' (emphasis in original). Like Orr, she insisted that to refuse Dworkin the belief and sympathy offered by feminists to women who speak about rape was cruel and politically suspect, but while the sympathy she offered was extensive, the belief was clearly curtailed. She suggested that the account might be the result of Dworkin's long-term PTSD from previous experiences of violence. In other words, like Dworkin's partner Stoltenberg, she 'looked for any other explanation' than accepting that what Dworkin insisted happened had really happened. The problem is, of course, that to accept Dworkin's sincerity without believing in the veracity of her account is to reproduce another legal trope around women, that of the hysterical or mad woman. Or, as the similarly sympathetic reader Suzie Bright (2000) put it: 'By the time you finish reading, you know she has finally lost her mind'.

The inability of even Dworkin's supporters to affirm their belief in the veracity of her account is due, I suggest, to its failure to match either general generic conventions of a rape story or readers' expectations of Dworkin herself. She presented herself as a woman traumatised by a violent and damaging sexual assault in ways that conflicted with and contradicted her public persona as an experienced feminist activist (Serisier 2013). For instance, she described this form of drug rape as 'fool proof': 'You can do this hundreds of times with virtually no chance of getting caught, let alone having anyone be able to make a legal case in any court of law'. In part, her decision that reporting would be futile was based, she wrote, on the fact that she knew 'too much': 'I know a lot about rape. I study it. I read about it. I think about it… I engage with prosecutors and lawyers and legislators'. Questioned later about points raised by Bennett, who argued that DNA and records of the men's movements could easily have been collected and used as evidence, Dworkin asserted that the problem was that she knew too little: 'You're in a country where you don't know the language or the way the legal system works. I didn't know anything about drug rape, which is the kind I endured. It's extremely confusing. You really don't know what's happening' (English 2002). Trapped between these two responses, Dworkin struggled to articulate herself as both a woman traumatised by rape and a feminist able to combat it, and she did not enable others to give her a role that made sense within the generic options available. She was speaking out, and thus, in some ways, positioned as the heroic survivor discussed in Chap. 3. But she also presented herself as unable to act on her own behalf in ways that left her positioned as a victim, unable to speak. Reconciling this with her identity as a prominent feminist campaigner seemed to leave her supporters with no coherent option for asserting the truth of her story and her ability and right to tell it.

The failure of the story to fulfil generic conventions of speaking out, especially from a prominent feminist, was most evident in what was, unsurprisingly, the most controversial paragraph of Dworkin's account:

> I go down the checklist: no short skirt; it was daylight; I didn't drink a lot even though it was alcohol and I rarely drink, but so what? It could have been Wild Turkey or coffee. I didn't drink with a man, I sat alone and read a book, I didn't go somewhere I shouldn't have been wherever that might be when you are 52, I didn't flirt, I didn't want it to happen. I wasn't hungry for a good, hard fuck that would leave me pummelled with pain inside. (Dworkin 2000)

The idea of the radical feminist Andrea Dworkin, the woman once described as the 'Malcolm X' of feminism, constructing a 'checklist' of victim-blaming stereotypes either was the ultimate symbol of the narrative as falsehood or was an indicator of Dworkin's mental instability (Levy 2007, pp. xix–xx). There are many reasons that Dworkin might have inserted the checklist, but it functioned primarily to deprive her narrative of believability and herself of credibility. While it is understood that victims of rape frequently engage in self-blame, the introduction of a checklist of crude victim-blaming stereotypes was, for Gracen (2000), 'contrary to everything a rape expert should know'. Dworkin's story could not compel belief on its own, but, ultimately, it was, even for her supporters, the failure of the narrative to align with her feminist identity that cast it outside the bounds of a 'true' narrative of rape, and therefore outside the bounds of speaking out.

In a warning of the consequences of failing to compel belief, even Dworkin's decision to speak out was taken as evidence of her unreliability. Her failure to report to the police was cast by Bennett (2000) as irresponsible: 'Is this bartender, with his accomplice, to be allowed to continue drugging and raping female guests?' She acknowledges that 'the reluctance of a rape victim to be further violated by examination and questioning is understood' but continues that 'if this is what prevented Dworkin from seeking help it does not seem consistent with her current decision to relive the ordeal, in vivid detail, for readers of the *New Statesman*'. Both her failure to speak in the legal domain and her decision to speak in a different genre are cast as suspect, reinforcing the sense that the law is the ultimate arbiter of truth and the appropriate generic home for true stories. The possibility that Dworkin, like many other women, might be seeking an outcome that she is unlikely to receive from the law is dismissed by Bennett. Instead, the decision to tell a story of rape in a different genre, with different truth criteria, is itself a reason for suspicion.

Dworkin's story draws attention to the risks of failing to meet the generic criteria demanded of feminist narratives and demonstrates how important the mobilisation of an audience that offers belief and support is for the success of speaking out. According to Dworkin, the disbelief that greeted her account was an injury that she would never recover from. In an interview the year before she died, she said that it 'was unbearable being disbelieved by my so-called sisters' (Bindel 2004). And the fact was that even her most vocal supporters stopped short of offering full belief, a sign that even when belief is constructed as an ethical imperative, there are still generic limitations and boundaries as to the narratives that will be given that belief. Dworkin's failure to produce a narrative that was read as believable left her without the support promised by speaking out. But if the disbelief that met Dworkin's account demonstrated the boundaries of belief and the importance of narrative conventions and expectations, in the remainder of this chapter, I explore the ways these very conventions and expectations, the 'generic' nature of narratives, can similarly be read as a cause or prompt for judgement and disbelief. I examine, in effect, the allegation that in constructing a genre or enabling a 'new literature' of rape, feminism has turned 'rape into fiction' (Roiphe 1991).

Turning Rape into Fiction

In 1993, Katie Roiphe, a graduate student in English literature at Princeton University, published *The Morning After: Sex, Fear, and Feminism*, an attack on the 'rape crisis feminism' that she believes had overtaken American university campuses. In the book, which received extensive media attention, Roiphe (1993, p. 7) positions herself as writing from the perspective of authentic and honest personal experience: 'I have written what I see, limited, personal, but entirely real'. Her personal experience is used to convey an image of campus feminism as 'alien, and even sometimes at odds with what I thought feminism was'. It is, for Roiphe, a completely 'authoritative discourse' (Bakhtin 1981), experienced by her as imposing a set of rules and taboos, and a 'rigid orthodoxy':

> I was surprised at how many things there were not to say, at the arguments and assertions that could not be made, lines that could not be crossed, taboos that could not be broken… You couldn't question the existence of a rape crisis, you couldn't suggest that the fascination with sexual harassment had to do with more than sexual harassment, you couldn't say that Alice Walker was just a bad writer, and the list of couldn'ts went on and on. (Roiphe 1993, p. 5)

In Roiphe's understanding, rape 'is a natural trump card for feminism' and key to the production of this new orthodoxy: 'By blocking analysis with its claims to unique pandemic suffering, the rape crisis becomes a powerful source of authority' (pp. 56–57). That authority is used to define women as victims and impose a restrictive definition of sexual ethics. Feminists, she writes, insist that sex should be 'gentle, it should not be aggressive; it should be absolutely equal, it should not involve domination and submission; it should be tender, not ambivalent; it should communicate respect, not consuming desire' (p. 60).

I am interested in *The Morning After* not so much as a political polemic but as a text deeply concerned with the production, reading and judgement of the feminist genre of personal narratives of rape. Roiphe uses her own 'authentic' story as a measure by which to judge the stories of rape she encounters in the text, and, on this basis, they are found wanting. They do not provide an 'internally persuasive' means of reflecting or understanding her experience (Bakhtin 1981). As she insists repeatedly throughout the book, the marches, speak-outs and workshops about rape and sexual violence are 'not me', they have 'nothing to do with me' (Roiphe 1993, p. 5). To access and speak her authentic truth, Roiphe must, therefore, reject the dogmatic and false genre of feminism. The stories she hears which partake in this genre are judged to be inauthentic because, firstly, they do not match Roiphe's experience, and, secondly, unlike her story, they are seen to be overly generic, the product of a restrictive, ideological mode of narrative that is incapable of producing authentic truth. In Roiphe's book, a personal story is used to enact a critique of the politics and genre of contemporary feminism through refusing belief to the stories that it enables and authorises.

The essence of Roiphe's (1993, p. 71) critique is that rather than enabling experiential truths, 'with all their noise about rape myths, rape-crisis feminists are generating their own'. The myths are about the nature of (hetero)sex, but they are also, myths of women as virginal, vulnerable and in need of protection from rakish and predatory men. Feminism has, she argues, in its desire to counter the stock plots and characters of law, shaped women's lives into Victorian 'stock plots' of 'passivity and victimhood':

> If you look at the scenes described in the plays, the poems, the pamphlets, the Take Back the Night speak-outs, the stories told are loss-of-innocence stories. We all know this plot: I trusted him – I thought people were good – then I realized – afterward I knew. The rape, or sexual assault, is the moment of the fall. (p. 71)

For Roiphe, the most pernicious effect of feminist distortions of reality is that they encourage, exhort and even coerce individual women into adopting these 'stock plots' to narrate and make sense of their individual experiences. In providing only these 'stock plots' for telling stories, feminism has constructed a genre of hackneyed and repetitive stories. Rather than providing them with 'semantic thickness', according to Roiphe, their generic nature detracts from their power and believability, especially when they are told in collective forums:

> The strange thing is that as the different girls – tall and short, fat and thin, nervous and confident – get up to give intensely personal accounts, all of their stories begin to sound the same. Listening to a string of them, I hear patterns begin to emerge. The same phrases float through different voices. Almost all of them begin "I wasn't planning to speak out tonight but…," even the ones who had spoken in previous years. They talk about feeling helpless, and feeling guilty. Some talk about hating their bodies. The echoes continue: "I didn't admit it or talk about it." "I was silenced". (p. 33)

At one level, this critique simply highlights the paradoxical nature of generic structures. As Derrida (1992) writes, genre is an enabling and a restrictive force. It provides a structure that makes narratives of rape tellable and recognisable to readers, but it also imposes limits on the deviation from this structure. As the example of Dworkin shows, readers' expectations about how rape narratives should look are strong, and the consequences for deviating from them are significant. Roiphe (1993, p. 36), however, makes conformity to generic structures itself a reason to refuse to believe or respond ethically to women's stories: 'Somehow the individual power of each story is sapped by the collective mode of expression. The individual details fade, the stories blend together, sounding programmed and automatic'. The fact that the narratives have recognisable generic conventions and similarities is taken as evidence that they cannot be authentic expressions of experience. What Roiphe's critique does not allow for is the fact that it is only these conventions that make the stories able to be told, heard and responded to.

Instead, for Roiphe, generic conventions simply mark the stories as inauthentic and taint the women who tell them as lacking the sophistication or discernment to reject these stock plots. Instead, in a point that Laura Kipnis will echo, they are women who 'want that melodrama. They want the absolute value placed on experience by absolute words' (Roiphe 1993, p. 82). Reliance on melodrama demonstrates the speakers' inability to confront reality: 'Words like "rape" and "verbal coercion" sculpt the confusing mass of experience into something easy to understand… [T]he fear of date rape offers a tangible framework to locate fears that are essentially abstract' (pp. 82–83). And ultimately, neither the narratives nor their speakers can be believed:

> In the heat of the moment, in the confessional rush of relating graphic details to a supportive crowd, the truth may be stretched, battered or utterly abandoned. It's impossible to tell how many of these stories are authentic, faithful accounts of what actually happened. They all sound tinny, staged. Each "I am a survivor and I am here to take back the night" seems rehearsed. (p. 42)

Ironically, Roiphe's assertion that feminists construct women through Victorian archetypes translates into her own characterisation of women who speak as prone to hysteria, mass delusion and an incapacity to recognise truth from falsehood, an equally Victorian archetype of women, used among other things, to argue against women's access to melodramatic, romantic literature (Radway 1991).

Roiphe ultimately insists that to be believed rape narratives must be effectively 'genreless', unshaped by shared conventions and locations of telling. Any sign of narrative convention or generic shaping renders them insufficiently authentic and therefore subject to doubt and disbelief. This is, of course, an impossible demand. Narratives are only tellable through the generic conventions that shape them in ways that are recognisable to readers and audiences. If genrelessness is an impossibility, the appearance of not being generically shaped is often based on a narrative conforming to dominant and traditional models of speech. This is evident in the single account of rape in the book that Roiphe accepts and responds to with sympathy. A friend tells her over coffee a story of having been raped at knifepoint and Roiphe (1993, p. 43) freezes: 'I felt terrible for her. I felt like there was nothing I could say'. Roiphe describes this story as 'worlds away from the spectacle of mass confession' that she finds 'unconvincing' and 'peculiarly aggressive' in the narratives that she discusses elsewhere in the book. The generic distinction she draws operates both on the level of narrative shaping and the type of story that is told. Her approval of her friend's mode of telling indicates a belief that rape is a 'private' and individual experience that should not be told publicly or in the realm of politics. It is a re-inscription of the pre-feminist belief, held by Susan Brownmiller (1976, p. 8) before her consciousness was raised, that rape victims have nothing to do with the public politics of feminism, but instead are the victims of an individual crime and a private tragedy. This definition simultaneously works to reinforce the distinction between the 'crime' of 'real' stranger rape and what Roiphe sees as the 'fantasy' of simple or acquaintance rape (Estrich 1987). The former is considered a legitimate subject of private conversations between women, and the latter a product of feminist mythology and the hysterical women who believe in it.

Contrary to Roiphe's self-presentations as a heroic speaker of common sense truth combating the ideological fictions of feminist orthodoxy, these distinctions highlight the discursive framing of her own experience and understanding. Where she accuses feminists of drawing on older tropes of gendered heterosexuality, Roiphe's starting point is a normative version of heterosexuality that presumes the existence of male sexual aggression and categorises women's stories of date rape as normal romance and (hetero)sexuality. For instance, she writes of her own history: 'thinking back on complicated nights, on too many glasses of wine, on strange and familiar beds', she 'would have to say', given the 'sweeping definition of rape' on offer, that not only has she been 'date raped', but that she wonders 'how many people there are, male or female, who haven't been date-raped at one point or another'. While Roiphe presents this musing as demonstrating the ridiculous over-reach of feminist rewriting of sex as violence, it might be read as problematising her own 'pragmatic' acceptance that certain levels of 'pressure' and 'manipulation' in sex are ordinary and harmless (Roiphe 1993, p. 79). Feminist analyses of date rape begin from a perspective that pressure and manipulation are not harmless and need not be accepted as normal, and, indeed as Sabine Sielke (2002) notes, in this way the feminist vision that Roiphe dismisses as anti-sex may, in fact, offer a more promising vision of female sexual pleasure. The vision of sex Roiphe offers says little about this pleasure, but instead presumes that a society where date rape is indistinguishable from 'too many glasses of wine' is the best that we can hope for.

Roiphe's self-representation is further complicated by the way in which she authorises her speech. Throughout she presents herself as an embattled truth-teller speaking the truth of experience. But, if that experiential truth relies on dominant and normative framings of gender and sexuality to render it 'common sense', Roiphe's authority to speak is similarly based on more than experience. Like Diane Bell in the previous chapter, she authorises herself not only to produce truth from her own story but to determine the meaning of the stories of others, and indeed to impose a meaning on these narratives that contradicts and denies the meaning that they give to it. Roiphe positions herself, bell hooks (1994) argues, as the inheritor of feminism based on white, middle-class entitlement. In other words, like Bell, she presumes her identity as a rightful 'custodian of feminism' (Yeatman 1993). She writes, for instance, that prior to university, feminism was something that she 'didn't spend much time thinking about' because it was 'assumed, something deep in my foundations' and passed on from her mother. On encountering a version of feminism that 'was not the feminism I grew up with', she insists that this other feminism must be wrong, constituting herself as the arbiter of acceptable feminist speech and politics through constructing her own subject position as authentic and outside of the realm of political and politicised genres (Roiphe 1993, pp. 4–5).

As critics such as Tanya Horeck (2004, p. 9) have suggested in relation to Roiphe, one can acknowledge and draw on her insights without accepting her conclusion that 'the views of 'rape-crisis feminists' are outdated and puritanical' or, I would add, her dismissal of women's narratives. As I noted in Chap. 2, discursive shifts do not enact completely new meanings and frameworks. Even radical attempts to challenge social meanings and understandings must draw on existing tropes, archetypes and cultural scripts, and frequently reproduce elements of these scripts. Read this way, Roiphe's cautions about the reproduction of sexist narratives of feminine passivity in feminist-authorised rape narratives are potentially useful, even if, as bell hooks (1994) argues, these and other critiques have also been made by other feminists who Roiphe erases in her attempt to present herself as a maverick. What limits Roiphe's analysis is the partiality and absolute nature of her critiques. Rather than exploring the generic conventions of women's narratives, she demands that they display no generic marks at all if they are to be read seriously, or only the generic markers of 'private' conversation. She sees only Derrida's (1992) 'law of genre', the marks and commonalities of sameness, and is unable to note the moments of generic departure, contamination and impurity that Derrida labels the 'law of the law of genre'. One feature of these 're-marks', as I showed in Chap. 3, is that many women who write or tell rape narratives are cognisant of the pressures of narrative conventions and the risks that their stories will only be read through the lens of generic commonality and reader expectation. In Roiphe's reading, this risk is realised. While she states that her book was written 'out of the deep belief that some feminisms are better than others', her dismissal of feminism as genre, and the stories of survivors, leaves her endorsing not a different version of feminism but traditional normative understandings of acceptable heterosexuality (Roiphe 1993, p. 7).

The Hijacking of Feminism by Melodrama

Like Roiphe's book, Laura Kipnis' (2017) *Unwanted Advances: Sexual Paranoia Comes to Campus* is concerned with the genre of stories of sexual violence enabled by campus feminism. The stories Kipnis is interested in are told within and as part of a changing environment of regulation of sexual misconduct, and, as Kipnis and others have noted, sexual activity generally, on campuses in the USA. These changes centre around the expanded remit of 'Title IX', a piece of civil rights legislation prohibiting gender discrimination in education. In 2011, the Obama Administration, following a wave of student activism, made preventing and responding to sexual violence and harassment a core element of universities' 'Title IX' responsibilities. In the years since, universities have been expected to develop 'Title IX' offices to investigate, adjudicate and respond to allegations of sexual violence and harassment in a process that operates in place of, or parallel to, the criminal justice system. Kipnis is among several academics who have criticised the new system as inherently unjust, damaging to academic freedom and as part of a new 'security' culture on academic campuses (e.g. Doyle 2015; Gersen and Suk 2016). On the contrary, many student activists, while they agree with some criticisms made of the system, argue that it has enabled students to speak out where they were previously silenced (Clark and Pinto 2016).

My interest, however, is not in Kipnis' critique of Title IX, but in the way in which her story of becoming a self-described 'whistle blower' is based on retelling the stories of two students who made Title IX complaints at her university against the same philosophy professor, Peter Ludlow (Kipnis 2017, p. 35). In her book, Kipnis critiques the generic basis of these stories, viewing them as evidence for her claim that feminism as a political genre has become 'hijacked' by melodrama. In labelling the narratives this way, she disputes their veracity, sincerity, credibility and authenticity. Like Roiphe, she contends that these are stories constructed out of feminist 'stock plots' that reproduce older generic tropes of women as sexually passive, and, based on these stories, she argues that feminism has become a producer of politically and generically flawed narratives.

Kipnis' book, like Roiphe's, enacts her critiques through her own experience of judging these stories and finding them wanting. She also, as the book documents, becomes a part of the story when a Title IX complaint is made against her. According to Kipnis (2017, p. 34), going 'through a Title IX investigation… made me a little mad and possibly a little dangerous', transforming her from a 'harmless ironist into an aspiring whistle blower'. The story begins with an essay that Kipnis (2015) wrote for the *Chronicle of Higher Education* about 'sexual paranoia' in academia. The essay argues that a new campus regulation at Northwestern, her institution, banning faculty-student relationships is symptomatic of a sexual culture which infantilises students as perennial victims, demonises faculty as potential predators, and instils a paternalistic regime of sexual regulation and protection. Within this critique, several paragraphs are devoted to a 'murky and contested' sexual harassment allegation made by an undergraduate student, who Kipnis would eventually call by the pseudonym Eunice Cho, against Ludlow. Following dissatisfaction with the Title IX process, Cho and Ludlow sued the university and each other. In addition, Ludlow sued several other people, including a graduate student that Kipnis writes he 'previously dated'. After the article was published, a protest was organised by students who saw it as dismissive of Cho's story and flippant about campus sexual harassment and violence more generally (Anonymous 2015). In addition, the graduate student mentioned in the essay, later named Nola Hartley in Kipnis' book, made a complaint against Kipnis for misrepresentation and, in the language of Title IX, 'creating a hostile environment' for student complainants (Kipnis 2017, p. 137). Following an investigation, Kipnis was cleared of wrongdoing. Ludlow, meanwhile, resigned during a dismissal hearing at which Kipnis acted as his faculty support. The book discusses these investigations but is particularly focused on the narratives told by the students which instigated them. Their centrality is indicated in the closing sentence of the introduction, 'thank you to my accusers: unwitting collaborators, accidental muses' (p. 34).

The central story told in the book is one of conflicts over the meaning of personal stories of sexual violence, and whose version of these stories should count as the truth. This is simultaneously a question of what genre is used to construct the narratives and their meaning: speaking out about violence, student-professor romance gone wrong or 'melodrama'. As a brief summary makes clear, it is, as in Chap. 4, not the facts that are at issue but the 'narrative glue' that holds them together and determines their appropriate generic location (Brooks 2008). Cho and Ludlow agree that they went out together off-campus, visited galleries, restaurants and bars, drank alcohol and shared a bed in Ludlow's apartment, but did not have sex. In Cho's story, Ludlow forced her to drink, flirted with her, made sexual advances which she rejected and refused to drive her home. She woke to find him groping her. In Ludlow's story, Cho flirted with and propositioned him and insisted on sleeping at his house. Nothing sexual happened between them. A Title IX hearing found Cho's story more plausible, and Ludlow was subjected to a variety of penalties but not termination. After hearing about Cho's case, Hartley disclosed to a professor that she had had an 'inappropriate' relationship with Ludlow. According to both, they were close, and she often stayed at his house. In her story their friendship was platonic, but Ludlow pursued her sexually with promises to help her career. They had sex once consensually, and on a different occasion, he raped her while she was drunk. According to Ludlow, they were involved in an on-going romantic and sexual relationship which Hartley ended, choosing to prioritise her relationship with her out-of-town boyfriend. The delay between these events, which occurred before the night involving Cho and Ludlow, and Hartley's complaint, made after Cho's complaint became public knowledge, was, according to Hartley, because Cho's narrative had forced her to rethink her own experience. In Ludlow's story, Hartley was involved, either innocently or deliberately, in a faculty plot to remove him from his position. A Title IX investigation did not uphold Hartley's allegation of sexual assault but found that Ludlow had engaged in sexual harassment (Kipnis 2017).

Kipnis believes that the Title IX investigation proceeded through a melodramatic framing that casts older male professors as cartoonish villains and young female students as virginal innocents. It thus believed Cho and Hartley over Ludlow because of generic conventions and expectations rather than facts or evidence. In response, Kipnis launched her own investigation, and much of her book is devoted to her own judgement of what really happened. The evidence she relies on to produce her narrative is public court records, records from her own Title IX investigation, an interview with Ludlow and a collection of his own records and documentation of the investigations which he was subject to. Kipnis never speaks to either Cho or Hartley, and so their narratives, and their interpretation of the 'evidence', remain completely inaccessible. Her story is produced instead from the point of view of the law, Ludlow and the Title IX investigation. This bias mirrors traditional media and legal rewritings of acquaintance rape narratives and produces similar effects. It shifts the genre of the story from the public realm of politics and violence into the private realm of romance gone wrong, and turns the story told by Cho and Hartley of male violence and female suffering and resistance into one of a man injured by women's lies or fantasies (Lees 1997).

Kipnis' story is produced through selective application of credibility and suspicion that reproduces older methods of doubting women, and is, ultimately, grounded in a generic preference for the private and 'nuanced' genre of romance rather than the public 'melodramatic' genre of gendered violence. The latter, she argues, is dominant in campus feminism, and on campuses generally. It relies on and reproduces a 'set of tropes' and a sense of 'narrative inevitability' that turns students and professors into 'stock characters in a predetermined story' where 'students are putty in the hands of all-powerful professors' (Kipnis 2015). Kipnis' distaste for this genre structures her responses throughout the book. She explains that she first learnt of Cho's story through a news item, which contained, she writes, quoting Barthes, a 'punctum', a small detail that grabs your attention in a way you don't understand, and which gave her a 'jab of irritation' (Kipnis 2017, pp. 51–52). The 'punctum' was the statement that Ludlow had 'forced' Cho to drink alcohol. For Kipnis, this claim 'is melodrama':

> I'm quite sure that professors can be sleazebags. I'm less sure that any professor can force an unwilling student to drink, especially to the point of passing out. With what power? What sorts of repercussions can there possibly be if the student refuses? (Kipnis 2015)

While Kipnis is undoubtedly correct that Ludlow does not have officially sanctioned power to force students to drink, she refuses to consider the other ways in which power might operate in this situation. Neither does she enact the same scepticism towards Ludlow's version of events. For instance, she could have experienced a similar 'punctum' at Ludlow's explanation that Cho ended up sleeping at his house because she 'insisted'. This claim might also produce the questions, 'with what power?' or 'what sorts of repercussions can there possibly be if the professor refuses?' Even though Kipnis believes Ludlow was 'naïve' to allow Cho to sleep over after drinking with her, she does not find it implausible that he went out drinking with a student and then allowed her sleep in his bed without any sexual or romantic interest or intentions, whereas she finds Cho's story that she was not sexually interested in Ludlow completely implausible (Kipnis 2017, p. 87).

The result of Kipnis' (2017, p. 74) selective suspicion and belief is not to produce, as she claims, an 'equally plausible but more nuanced' story of the events and their characters. Rather, it relies on a set of opposing stock characters which are equally open to doubt and just as melodramatic as those she rejects. In Kipnis' telling, Cho is transformed from a helpless victim to a gold-digger whose story is 'ratcheted up' with each telling, while Ludlow is turned from a predator into the bumbling prey of manipulative women (p. 68). Far from a professionally successful academic who is able to wield formal and informal institutional power,

Ludlow in Kipnis' version is an innocent, guilty of being too 'trusting' (p. 87) and hopelessly naïve: 'so much an outsider' that he 'didn't know there was an inside and outside' (p. 82). He is now the passive 'putty' in the hands of the all-powerful students. This reversal provides Ludlow with a form of 'narrative immunity', while Cho is consistently 'tainted' with doubt and imputation of bad intentions (Waterhouse-Watson 2013; L. Gilmore 2017). These processes occur even in relation to the same actions. For instance, Cho's lawsuits demonstrate her tendency to exaggerate in pursuit of financial gain, while Ludlow's more numerous lawsuits are simply reasonable attempts to clear his name. Ludlow's taking Cho out, buying her drinks and telling her about his preference for younger women are reported as reasonable actions. On the other hand, Cho, Kipnis argues, was likely riven by ambivalence, so that she simultaneously flung herself at Ludlow and felt 'victimised' by doing so. This type of behaviour, she informs her reader, is 'often found in those who've been diagnosed with what's known as "borderline personality disorder"', so that Cho is cast as not merely bad but potentially mad (p. 75). Melodrama as a genre is at least equally present in the version of events provided by Kipnis, but with the roles of villain and victim reversed, a generic reframing common to the legal narratives discussed in Chap. 4.

The same generic reversal is found in Kipnis' rewriting of Ludlow's relationship to Hartley. Here, Hartley is a femme fatale, who possesses such power over Ludlow that he even drives her to the airport so that she can visit her other boyfriend. For Kipnis (2017, p. 94), 'everything I learned about their relationship throws into question easy assumptions about institutional roles alone determining who has more power in romantic entanglements'. Everything she learns is, of course, through Ludlow, and it produces a reality where rather than being the sole determinants of power, institutional roles appear to have no bearing on interpersonal power dynamics. Further, all of Hartley's speech is subject to doubt and speculation except for the romantic speech reported by Ludlow which Kipnis takes as a direct reflection of Hartley's thoughts and beliefs. So, Ludlow's production of affectionate text message exchanges between the two of them after the night that Hartley claims Ludlow sexually assaulted her demonstrate that the assault never happened. Kipnis links these messages to an anonymous quote in an article about sexual harassment in philosophy: 'It was consensual, but I didn't have any choice – he has too much power in the discipline – and at points I have hated him so much for taking advantage of the power asymmetry that I have plotted revenge against him' (p. 237). Aware that the author is a supporter of Hartley's and finding similar language in the report of the Title IX investigator, Kipnis concludes that she is 'most likely' the source of the quote, and that the use of the word 'plotted' rather than, for instance, 'fantasised', supports Kipnis' belief that Hartley could plausibly concoct a 'false or pumped-up rape charge … to get a supposed predator ousted from academia' (p. 238). While she accepts that there is 'no way to say' whether this speculation is true, what 'can be said' is that Hartley went from believing her relationship with Ludlow was consensual to seemingly believing the opposite. In the generic logic of romance gone wrong deployed by Kipnis, it is plausible that Hartley enacted a complicated revenge plot involving a concocted rape charge against a man she had dated and dumped. It is, however, implausible that she may have concealed her true feelings from Ludlow in a series of text messages following an experience of sexual violence, or even an ambivalent sexual encounter.

Kipnis clearly believes that Cho and Hartley have wronged Ludlow and herself through the production of false allegations. But she does not simply or straightforwardly accuse either student of lying, as indicated by her statement that Hartley changed her beliefs. She disputes the veracity of their claims but is willing to accept that the feminist discourse they have adopted of gendered violence and institutional power differentials has caused them to rewrite their own reality. Using this framework to tell their stories locates them generically as stories of gendered violence rather than of romance, or flirtation and attraction. For Kipnis, telling their stories in this genre is unfair to Ludlow, and, in the end, also to themselves. They produce themselves as characters whose roles are defined by violence and victimisation rather than sex, romance and empowerment. In so doing, they trap themselves, Kipnis argues, in a narrative role of victim even as they think and are told that they are making themselves into heroic survivors. She writes, for instance, of Cho that she 'entered campus mythology as a survivor, a plucky heroine standing up to the university's indifference, just as she'd stood up to the sexual predator', but that she 'could only see Cho as the unlucky product of a system devoted to persuading a generation of young women that they're 'helpless prey' who was unfortunate 'enough to have her story of violated femininity enforced by officialdom' and become 'interred in the same aggrieved passivity that entrapped females worldwide have perfected over the centuries' (Kipnis 2017, p. 90). While it is the 'system' that has damaged Cho, Kipnis lays the blame for Hartley's transformation at the feet of a 'trio of feminist advisors'. They turn her from the powerful young woman who dominates Ludlow into a 'not very bright child or a chronic dissembler' (p. 125). This is the ultimate outcome of convincing her that her relationship *couldn't* have been consensual' (p. 120). In the final twist, the true villain of Kipnis' story of romance gone wrong is feminism, a political movement that has become devoted to producing melodramatic narratives of victimisation and forcing them onto young women. Kipnis, on the other hand, rather than engaging in victim-blaming or denial, positions herself as their potential saviour through her refusal to accept this damaging discursive and narrative logic.

However, as discussed in Chap. 3, the genre of speaking out produces stories that are simultaneously about victimisation and transcending that victimisation through speech. It is Kipnis, not Cho and Hartley, who insists that they can only tell one or another story but not both. That insistence means she can 'only see' Cho and Hartley in specific ways. 'Campus mythology', for instance, is correct that Cho stood up to the university and Ludlow through her complaints and lawsuits and even through her eventual decision to cease to co-operate with the Title IX process. She may see herself as a victim, but she is clearly not reduced to passivity by this status. Kipnis might criticise or disagree with her actions, but her agency is undeniably part of the story.

The significance of Kipnis' own generic preferences and desires is made most clear in her depiction of Hartley. She writes that she liked Hartley at the beginning of the story when she was 'confident, funny and in control' and wrote clever, flirtatious text messages. In the other story, 'she'd come to view herself through a scrim of bathos', and describes herself through clichés, stating, for example, that she is a 'shadow of her former self'. This use of generic conventions renders her speech suspect. Kipnis writes that she can't understand 'how someone who'd once had a lot of spunk and originality could have spoken such a canned sentence unless she were playing a role' (p. 125). But Kipnis provides no logic for her decision to see the flirtatious, spunky student impressing the older professor as any less a clichéd role, except that it is a story, and a character, that she prefers. Rather than seeing Hartley's use of 'canned' language as a possible consequence of her experience of violence or considering the limited linguistic resources that women have to speak of such violence, Kipnis simply seems to want Hartley to stick to telling the story that she prefers. This disavowal of the reality of Hartley's story makes Kipnis blind to the effects of her insistence on rewriting it in a way that she likes better. Writing anonymously, a graduate student friend of Hartley's describes how, 'just when she wanted to put the most traumatizing part of her life behind her and move on with her education', she 'had a professor of her own university take to national media to publicly misrepresent what happened to her':

> She knows what happened to her, and she will never recant her story, but nonetheless, she regrets coming forward. She regards it as nothing less than a life and career ruining decision. Hold these two facts together in your mind: she believes she was assaulted, and she regrets having ever told another soul. This is the world we live in. It's not melodramatic; it's heartbreaking. (Anonymous 2015)

As Kipnis (2017, p. 84) writes at one point in reference to Ludlow's fate, 'casting real people in fictive roles isn't harmless pastime'. They can 'end up jobless and destitute'.

Casting real people into fictive roles is precisely what Kipnis' book does in order to construct a morality tale of the contemporary university. She argues that Ludlow has been jettisoned as a heretic, guilty of 'thinking women over the age of consent have sexual agency', while feminists are depriving them of that agency by casting them as victims in a melodrama (Kipnis 2017, p. 239). Despite Kipnis' calls for nuance, this is a narrative that insists women are either victims or agents and, in parallel, men are either villains or good guys. At one point, Kipnis (2015) says that she believes 'bona fide' harassers should be 'chemically castrated'. While the comment is clearly meant facetiously it does give insight into the black-and-white story that Kipnis is telling. A nuanced engagement would demand due process regardless of innocence or guilt, or even ask if the Title IX system is adequate for dealing with gendered harm without denying that that harm exists. It might include elements of Kipnis' critique about unidimensional understandings of power without presuming that agency or power exercised by Hartley or Cho means that Ludlow does not have any.

As I discuss in the concluding chapter, insisting on women's ability to construct narratives that challenge the inevitability of male violence is important (Marcus 1992). Also important is the production of narratives that do not presume that the outcome of a rape story is a necessarily and permanently damaged subjectivity (Gavey and Schmidt 2011; McKenzie-Mohr 2014). At their best, Kipnis' arguments highlight that speaking out about sexual violence is a political practice that is ambivalent. It produces both vulnerability and empowerment. It can challenge and reify traditional understandings of sexual violence. In this sense, Kipnis (2017, p. 36) is right that due to the limits of narrative and discursive change, feminist genres of sexual violence enact a 'hodgepodge of gender progress and gendered conventionality' that simultaneously contest and draw on older genres and discursive frameworks. As I have suggested, the same might be said about Kipnis' own constructions of Cho, Hartley and Ludlow, or, indeed, her general characterisation of sexual violence.

In Kipnis' case, this can feel not only like gendered conventionality but a refusal to allow that these conventions could be overturned. For instance, in an example of 'being drawn to what you're not supposed to say' on contemporary campuses, Kipnis recounts a conversation with a friend whose sister got drunk and fell asleep in a frat house, only to wake with a 'guy on top of her'. After remarking that 'you couldn't see that coming', Kipnis and her friend laugh (pp. 185–186). It is hard to disagree with Kipnis' point that only a 'dim-witted feminism' would want 'to shelter women from the richness of our own mistakes' and 'ambivalences'. However, accepting these ambivalences and mistakes does not have to mean denying or excusing violence or harassment, or that making mistakes disqualifies women from making claims for justice. A woman can make a mistake in falling asleep at a frat house but still refuse to accept that waking up while being sexually assaulted is her fault. The problem is that for Kipnis, her demand that women enact a 'grown-up feminism' becomes a discourse where only women are required to take responsibility and men's actions are removed from scrutiny. She refuses the 'nuanced' but 'plausible' interpretation that women may make unwise or bad choices and still have a right to bodily autonomy. But, more importantly, she neglects the aspects of the feminist story that are predicated on making change through narrative. Kipnis does not appear to accept that refusing to blame oneself for falling asleep in a frat house might also be about insisting on a possible version of this story where falling asleep in a frat house might no longer be a risky act. To presume that it necessarily is and always will be is itself a form of 'gendered conventionality'.

The Political Implications of Generic Judgement

In creating a generic space and framework for women to tell stories of sexual violence, feminism created the potential for these stories to be told, heard and believed rather than met simply with denial and doubt. Feminist spaces and audiences offered the promise that stories of sexual violence told within this genre would be heard and believed, and would themselves strengthen the genre, allowing more women to speak. Ultimately, this, it was believed, would enable and ensure the political efficacy of this speech. Each of the examples discussed in this chapter complicates these assumptions about the connections between feminism, speaking out and practices of judgement, genre and belief. Just as I argue that speaking out is both a form of narrative and a form of politics, the judgements operate simultaneously as political contestation and literary critique. At their worst, they seek to enact and enforce a 'law of genre' that casts certain narratives as unspeakable, demands narratives reach an unattainable level of authenticity and 'genrelessness', or insists that narratives be told in a different genre altogether.

As Derrida (1992) makes clear, the process of genre construction enacts boundaries and limits at the same point as it enables speech. The 'do' of genre is always accompanied by a 'do not' and, as I discuss in Chap. 3, both may be experienced as coercive demands. What this chapter shows is that these processes are enacted and enforced largely through the expectations and demands of readers. Readers insist that rape narratives, like other autobiographical stories, meet standards of credibility and authenticity that are based on their relationship to other texts in the genre, and the audience's perception of the teller. When a story seems to conflict with or undermine that perception, the audience may refuse it credibility. This is equally true in relation to prominent public figures such as Andrea Dworkin and the 'stock characters' that audiences use to grant or deny belief to stories told by unknown women. What these examples show is that either conforming to or failing to conform to generic standards and conventions can be a cause for disbelief and the refusal of sympathy and support. To gain belief and sympathy, narratives must meet readers' generic expectations, even where those expectations are that the story not display any markers of generic belonging. I do not mean to infer that even among feminists, women's stories only meet with doubt and disbelief. This is clearly not true as the examples throughout this book have shown. What I do insist is that the experience of doubt and disbelief remains a risk in feminist genres and among feminist readers. These cases, each in their own way, demonstrate that belief is a political question, and one that speaks to the limits of the politics of speaking out. Each example also shows that even among feminists the project of establishing an ethics of response and of belief is an on-going project (Serisier 2015).

As discussed in Chap. 5, these debates have become increasingly urgent with the growth of women's speech online. The story of Dworkin represented an early example of the way that the internet may facilitate doubt and debate around women's narratives through similar processes to those discussed in relation to Dylan Farrow. The success of #MeToo in targeting individual men and their careers has raised similar concerns to those articulated by Kipnis, and she continues to insist that the genre of speech about violence endangers other categories of speech, such as seduction (Kipnis 2018b). In keeping with the bifurcation that she draws in her book, Kipnis (2018a) argues both that #MeToo has gone 'too far' in terms of rewriting private incidents that women 'should just get over' as public accounts of violence and 'not far enough' in reclaiming control of women's bodies from those she might call 'bona fide' harassers. In keeping with this distinction, she describes 'fumingly' tweeting in response to a story about a 'Powerful Literary Man' told in the *New York Times* that the man was an 'arsehole' and not a 'predator' as the author characterised him, and disputing details of the story. Roiphe (2018) has similarly extended her critique into this era. She has declared herself 'exhilarated' by the movement to hold men accountable, but her writing remains far more preoccupied with the 'chilling effect of feminist orthodoxy' and its use of generic strictures and inauthentic narratives to silence those who might be ambivalent or cautious about the new movement. The 'sense of viciousness lying in wait, of violent hate just waiting to be unfurled', she writes, '… leads people to keep their opinions to themselves, or to share them only with close friends'.

The reproduction of these questions in contemporary settings makes clear that they are not isolated examples but on-going concerns about what it means to politically engage with narratives of sexual violence. The tendency that they reveal is for political debates to be supplanted by questions of generic judgement and belief. These questions are to do with what stories do and don't belong in feminist genres, and with the legitimacy of the genres themselves. They also revisit the question, addressed in Chaps. 5 and 6, as to who is able to have these discussions and who is able to institute or demand certain generic boundaries around acceptable speech. The judgements I discuss in this chapter primarily involve white women and rarefied media spaces or elite college campuses. The Victorian and melodramatic structures that Kipnis and Roiphe point to are predominantly narratives told by and about white 'respectable' women. The points and arguments they raise are far less relevant to women who are unable to access these genres or this speaking position.

Nevertheless, these examples raise questions about the political strategy of constructing a genre of stories as a political tool. They are cautionary tales about the ability of speaking out to fulfil its core tenets of individual and collective empowerment for survivors and wider cultural change even within feminist spaces and among feminists. The critiques offered by Roiphe and Kipnis suggest that there is something inherently flawed in this literary politics and that it is not enabling the kinds of stories that can or do assist women's empowerment or institute progressive cultural changes around the intersection of sex and violence. I would suggest that a more productive approach is to interrogate and intervene in practices of belonging and exclusion rather than simply enforcing them. Doing so would also enable attention to what Derrida (1992) describes as the 'principle of contamination and impurity', which means that all narratives simultaneously participate within and exceed the genres through which they are told. Processes of generic judgement and the imposition of expectations and conventions on narratives cannot be eliminated. But as I argue in the Conclusion, feminists might use the tools of generic analysis to enable the telling of new stories which decentre these questions of judgement and belief. One way of beginning to do this, I suggest in the following chapter, is to focus attention more clearly on the politics of listening alongside the politics of speech.

8

That Which Must Be Broken: Silence and the Politics of Listening

Silence has surrounded and engulfed women's experiences of sexual violence throughout history. The condemnation of this silencing is perhaps the most powerful and resonant element of second-wave feminist responses to rape. To be silenced, to not have one's speech, precludes political action and prevents survivors reclaiming and rebuilding their subjectivity through speech. As I showed in Chap. 3, silencing is the main villain in the core narrative of speaking out, decentring the rapist and his actions. Silence, as a villain or political opponent, features repeatedly in this book as the 'other' of speaking out, as that which must be overcome through survivor speech and feminist activism. To be silent, then, is either to be victimised or to be passive and complicit, while to engage in silencing is to enact a form of violence. In the highly antagonistic Bell debate discussed in Chap. 6, one of the most common, and most damning, of the allegations made was the accusation of silencing. Diane Bell (1991a) accused 'political' Aboriginal women and their allies of silencing women's stories of intra-racial rape in Indigenous communities. The Indigenous women who opposed Bell accused her of enacting a form of white feminist silencing (Huggins et al. 1991). The editors of *Women's Studies International Forum* claimed that white anthropologists who wished to write about gendered violence in Indigenous communities were victims of a 'silencing process' (Rowland 1991–1992, p. 430). The over-riding logic of both sides of the debate, and of much feminist analysis generally, was perhaps most eloquently expressed by Bell (1991b, p. 508) when she wrote that 'silence kills women'. The central location of silence in the politics of speaking out calls for closer attention than it is usually given, and that is the task of this chapter.

In feminist discourse around rape, silence frequently figures as a synecdoche for the effects of patriarchal power on women, a shared trope even among those who agree on little else. Women's speech is, therefore, inherently oppositional and liberating, raised up against power and capable, ultimately, of breaking silence. Parsing Foucault's (1998, p. 6) famous formulation of the 'speaker's benefit', feminist discourses presume that because women's speech about rape 'is repressed, that is, condemned to prohibition, nonexistence, and silence, then the mere fact that one is speaking about it has the appearance of a deliberate transgression'. To speak, or to speak out, is to place oneself 'outside of the reach of power', to 'upset established law' and to anticipate 'the coming freedom'. In this chapter, I follow Wendy Brown (2005, p. 85) in interrogating the 'oddly non- or pre-Foucauldian quality' to most feminist discussions of silence in relation to sexual violence. Like Brown and Foucault, I do not do this to call for a return to silence, but rather to more precisely articulate what kinds of silences are harmful, and why. Disaggregating notions of silence and silencing, I suggest, opens the possibility for thinking about how certain kinds of silences at certain moments might not be harmful but may even be strategically useful in feminist responses to sexual violence.

Another way of phrasing this is to ask what kinds of understandings the powerful and omnipresent metaphor of 'breaking' the silence precludes, and what understandings might be enabled by thinking about the relation between speech and silence in different terms. One answer to this is suggested by the Canadian writer and activist, Elly Danica. Danica (1988) published *Don't: A Woman's Word*, a memoir about her experience of childhood sexual abuse by her father, in 1988. The memoir achieved some commercial success, and Danica, like Nancy Ziegenmeyer and Jill Saward discussed in Chap. 2, experienced a period of being known as a 'public survivor' in Canadian public culture in the late 1980s and early 1990s. However, as she chronicles in the sequel to this book, *Beyond*

Don't: Dreaming Past the Dark, published eight years later, the political effects of her speech were not what she imagined (Danica 1996). She felt that after the interest in her story as a spectacle had evaporated it was as if the impact of the story similarly evaporated, leaving a situation where it was as if it had never been told in the first place. As she writes, 'I now see that I and numerous colleagues over the years have been breaking the silence over and over again, only to have it subsequently swallow us up again moments after we speak' (Danica 1996, p. 141). Rather than breaking through the silence like a rock through a pane of glass, her speech was more like a rock thrown into a pond, creating a splash and ripples which gradually faded away, leaving the surface of the pond the same as before. Many of the examples discussed in this book might be seen having been similarly swallowed. There is little public memory, for instance, of Nancy Ziegenmeyer and the media event that surrounded her story, or even of some of the hashtag campaigns that preceded #MeToo, discussed in Chap. 5. If feminist and survivor speech can draw significant public attention for a brief time before fading from public memory, then, as Danica suggests, the feminist exhortation to 'break the silence' needs to be rethought.

In the remainder of this chapter, I draw on discussions of silence in survivor narratives to develop a more complicated understanding of silence, its relationship to speech and its political potential. In the first section, I return to Lyotard's (1988) concept of the *differend*, introduced in Chap. 4, to articulate the harms of silence and what is at stake in the attempt to overcome it. The second section returns to survivors such as Danica who have discussed the limitations of speaking out to consider how speech might co-exist with, and even enable, certain forms of silencing. In the third section, I suggest that some kinds of silences might be necessary for speech, and for an effective politics of speaking out. The concluding section turns to the future, a theme continued in the Conclusion which follows this chapter. It asks what an 'after' might look like in relation to silence and silencing. It articulates the necessity of silence for a politics of listening and the importance of imagining a world in which speech about and against sexual violence might not be so necessary. Complicating discussions of silence, I argue, is important for producing a more effective politics of speech.

Kill the Silence

In the survey of rape memoirs provided in Chap. 3, I noted that their titles provide a useful insight into the politics of speaking out. These titles produce a multitude of variations on the theme of silence. It is seen as a second stage in the harms of rape, *Hours of Torture, Years of Silence: My Soul Was the Scene of the Crime*; as something that must be endured, *Surviving the Silence: Black Women's Stories of Rape*; and, of course, as something that must be overcome for personal and collective liberation, *Diary of a Rape Victim: Breaking the Silence to Break Free* (Lauer 1998; Pierce-Baker 1998; Van Godwin 2000). The central quest narrative that the genre enacts is one of reconstituting subjectivity through speech and against social and institutional forms of silencing. Nancy Venable Raine's (1998) memoir, *After Silence: Rape and My Journey Back*, describes a descent into a realm of silence that she must literally journey out of and away from. Coming 'back' means reconstituting her subjectivity and re-entering the social world. Monica Kørra's (2015) *Kill the Silence: A Survivor's Life Reclaimed* similarly evokes the framework of a quest narrative in which silence must not only be overcome, but in fact killed, in order for her to reclaim her life. Slaying the forces of silence enables her to transform herself from a victim into a heroic survivor.

Silence in these texts means far more than the absence of speech. It therefore requires more than a simple act of speech to overcome it. If speaking out is, as I contend, a politicised form of speech that can create cultural and social transformations, the silence it opposes needs to be understood in similarly political and social terms. Rather than reacting against silence itself, survivor stories confront social silencing as an active force. This silencing is not coterminous with silence as in a simple lack of speech. It is more effectively understood through Lyotard's concept of the *differend*, introduced in Chap. 4 (see also Stringer 2013; Waterhouse-Watson 2013). As Lyotard explains, a *differend* is not about literally stopping someone from speaking in the form of making words, but rather, in obtaining 'deafness' from those who might hear that speech, rendering the testimony meaningless: 'You neutralise the addressor, the addressee, and the sense of the testimony; then everything is as if there were no referent (no damages)' (Lyotard 1988, p. 8). The *differend* turns plaintiffs, who are able to speak of the harm done to them and demand justice, into victims, who are unable to be heard and can achieve no meaningful redress. In her memoir, *Aftermath*, Susan Brison (2002, p. 85) poignantly articulates the experience of being subject to a *differend* through the Bertolt Brecht poem, 'When Evildoing Comes Like Falling Rain', which introduces her chapter on silence and forgetting: 'Like one who seeks to warn the city of an impending flood, but speaks another language. ... So do we come forward and report that evil has been done to us'. The poem concludes: 'When sufferings become unendurable the cries are no longer heard. The cries, too, fall like rain in summer'. The experience of cries falling like rain in the summer which almost immediately evaporates echoes Danica's experience of her speech being swallowed up again, and it gives insight into the harms of experiencing silence as a *differend*.

A detailed accounting of how the individually violent act of rape becomes the socially and politically harmful experience of a *differend* is provided by Nancy Raine (1998, p. 6):

> The words *shut up* are the most terrible words I know. I cannot hear them without feeling cold to the bone. The man who raped me spat these words out over and over during the hours of my attack – when I screamed, when I tried to talk him out of what he was doing, when I protested. It seemed to me that for seven years – until at last I spoke – these words had sunk into my soul and become prophecy. And it seems to me now that these words, the brutish message of tyrants, preserve the darkness that still covers this pervasive crime.

For seven years, this coercive silence persisted: 'I had been a writer, yet since the rape I had written very little, and finished nothing... I had written nothing at all about what was, in fact, the most profound experience of my life' (pp. 3–4). The problem was not that she could not or did not want to speak of her experience, but that words 'had turned as brittle as the leaves that minutes before had called the memory of rape out of the wind' (Raine 1994). While the ways in which the experience of trauma disrupts the representative capacities of language cannot be underestimated (Herman 1992), neither, I argue, can the effect of the various mechanisms of social silencing, from explicit commands to shut up, to the legal production of women as liars discussed in Chap. 4, to conventions of politeness and civility. These different mechanisms work together to produce the 'incoherence' of survivor testimony and the 'deafness' of others to it.

Cultural and social forms of silencing may be more subtle than the violence of rape or even the injustice of the law, but they enact similar damage. They may even be more effective precisely because their apparent reasonableness functions to render the survivor and her speech as the cause of social disruption or discomfort rather than as a legitimate call to recognise social injustice. It is no coincidence that the chapter in Raine's book which describes the insidious function and profound effects of the *differend*, 'The Woman in the Amber Necklace', is also the longest (Raine 1998, pp. 118–135). The chapter begins shortly after Raine has published her first piece of writing on rape, 'Returns of the Day', an essay which writes of the difficulties she faces on each anniversary of the day she was attacked. She attends a lunch where she is seated next to a woman in an amber necklace. After introducing each other, Raine mentions the article and her book project before they are interrupted by welcomes from the host:

> The woman with the amber necklace turns to me again and says, as if she's been thinking about it while the toasts were being made: "I thought your article was well-written." I am smiling. "But let's face it, no one wants to hear about such terrible things."

In the moment, Raine is unable to reply. 'The next day I can't get back to the book, which I have been working on for several months. And the day after that. A week passes, then six' (p. 119). She ponders the wider implications of the conversation and its effects:

> Attempts to dissipate the shame by giving words to the unspeakable seem only to increase it. The shame is mirrored by the listener, sometimes quite obviously by a blush, an averting of the eyes, or a hunching of the shoulders, sometimes by silence. The telling then feels like a confession, an admission of wrongdoing, and the sense of blame is deepened. (p. 131)

In a classic function of the *differend*, Raine is no longer a plaintiff, able to be heard about her experience of victimisation by sexual violence, but a victim, punished for her attempt to speak and demand witness. The conversation returns her to the way she felt immediately after she was raped, a state characterised by the unavailability and incapacity of language. She is a language without punctuation of structure. 'Verbs dangled at the end of sentences, tenseless. Subjects began to drop out altogether' (pp. 24–25). Her experience highlights a theme of this book: to be successful, political storytelling must have an audience who will hear and respond: 'How can I make a sum of everything I remember – a self – if that self does not exist in relation to others?' (p. 121).

The question of how to make a self that can acknowledge and account for sexual violence and be recognised is also a central concern of Monika Kørra. For her, it is a question of what it means to 'kill the silence' that surrounds sexual violence. Kørra was a Norwegian exchange student at a university in Texas when she was abducted from a party by a group of men who raped her before leaving her on the side of the road. Her book documents her experience and its aftermath, the trial of her assailants and the gradual emergence of her determination to become an activist against sexual violence. It is this determination that gives the book its title:

> From the very first days when I thought about coming forward, a phrase had kept running through my mind: "Kill the silence"… I'd been silent for far too long, and I knew that it was the silence that prolonged the pain for many rape victims; it was a silence whose source was shame and humiliation, a severe form of the desire to be treated as "normal." (Kørra 2015, p. 277)

In addition to writing her book, Kørra established the 'Monika Kørra Foundation', whose mission statement is 'working to kill the silence around rape and abuse' (Monika Kørra Foundation 2015). Kørra's story is not so much a story about rape as a quest to 'kill' the silence that surrounds sexual violence and that enacts shame and humiliation on survivors.

As Raine suggests, overcoming silence is not as simple as generating speech. This becomes clear when Kørra participates in a restorative justice programme with one of the three men who attacked her. As the conversation progresses, she becomes increasingly frustrated with his oblique descriptions of the sexual assault as 'what I did to you' and his avoidance of more specific language. She insists that he name his actions as rape before she will continue the conversation. Reflecting afterwards on this insistence, she notes that from 'the very first speech I did after deciding to come forward, I had in my mind the idea of killing the silence', but that not just any speech about rape would suffice to do this. A violent act, she writes, required recognition in violent words:

> Ending it [silence] wasn't enough. It was going to take something more drastic than that, something that had more finality… Some people needed to have their attention grabbed… We'd tried subtlety and indirection. There was nothing subtle about rape. (Kørra 2015, pp. 293–294)

For Kørra, her eventual success in making him use the word 'rape' signals a 'starting point' in her goal of killing silence. In her interaction with the man who raped her, Kørra refuses to speak a different language or to allow her cries to fall like rain and melt away. Her insistence on the word 'rape' signals her determination that the harm done to her be named and recognised. There is, to use Lyotard's (1988, p. 8) phrasing, a 'referent' that registers the harm and injustice of the act of rape. Breaking or killing the silence goes beyond speech, simply understood. It contests the *differend* and enacts a self in relation to others. However, as the opening quote from Danica indicates, a single moment of contestation is insufficient to achieve this. In the following section, I consider how rethinking silence can lead to a more critical investigation of the politics of speech.

The Silences of Speaking Out

Feminist speech around rape is, as I posit above, primarily understood through the lens of what Foucault (1998) labelled the 'speaker's benefit', the notion that in relation to a social taboo such as rape, to speak, and particularly to speak of one's experience, is to take a position against power and for freedom. In this section, I question this assumption by asking about the silences that feminist and survivor speech might contain or produce within and alongside it. Feminist and survivor speech around rape, I argue in this section, cannot be automatically presumed to be transgressive or oppositional. I make this case initially through the reflections of Elly Danica and another 'public survivor', Louise Armstrong, two women who achieved public recognition for their stories of familial child sexual abuse in the 1980s, but who came by the mid-1990s to question the political efficacy of their speech and of speaking out in general. Danica doubted if speaking out as a political strategy could overcome the on-going and recurrent practices of social silencing, while Armstrong offered an even stronger critique which suggested that speaking out might in fact produce its own *differends* in relation to sexual violence.

In 1978, Armstrong published *Kiss Daddy Goodnight: A Speak-Out on Incest*. The book told her story alongside the stories of other women she had solicited through advertisements in feminist media. It used these stories, in the tradition of second-wave feminist consciousness-raising practice, to produce a political analysis of incest as an essential feature of the patriarchal family. The book received significant attention, and Armstrong made various media and conference appearances, becoming, as she later saw it, a spectacle rather than a political activist, the 'World's First Walking, Talking Incest Victim' (Armstrong 1994, p. 2). Ultimately, she argued, the politics of speaking out were incorporated and co-opted within the wider backlash of the 1980s, making survivor speech meaningless by erasing its political content:

> But not very gradually, the decade of the 1980s brought an ever greater denial of feminist voices. A new veil of silence began to descend, woven of a magical new hi-tech fabric. This fabric was permeable by the personal, but it acted as a filter, blocking out the political. All that began to get through were stories: battered women's stories, rape victims' stories, incest victims' stories. (p. 76)

These stories were no longer recognisably feminist, in the sense of promoting a collective politics of social change, but were merely personal stories of individual growth and recovery, marketed by a burgeoning 'incest and trauma industry' that relied on the production of women as disempowered and individual victims. In this context, survivor narratives became 'I-Stories', which, rather than insisting that the personal was political, reduced the 'political to the merely personal' (Armstrong 1990, p. 3). This was not, or was no longer, speaking out as a form of feminist activism but an anti-feminist form of speech that rendered political speech unhearable, and reduced survivors collectively from political plaintiffs, able to make claims on their own behalf, to victims unable to testify to the structural and systemic basis of the harm they experienced. Ultimately, she concluded that 'breaking the silence' as a political project had 'come to seem bankrupt' (Armstrong 1994, p. 204).

When Armstrong first made this argument in the *Women's Review of Books*, she generated significant controversy. Letter writers accused her of 'falling into a blame-the-victim approach', 'trivialising survivors' experiences', and forgetting that 'every woman's narrative has a place in the feminist view of the world' (Mitchell et al. 1990). Twenty years later, however, her points about the dangers of presuming the political efficacy of women's speech can seem prescient. They prefigure contemporary feminist discussions about the shaping of personal stories through neoliberalism (e.g. Phipps 2016; L. Gilmore 2017; Crawley and Simic 2018). Her critique of the depoliticising effects of psychological discourses has also been raised by contemporary critics and has strong resonances with my discussion of the continuing influence of criminal justice discourse in survivor narratives (Sersier 2005; McKenzie-Mohr 2014). And, at least some survivor narratives seem to fulfil her prophecy, making use of self-help discourse to explicitly disavow any collective political content to their stories. Trisha Meili's (2004) *I am the Central Park Jogger: A Story of Hope and Possibility*, for example, is told through the framework of Meili's profession as a motivational speaker. Meili writes that she 'never really identified strongly' with other rape survivors and insists that the true lesson of story is to do with individual resilience and overcoming, an archetypal example of what Leigh Gilmore (2017) labels 'neoliberal life narratives'.

Armstrong's critique resonates with the call by feminist scholars such as Tanya Horeck (2004, p. vi) to rethink the politics of volubility around rape: 'Susan Griffin's call to break the "conspiracy of silence" surrounding rape was once feminism's goal; it now seems that the main challenge facing feminist cultural critics approaching the topic of rape in the twenty-first century is how to deal with the intense publicity trained on the crime'. As Armstrong and Danica make clear, the question of publicity is intimately tied to problems of co-optation through commodification and spectacularisation. Danica (1996, p. 141), for instance, writes of her distress at seeing sexual violence survivors presented as a 'freak show on the talk shows every afternoon'. As long as this mode of representation dominates, 'any call for change, however passionate – and eventually any reporting of abuse, however horrible – will be effectively silenced, slotted as it is, in between advertisements for new tampons, hair colour and the latest super-clean, non-polluting, biodegradable detergent'. A less absolute conclusion is suggested by Alcoff and Gray (1993), who contend that, while spectacular media formats like television talk shows commodify and co-opt survivor speech, they are unable to completely silence the political impacts of that speech and the calls it makes for change. For them, the appropriate and necessary response to Armstrong's argument is to investigate how the 'transgressive potential' of this speech can be maximised 'in such a way that the autonomy and empowerment of the survivor who is speaking as well as of survivors elsewhere will be enhanced rather than undermined' (p. 282), and they insist that this outcome is possible. They use Foucault to outline the methods by which women's speech is rendered 'confessional' rather than political, and how its meaning is framed and delimited by experts with the voices of survivors reduced to the 'raw experience' of spectacle and emotion (Alcoff and Gray 1993, p. 280). Unlike Armstrong, however, they insist that political speech is possible, even in the compromised forums of media such as television talk shows.

Where Armstrong and, to a lesser extent, Danica, see questions of political success and co-optation in the form of binaries and absolutes, Alcoff and Gray contend that these are strategic questions. Thinking strategically, they recognise that there are moments when it is necessary or better to remain silent: 'survival itself sometimes necessitates a refusal to recount or even a refusal to disclose and deal with the assault of abuse, given the emotional, financial, and physical difficulties that such disclosures can create' (1993, p. 281). This statement, however, is more of a recognition that survivors are not always able to speak than an assertion that silence may sometimes be a point of resistance. They insist that feminists and survivors should not 'retreat … from bringing sexual violence into discourse but, rather … create new discursive forms and spaces in which to gain autonomy within this process' (p. 287). Alcoff and Gray thus offer an important corrective to the perspective of Armstrong and Danica in their insistence that co-option is not an absolute or irreversible process. At the same time, they insist that survivor speech is not positioned in 'an oppositional but still harmonious complementarity with the dominant discourse but rather in violent confrontation with it' (p. 269). In other words, it is necessarily and always transgressive. As Armstrong and Danica argue, and as I have attempted to show throughout this book, that cannot always be presumed, and it fails to account for the ways that even political speech may be 'filtered', as Armstrong implies, so that only the personal elements are able to meaningfully register.

Finally, I suggest that the analyses of Alcoff and Gray, as well as those of Armstrong and Danica, fail to consider the ways in which oppositional speech may adopt and reproduce the silences of dominant discourse, not as a result of recuperation, but because it reproduces and shares fundamental assumptions of that discourse. A primary example of this is the way in which feminist speech may reproduce radicalised discourses of criminality and victim hierarchies that silence the speech of women of colour. An example of this type of silencing can be found in Armstrong's own book-length 'speak out'. Because she wanted to produce a collective, 'political' text rather than a personal account, she included the experiences of other survivors alongside her own. After advertising, 'primarily' in the feminist press, she received 'hundreds' of responses. She spoke with 183 women and eventually included 16 of their stories in her book (Armstrong 1978, p. 16). All except one of these were from white women. Armstrong attributed this primarily to 'self-selection' in that the overwhelming majority of responses she received were from white women. This may, of course, say more about the racial make-up of the audiences of feminist publications than it does about self-selection, although both were probably a factor. But as Armstrong admits, she still played an active role in selecting her subjects: 'I do concede some bias against playing into that need for melodrama, for "victims", which I sense in the world'. The women she chose are:

for the most part ... people I felt the majority of readers might think of themselves as working next to, shopping alongside of, living in the neighbourhood of (and ending sentences and prepositions with). They are not, in the main, what society would cast as losers, for I quickly learned that most people have no difficulty believing that sexual abuse happens among the dimwitted, the poor, the morally obtuse, the overcrowded. (pp. 232–233)

There is much that could be said about the processes of judgement and categorisation that inform Armstrong's 'bias' and link race, class, intelligence and morality to produce a representable feminist subject. Leaving this aside, my point is simply that to see silence and silencing as necessarily or always imposed on survivor narratives from the outside ignores the discursive framing of experience and the racial and class politics that trouble feminist stories of gender universalism. It also ignores Foucault's political caution about the speaker's benefit and the way that it can enable and produces new silences and unintended political consequences. Thinking instead about silence as a part of discursive politics enables us to interrogate how speech can nurture harmful silences and to think about how silence might, at least in some circumstances, work to enable other forms of speech and new possibilities. This is the question that I turn to now.

Silence in Discourse and Dialogue

To this point, the discussion in this chapter has complicated understandings of silence but not disputed the fundamental valuation of silence as negative and speech as positive. The authors discussed have largely accepted the 'common conceit' that speech and silence are inherently opposed. This conceit 'enables both the assumption that censorship converts the truth of speech to the lie of silence and the assumption that when an enforced silence is broken, what emerges is truth borne by the vessel of authenticity or experience' (Brown 2005, p. 83). From a Foucauldian perspective, however, both speech and silence are complex domains of power and resistance:

> Discourses are not once and for all subservient to power or raised up against it, any more than silences are… Discourse transmits and produces power; it reinforces it, but also undermines and exposes it, renders it fragile and makes it possible to thwart it. In like manner, silence and secrecy are a shelter for power, anchoring its prohibitions; but they also loosen its holds and provide for relatively obscure areas of tolerance. (Foucault 1998, pp. 100–101)

As Wendy Brown (2005, pp. 92–93) argues, we expand the number and type of questions that we can ask about the relationship between speech, silence and power if we begin from the perspective that they 'aren't really opposites'. We can consider if 'to speak incessantly of one's suffering is to silence the possibilities of overcoming it, of living beyond it, of identifying as something other than it'. At the same time, we can posit that 'a certain modality of silence about one's suffering' might articulate 'a variety of possibilities not otherwise available to the sufferer'. Brown points out that incessant speech might equally overwhelm 'the experiences of others' and 'alternative (unutterable, traumatized, fragmentary, or unassimilable) zones of one's *own* experience' (emphasis in original). In this section, I draw on this analysis to think about first how silence on the part of survivors enables political possibilities of speaking out, and second, how silence on the part of feminist audiences is similarly essential to this politics.

Crucial to this unpacking is a cognisance of different types or modalities of silence. Nancy Venable Raine, for instance, experiences the silence of the *differend* with the woman in the amber necklace, but she also writes of other modalities of silence that are chosen rather than imposed. These modalities are an important part of her journey out of and away from the silence of the *differend*. Raine (1998) returned to her book several months after her conversation with the woman in the amber necklace. A short while later she abandoned the book for a second time. In this 'two-year period of change and construction' she met and married her second husband, immersed herself in other work and 'thoughts of the rape disappeared completely' (p. 170). At the end of two years, her traumatic symptoms returned, and she returned to the book. But, she contends, her ability to complete the project was dependent on this period of silence:

'I believe I was granted (by whom or what I cannot say) a full but temporary pardon that permitted me to construct the hull of the vessel that would carry me here, to words themselves, the witnessing of my own survival' (p. 174). This distinction speaks to Lyotard's (1988, p. 10) insistence that silence is not coterminous with the *differend*:

> Not to speak is part of the ability to speak, since ability is a possibility and a possibility implies something and its opposite... That the opposite of speaking is possible does not entail the necessity of keeping quiet. To be able not to speak is not the same as not to be able to speak. The latter is a deprivation, the former a negation.

The *differend* deprives subjects of the ability to speak rather than speech itself. Silence, in the context of a wider ability to speak, for Lyotard, is simply a 'phrase' and a necessary component of language (p. 12). As Raine's story indicates, interpreting silence requires looking beyond the simple fact of the absence of speech: 'If the survivors do not speak, is it because they cannot speak, or because they avail themselves of the possibility of not speaking that is given them by the ability to speak?' (p. 10).

The choice not to speak is, according to the feminist author, Dorothy Allison, crucial to a politics of speech. It is, she insists, essential to survivors to be able to exercise control over their stories: 'I am the only one who can tell the story of my life and say what it means. I knew that as a child. It was one of the reasons not to tell' (Allison 1996, p. 70). To tell a story without the ability to control its meaning, as I have argued in previous chapters, produces a *differend* that mirrors the experience of being unable to speak. Allison (1996, pp. 43–44) writes that her ability to control her stories of childhood sexual violence was built on a foundation of 'years of silence':

> I had to learn how to say it, to say "rape," say "child," say "unending," "awful" and "relentless," and say it the way I do – adamant, unafraid, unashamed, every time, all over again – to speak my words as a sacrament, a blessing a prayer. Not a curse. Getting past the anger, getting to the release, I become someone else, and the story changes.

The transformative potential of speaking in this way is contrasted by Allison to the trap of being compelled to tell the story 'the world wants, the story of us broken, the story of us never laughing out loud, never learning to enjoy sex, never being able to love or trust love again, the story in which all that survives is the flesh' (p. 10). She tells the story she does so she never has to tell that story. It is only through being able to recognise that which is inarticulable, suggests Allison, that experience may usefully and politically be brought into the realm of the political, and, in the years of silence and the speech that follows them, the story itself changes.

Control over one's story is also something that is granted by or extracted from an audience. Or, as I discussed in the previous chapter, something that may be refused, even by feminist audiences. The willingness or refusal, or ability or inability, of an audience to listen is an important but undertheorised element of the politics of speaking out. As Walter Benjamin (2002, p. 149) reminds us, the 'community of listeners' is the 'web in which the gift of storytelling is cradled', and so, listening forms an essential part of any progressive politics of speech (Lacey 2013). Attentive silence is a precondition of the act of listening, or reading, or in other ways taking on the role of audience for a speaker. When it comes to stories of sexual violence, the act of listening or hearing in ways which do not devalue or deny the speaker requires the audience to open themselves to a traumatic experience and to refuse to hear it through the social filters that prevent and disallow women's narratives of sexual violence. It is, to return to the woman in the amber necklace, to push beyond the sense that the listener does not want to hear 'such terrible things'. Survivor stories are not only hard to tell, but they are, as survivor and author Migael Scherer (1992, p. 84) reflects, thinking of her family and friends, hard to hear and even harder to hear well. This does not preclude discussion or even disagreement with aspects of the interpretation offered by the teller but locates this debate after the gift of listening. To insist on listening as the counterpart of speaking emphasises the collective nature of the project of speaking out and helps to avoid the individualising tendencies critiqued by Armstrong above.

The politics of listening, and the silence it requires, have been central to the discussions of the previous two chapters. Both the overt refusals of witnessing discussed in the previous chapter and Diane Bell's insistence on speaking for or over the stories of raped women, represent, in different ways, a failure of listening. Feminist valorisation of the figure of the heroic speaking woman obscures the fact that, at times, listening may be the more important and even more challenging feminist act. Attentive listening means listening for and beyond the conventions of genre, to accept different narratives of violence as legitimate participants without only hearing their participation in the genre and not their particularity. An example of that kind of well-intentioned non-listening was provided in Chap. 4 in Alice Sebold's (1999, p. 155) description of Tricia, at the rape crisis centre, who appeared only to see in Sebold the generic characteristics of raped women as a group.

A more nuanced politics of listening would refuse the presumption that political solidarity arises automatically from stories of rape and sexual violence. It could focus instead on the way in which collective and reciprocal practices of listening might work to build that solidarity between and around the differences as well as the similarities of these stories. Building this solidarity might require, as I suggest in Chap. 5, pausing before saying 'me too', or listening for the ways in which the experiences of others are strange and unfamiliar rather than always and already known and knowable. This is crucial for a politics of speaking out that avoids assuming the experiences of white middle-class women are representative or can be universalised. Writing of the ethical responsibilities of white feminists in the Bell debate, Sara Ahmed (2000, p. 64) insists that interventions by marginalised women, such as the group of Indigenous women who wrote to Diane Bell, can and should be seen as a 'gift' to white feminism. She argues that 'in receiving that gift, white feminism would not be forced into silence', labelling this a 'perverse response' that 'refuses responsibility' for power relations and political implications. But I would suggest that this only considers one modality of silence, presuming it to signify a withdrawal from engagement rather than a necessary precondition. A silence that is engaged and listening, and open to learning and hearing something new and unexpected, may be the only way to produce political solidarity and shared action from the genre of survivor narratives that this book is concerned with. As Linda Alcoff (1991, p. 17) suggests, sensible use of the 'retreat response', especially by relatively privileged women, may be the only way to build a politics based on shared goals and mutual understanding.

After Silence?

To return to the title of Nancy Venable Raine's (1998) book, *After Silence*, I ask what a collective or political 'after' to silence might look like in relation to sexual violence. This 'after' is implicit in the exhortation to break the silence but, as I discuss above, the social silencing of rape survivors has evidenced a profound ability to persist and return. To be after silence, then, means moving beyond the *differend* of imposed silence and the cycle of speech, silence and forgetting alluded to by Elly Danica in her metaphor of silence swallowing those who speak back up. As Sabine Sielke (2002, pp. 4–5) writes, 'the central paradigm of a rhetoric of rape is not simply one of rape and silencing ... insinuating that this silence can be broken' but rather one of 'rape, silence and refiguration'. Viewed in this way, the central point of political action is not breaking the silence but intervening in the process of refiguration. This offers the possibility of disrupting what Lynn A. Higgins and Brenda R. Silver (1991, pp. 1–2) label the 'most profoundly disturbing pattern' in representations of rape, the repetition of 'an obsessive inscription – and an obsessive erasure – of sexual violence against women':

> The striking repetition of inscription and erasure raises the question not only of why this trope recurs, but even more, of what it means and who benefits. How is it that in spite (or perhaps because) of their erasure, rape and sexual violence have been so ingrained and so rationalized through their representations as to appear "natural" and inevitable, to women as to men?

To envision ourselves as 'after' silence is, first and foremost, to imagine an after to this cycle, where in the words of Danica, silence may swallow us up again moments after we speak, and where rape and sexual violence are no longer allowed to appear natural and inevitable.

Obsessive cycles of inscription and erasure might be considered a general feature of the contemporary social media era, including the waves of hashtag campaigns against gendered and sexual violence that have emerged and faded in the last five years, from #EverydaySexism and #YesAllWomen to more recent examples such as #MeToo, or #NotOkay, the hashtag that emerged following the release of a video that showed the then Presidential candidate, Donald Trump, bragging about sexually assaulting women. While I return to this election campaign in the Conclusion, here I am interested in the hashtag which was started by Canadian writer, Kelly Oxford (@kellyoxford), who asked women to tweet their first experiences of sexual violence accompanied by #NotOkay. The hashtag went viral, trending for over 48 hours (Megan et al. 2018). Following its success, Oxford partnered with the Canadian branch of the YWCA to launch a website based on the hashtag. The section 'what can I do' listed four options: 'When you see something that's not okay tag it #NotOkay'; 'Turn your Facebook or Twitter profile into a symbol for change'; 'Use social media posts to speak out'; and 'Spread the word. Ask your friends to do the same' (YWCA Canada 2016). As in the follow-up campaign to #MeToo launched by Alyssa Milano, #KeepTellingPeople, discussed in Chap. 5, each of these options is in fact a variant on the same theme: continuing to speak. This politics continues attempts to intervene in the process of refiguration, but it focuses far more on the fact of speech than on its political shaping, and it is the shaping of speech that Sielke rightly suggests requires attention and focus. We need to think about what is said and how, alongside the way speech might be accompanied by other forms of action, or 'work', as 'Me Too' founder Tarana Burke describes it in Chap. 5.

This is not only a question of political efficacy and focus. It is about the need to envision speaking out and other political actions against rape as working towards their own redundancy. In other words, rather than naturalising the existence of rape through projecting the need for incessant and unending speech about it, we might instead build a politics that keeps the image of a world without rape present. The alternative is an eternal present with unending acts of speech that are unable to effect real change. To speak with no effect is not that different from the *differend* that renders speech ineffective and unintelligible. Imagining an after to the forcible silencing of the *differend* allows for the possibility of a different kind of silence. Writing in the conclusion of her autobiography, Monica Kørra notes that after she established her foundation, 'killing the silence' was no longer an obsession. Instead, her speech about sexual violence became one part of a life that has many other facets. She no longer views her life through the prism of speech or the quest narrative of speaking out. In fact, she is often silent about sexual violence so that she can tell and live other stories in which, increasingly, her life is something other and beyond speaking out. To allow the story of speaking out to reach an end or a pause may be a sign of political success, both individual and collective. To imagine a world 'after silence' is paradoxically not necessarily a world with more or even different speech around rape, but rather one in which we do not have to speak of rape so much, or, perhaps, one day, even at all.

9

Conclusion: Break the Silence, End the Violence? A Politics of Narrative

On October 9, 2016, speaking out burst into the centre of traditional partisan politics in the USA. The second debate in the Presidential election contest between Democratic candidate Hillary Clinton and Republican Donald Trump occurred two days after the release of a 2005 video that showed Trump bragging about sexually assaulting women: 'And when you're a star, they let you do it, you can do anything … grab them by the pussy'. In an attempt to contain the political damage of the tape, Trump brought four women to the debate, three of whom had accused Bill Clinton of sexual misconduct, and one who accused Hillary Clinton of mistreating her when Clinton acted as a defence attorney for the man who raped her as a child. Among them was Juanita Broaddrick, who has publicly claimed for over 20 years that Bill Clinton raped her in a hotel room when she was a volunteer for his Gubernatorial campaign. Trump held a press conference with the women prior to the debate, which they attended as his guests. When asked during the debate about the *Access Hollywood* tape, he dismissed it as 'locker room talk', claiming that where he was guilty of speaking, Bill Clinton was guilty of acting (BBC 2016). In the weeks and months following, however, a number of women came forward to share their stories of assault and harassment by the man who very soon would become the President of the USA (e.g. Twohey and Barbaro 2016).

In this conclusion, I draw on the discussions of the preceding chapters to consider more closely the political uses of narratives of sexual violence and the strengths and weaknesses of the public production and dissemination of these narratives as a strategy of feminist politics. I begin with the October 2016 Presidential campaign as a point of intersection between politics as traditionally understood and the political project of speaking out. This intersection can help to clarify what it means to view women's experiential narratives of sexual violence as political and point to some of the paradoxical manifestations of this politics. The mobilisation of women's speech about violence in the context of electoral politics can be read as a cautionary tale and a contrast to the more transformative political claims that are made for speaking out. It is these claims that I turn to in the second half of the conclusion. The contrasting visions offered here of speaking out as politics are equally part of the cultural landscape which shapes the possibilities and limitations of speaking out as a form of discursive activism and narrative politics.

As I noted in the Introduction, any contemporary assessment of feminist anti-rape activism and politics must reckon with a paradox that Rose Corrigan (2013) describes as the 'failures of success'. As a form of discursive activism, feminist politics around rape has been extraordinarily influential. It has shifted media representations, initiated legal and medical reforms, introduced education programmes and begun necessary conversations about normative behaviours of heterosexuality. It has even, as I discuss below, entered the arena of US Presidential politics. But this influence sits alongside a profound lack of change. As two researchers put it in a review of decades of anti-rape scholarship, '[p]revalence studies today yield nearly the same numbers' (Campbell and Wasco 2005, p. 129). So too do conviction and attrition rates which remain stubbornly low and high, respectively. The experiences of contemporary survivors in court, in their treatment by the media and in the on-going experience of social stigma and shame mirror all too closely the experiences of Sara Pines and others who told their stories in the consciousness-raising groups and speak-outs of the 1970s.

The political problem of sexual violence is thus characterised, as Corrigan notes, simultaneously by success and failure. I suggest, alongside many other feminist scholars and critics, that there is a need to rethink some of the central strategies and assumptions that have characterised feminist responses to sexual violence from the 1970s to the present day. Corrigan and others such as Yvette Russell (2016) argue that it is time to face what Russell describes as the 'limits of legal reform' in relation to the law. Beth Richie (2012) and Kristen Bumiller (2008), among others, have similarly insisted that accepting a punitive carceral response to rape has not only failed to make women safer but may even increase the amount of sexual violence enacted on women, and particularly on low-income and minority women. Laura Kipnis (2017), discussed in Chap. 7, is joined by other feminists to warn of the negative consequences in feminist embrace of a uniform and hegemonic trauma narrative of rape, and the need for a politics that promotes and enacts women's agency at the same time as recognising and responding to their suffering (Gavey and Schmidt 2011; McKenzie-Mohr 2014; Mardorossian 2014). In the realm of public speech and representation, scholars such as Tanya Horeck (2004) and Sabine Sielke (2002) have insisted on the need to focus on the intense publicity accorded to rape rather than still thinking in terms solely of breaking silence.

The 2016 US Presidential election evidenced this paradox and the need to rethink assumptions around feminist politics and, in this case, specifically around speaking out. In the campaign, women's narratives were mobilised politically in ways that were unthinkable in the 1970s or even 20 years ago when Juanita Broaddrick first told her story. As with other stories of famous men discussed in Chap. 5, it was not the stories about Trump and Clinton that were new but rather the ways in which they were able to register in electoral politics and wider public culture. This hearing, however, was incorporated within the framework of existing partisan politics rather than significantly disrupting this frame, or, indeed, preventing a man who boasted of and committed sexual assault from being elected President. I consider the ways in which, in its 'politicisation' within the election campaign, speaking out was highly influential but the forms of this influence were strictly curtailed. In the second half of the conclusion, I engage in a more speculative conversation about political possibility. I use the archive of stories of sexual violence, and the stories of telling these stories, discussed throughout the book to articulate the possibility of telling a utopian, future-oriented story of a world without endemic rape and sexual violence.

Politicising Speaking Out and Electing the Predator-in-Chief

On Friday, October 7, 2016, Donald Trump's Presidential campaign was thrown into crisis by the release of the now infamous *Access Hollywood* tape that showed Trump bragging about sexually assaulting women. Following calls by several senior Republicans for his disendorsement, Trump began his campaign to address the damage caused by the tape (Bash and Kopan 2016). The first element of this campaign was to dismiss the recordings as simply 'locker room' talk and the second was to divert attention onto his opponent, Hillary Clinton, through the long-standing public allegations of sexual assault and harassment against her husband, former President Bill Clinton. He contended that the things he said on the tape were not as bad as the things that Clinton had done. Further, he suggested that, in her efforts to support her husband, Hillary Clinton had 'bullied, attacked, shamed and intimidated his victims' (Trump 2016). His attempt to link Hillary Clinton's candidacy to Bill Clinton's sexual misconduct continued two days later at the second Presidential debate. Trump held a pre-debate Press Conference where he introduced four 'victims' of the Clintons. As many commentators noted at the time, however, the stories of Juanita Broaddrick, Paula Jones, Kathleen Willey and Cathy Shelton are very different. Shelton claims that Clinton mistreated her as a witness while defending a man who raped her at the age of 12. Jones and Willey have accused Bill Clinton of sexual harassment, although a judge has ruled that Jones' allegations do not meet the legal definition of harassment. Broaddrick, finally, has consistently claimed that Bill Clinton raped her in 1978, including in a lengthy television interview on NBC's *Dateline* in 1999 (Baker 2016b). Trump explained his decision to host the women at the debate by emphasising their agency and the importance of their speech, stating: 'These four very courageous women have asked to be here, and it was our honour to help them' (BBC 2016).

Trump's assertion that the *Access Hollywood* tape was trivial compared to the allegations against the Clintons was supported by the women at the press conference. As Broaddrick stated in response to a question about the tape: 'Actions speak louder than words. Bill Clinton raped me, and Hillary Clinton threatened me' (BBC 2016). As is now well-known, this distinction between Trump's words and Bill Clinton's actions did not take long to unravel. On Wednesday, October 12, three women publicly accused Trump of harassment and assault. In the *New York Times*, Jessica Leeds described Trump groping her and grabbing her breasts on a flight in the early 1980s: 'He was like an octopus. His hands were everywhere. It was an assault'. Her account was joined by Rachel Crooks, who told the paper that when she met Trump in an elevator of her office building in 2005, he began kissing her on the cheeks and the mouth (Twohey and Barbaro 2016). Natasha Stoynoff (2016), a reporter for *People* magazine, wrote about an assault that occurred while she was on an assignment at the Trump residence. Suddenly, she wrote, he was 'pushing me against the wall and forcing his tongue down my throat'. Soon, their accounts would be joined by many more, making Trump's history of sexual misconduct a key element of the election campaign that he would ultimately go on to win, leading him to be christened the 'Predator-in-Chief' by many of those who opposed his candidacy.

My purpose is not to compare the number, severity or credibility of the stories told about Bill Clinton and Donald Trump. Rather, I am interested in what this unprecedented focus on women's narratives of sexual violence during a US Presidential campaign might tell us about the politics of speaking out. In this campaign, women's speech was caught between different modalities of 'politics'. The public interest in this speech reflected significant shifts in cultural politics that allowed stories of events that had happened years or decades earlier to register and resonate in new ways across traditional political boundaries. At the same time, the register in which these stories were understood and heard might more accurately be described as that of the spectacular partisan politics of 'scandal' rather than feminist political interrogations of the links between gender, power and violence (Thompson 2000). There is huge significance to the fact that both the progressive and conservative elements of US politics, symbolised by Democrats and Republicans respectively, championed the speech of some women while seeking to dispute and deny the speech of others. I do not wish to assert that all these responses were equally sincere or to dispute the allegations of political opportunism made against Trump especially. For my purposes, the more important point is that across the political spectrum, the most effective political weapons, or the best political opportunities, were believed to be women's stories of sexual violence. In other words, the fact that Donald Trump was almost indisputably motivated by self-interest at the second debate matters less to my argument than the fact that he believed the best way to further his self-interest was through selectively aligning himself with women's speech about sexual violence. This fact reflects the paradoxical impact of speaking out traced in this book. Speaking out about sexual violence has become a significant feature of cultural and political landscapes and has, in that way, changed the dynamics of political speech around gender, sexuality and violence. Women's stories of violence, where they are accepted as true, occupy a position of significant moral and political authority. However, this authority means that in situations like the Presidential election there may be significant political consequences to accepting their veracity and sincerity. The political and ethical acts of speaking and hearing accounts of sexual violence can then be subsumed within narrow senses of politics as usual, and even, in the case of Trump, as political tools mobilised towards clearly regressive and even misogynist ends.

As noted above, many of these stories did not emerge in October 2016. Rather, they became politically important. Several of the women had spoken publicly years earlier, but their stories were now deemed newly relevant. While it was common to attribute this simply to a teleological story of feminist progress, this is complicated by the way in which they entered the campaign during a wider period of public discussion of sexual violence, particularly on university campuses. The stories first entered the realm of the campaign in late 2015 after Hillary Clinton (@HillaryClinton) tweeted, in September and again in November, about sexual violence, stating that every survivor 'deserves to be heard, believed and supported'. When questioned at a campaign event as to whether this included Bill

Clinton's accusers, Clinton replied: 'Well, I would say that everybody should be believed at first until they are disbelieved based on evidence'. A month later, Juanita Broaddrick (@atensnut) tweeted: 'I was 35 years old when Bill Clinton, Ark. Attorney General raped me and Hillary tried to silence me. I am now 73....it never goes away'. The tweet went viral and by the time of the election, had been retweeted over 100,000 times and favourited over 80,000 times (Baker 2016b). In May 2016, the *New York Times* published a story, 'Crossing the Line: How Donald Trump Behaved with Women in Private'. The article, based on interviews with 50 women, showed a pattern of harassment and assault by Trump in the workplace and elsewhere (Barbaro and Twohey 2016). In keeping with his response to the *Access Hollywood* tape, a week later Trump released an online ad which played audio taken from a 1999 television interview of Juanita Broaddrick describing Bill Clinton sexually assaulting her before cutting to a clip of Hillary Clinton laughing, framed by the slogan, 'Is Hillary really protecting women?' (Baker 2016b). In July, the *Guardian* published a detailed interview with Jill Harth, a woman who had previously sued Donald Trump for attempted rape (Graves 2016). The journalist who interviewed Harth later noted that the story provoked very limited interest prior to the October 9 debate (Vernon 2016).

While stories of sexual violence were present in the campaign well before the *Access Hollywood* tape, it was only after Trump himself seemed to confirm the allegations against him and give his patronage to the women who spoke about Clinton that their stories collectively became a major force. They were only fully heard, in other words, because of Trump's verification. This mobilisation was experienced by at least some women as a validation, or as *People* journalist Natasha Stoynoff (2016) wrote, a relief: 'I finally understood for sure that I was not to blame for his inappropriate behaviour. I had not been singled out'. The recording of Trump gave Stoynoff the courage to come forward, an act that made her vulnerable to the practices of judgement, belief and denial discussed throughout this book. Responses to her story were political in the sense that they corresponded broadly with divisions within electoral politics. She received significant public support, especially from Democrats and liberals, but had her narrative and her character doubted, denied and attacked by Trump and his supporters. Broaddrick has also complained about these processes of partisan support, but her position is the reverse of what would generally be expected or presumed. She feels that she has been attacked by Democrats and ignored and abandoned by feminists since she first spoke publicly in 1999. This includes public feminist and anti-rape activists, such as Susan Estrich (2001, p. 182), Democratic party activist and author of the book *Real Rape*, who has stated publicly that she doesn't believe Broaddrick's story and doesn't think it warrants public consideration. Even in 2016, she notes, many of those on the left who displayed outrage about Trump were reluctant to support or acknowledge her story. She told *Buzzfeed* journalist Katie Baker (2016b), 'I just wish some of the people who are high on the list of supporting victims would come forward and say, "Yes, I believe her"… But they won't even say they're sorry for me. They just say, "It's not Hillary's fault"'. The story of the 2016 election campaign is both one of the influence of speaking out and of that influence being contained by male validation and constrained by partisan political allegiance. In this divisive campaign there were very few public voices for whom a feminist commitment to speaking out and belief of survivors overshadowed attitudes to the candidacy and potential presidency of Donald Trump.

Juanita Broaddrick has emerged as a polarising figure who raises important questions about disentangling feminist imperatives to respond ethically to women's speech from political disagreements with the conclusions they draw from their experiences and the purposes for which they mobilise their stories. Broaddrick represented a problem for Hillary Clinton's campaign and for Democratic politics more generally. While I return to this below, the problem is perhaps most effectively symbolised by one effect of her January 2016 tweet. A section on sexual violence and survivors was added to Hillary Clinton's campaign website in late 2015, and this section was linked to in her tweets about supporting survivors. Shortly after Broaddrick's tweet the section was removed, although Clinton has never confirmed any connection between the two events (Baker 2016b). Broaddrick has continued to be a difficult, and even irreconcilable, figure following the election. She claims that she was interviewed for *Time* magazine's profile of 'Silence Breakers' discussed in Chap. 5 (Halper 2018). However, she and her comments are absent in the published article, although it does contain a reference to the difficulties feminists have faced in coming to terms with the allegations against Clinton (Zacharek et al. 2017). It is easy to understand why Broaddrick feels that many feminists and progressives have wanted her and her story to disappear. This is, she says, a significant part of the reason she has become closely associated with right-wing Republicans and Trump. She supports Trump, she told an interviewer, because he 'gave Bill Clinton's victims a voice that we had been denied for two decades' (Halper 2018). Broaddrick even goes so far as to state that Trump helped her come to terms with her experience and to name it as rape. She says she never conceptualised Clinton's actions in this way until Trump used the word to describe her claims on *The Sean Hannity Show*. This, she said in an interview, made her realise she couldn't 'skirt around it anymore' as it was the 'correct terminology' (Baker 2016b). Trump's comments gave her the courage to confront Clinton after she heard her speaking about the need for rape survivors to be believed. In the period since, she has become a Republican activist and joined supportive communities of rape and sexual assault survivors online.

Juanita Broaddrick challenges many of the assumptions of speaking out through her combination of public support for Trump and a strongly stated commitment to the principles of speaking out. She challenges presumed automatic links between survivor speech and progressive politics, not only in her political conservatism but in the divergent responses that she garners from feminists and conservatives. While she demands an ethical hearing, her story has frequently been ignored and denied and her interpretation of it has garnered allegations of hypocrisy and naivety. Responding to these allegations in an interview, she argued that she supports the rights of Trump's accusers to speak out and that if she heard a story about him that was of a similar gravity to hers she would cease to support him (Halper 2018). This position clearly imposes hierarchies of victimisation, but, as I have shown in this book, it does not make Broaddrick unique within the political spectrum of speaking out. In answer to the suggestion in an interview that she had been used by Trump, Broaddrick stated simply that she doesn't care: 'Whatever his reasons were when he asked us to the second debate, I thought I would finally be able to tell my story to millions of people who had never heard it before. That's why I went' (Halper 2018). She has, at times, enacted critiques of Trump, including in a response to an interview question about the campaign ad in which he used her voice without her permission: 'You take the most awful part of my Dateline interview, where I'm crying, trying to relate what had happened to me, and put that in a campaign ad? I thought it was very tasteless' (Baker 2016b). However, for Broaddrick, this does not eclipse or outweigh the fact that Trump has enabled her speech to be heard by others, and to garner increasing levels of belief.

The different registers of politics speak to the need to grant a figure like Broaddrick belief, support and even respect for the meaning she makes of her narrative without disallowing the possibility of disagreeing with her broader political perspective. Indeed, such disagreement is essential to build a feminist politics against sexual violence that can respond not only to the reality of Trump's abuse of women but also the effects of his wider political platform. Ethical responses require a disaggregation of modes of responding to women's speech. Disputing wider political perspectives of individual survivors should not preclude a political commitment to hearing and responding to their stories. Both processes are necessary for building an anti-rape politics and not only in relation to survivors such as Broaddrick with clearly conservative politics. As I have demonstrated throughout the book, even more straightforwardly feminist narratives make use of different discourses and are capable of reproducing elements of conservative or anti-feminist politics, and feminist politics itself is well-known for, at times, drawing on and reproducing class and racial biases. Rather than seeking politically pure survivor narratives and seeking to cast stories like Broaddrick's outside of the genre of speaking out, Broaddrick's story and others like it deserve an ethical hearing and demand political engagement.

The other major figure in the campaign who troubled the political assumptions of speaking out was Hillary Clinton. Clinton is widely understood as a 'feminist' within US politics. She claims this speaking position for herself, and she ran an avowedly feminist campaign which emphasised the possibility and significance of her becoming the first female President. As mentioned above, she sought to represent herself as a supporter of survivors of sexual violence. Paradoxically, her public identification with feminism meant that allegations of complicity in silencing the women who accused her husband of sexual misconduct 'stuck' to

Clinton more effectively than allegations of actual violence affected Trump (L. Gilmore 2017). Clinton is not the only woman who has been scrutinised over her response to allegations of sexual violence against her husband, but she is unique in facing this scrutiny as the 'feminist' candidate in an election deeply polarised around questions of sexism. Clinton thus found herself in a paradoxical position in relation to speaking out and sexual violence, a paradox exemplified by the addition and subsequent removal of the sexual assault section on her website.

Her memoir of the election, *What Happened*, similarly enacts this paradoxical position. Clinton (2017, p. 139) only briefly mentions Broaddrick, referring to her as one of the women who accused her husband of 'bad acts decades ago' and who were used by Trump in an 'awful stunt' that was a 'distraction' from the debate and wider campaign. In contrast, Clinton writes that she was disturbed by the fact that the question of 'sexual assault' was obscured in the *Access Hollywood* tapes, with too many people focusing on Tump's boorishness and vulgarity (p. 138). Elsewhere in the book she pays tribute to the politics of speaking out, referring to examples such as #YesAllWomen, which 'spoke to me like so many others' and made her remember the 'million defensive habits' that were part of her daily reality as a student and her early experiences in the Democratic party (p. 139). She juxtaposes the *Access Hollywood* tape with the statement released shortly beforehand by Emily Doe, writing that she hopes she 'can meet the author someday and tell her how brave I think she is' (p. 140). She even evoked Doe's statement in her concession speech, deliberately echoing it in her opening sentence: 'To all the little girls who are watching this, never doubt that you are valuable and powerful and deserving of every chance and opportunity in the world to pursue and achieve your own dreams' (p. 141). In Clinton's self-framing, Broaddrick is an exceptional figure whose speech is simply outside the genre of speaking out to which Clinton is politically committed. Her act of generic exclusion is performed through obscuring the specificity of Broaddrick's narrative and classing it as a 'stunt' engineered by Trump rather than the political speech of a survivor. These exclusions follow her earlier response which asserted that the story had been disproven and so was not true. In her various characterisations, Clinton renders Broaddrick's speech lacking in veracity, sincerity, credibility and authenticity, the primary criteria of generic judgements of survivor narratives.

I do not raise this to accuse Clinton of individual hypocrisy. As I noted above, her response was shared by many feminists and progressives. Rather, I suggest that she, like Broaddrick, was positioned during the campaign in a way that troubled the politics of speaking out. Broaddrick was a right-wing survivor supporting a misogynist for President and Clinton was his feminist opponent, selectively believing and denying the stories of survivors. The difficulties raised for both were to do with their identities as women, survivors and feminists, and how these identities figure in relation to speaking out. What is significant about Trump's actions, in contrast, is not so much that they demonstrate his cynicism in relation to feminist politics, but that they were so effective.

The 2016 election campaign might be judged among Corrigan's (2013) 'failures of success'. Women's narratives of sexual violence sat at the heart of the election campaign to decide one of the most powerful positions in the world. This campaign ultimately elected a man now publicly known to have sexually assaulted numerous women and to have bragged about doing so. The legacy and implications of this campaign are still playing out in the policies and interpersonal politics and scandal of Trump's Presidency and in cultural politics including #MeToo. Broaddrick's story is now receiving wider attention and there are movements towards rethinking the political legacy of Bill Clinton and his support by feminists. Monica Lewinsky (2018), the woman whose affair with Clinton launched a political crisis, has, like Broaddrick, found a new audience and has been able to speak about the complexity of her situation, which she characterises as simultaneously consensual and an abuse of power by the then-President.

Broaddrick herself sees the growing influence of speaking out as the main message of her story. She told journalist Katie Baker (2016b) that things have changed incredibly from the 1970s when she was assaulted and 'no one' talked about rape, and even from the late 1990s when she first told her story: 'Women thanked Broaddrick for telling her story on *Dateline* in 1999, but weren't explicit. Now, teenagers describe their sexual assaults to her in private messages'. These same teenagers tell her she is an 'inspiration' and a 'hero', and even though Broaddrick says 'she can't imagine being something that inspires them', she leaves the possibility open, saying 'I haven't gotten there yet' (Baker 2016). The strength of the teleological narrative of speaking out is evidenced by the fact that Trump's opponents also tell it. As a *New York Times Magazine* article asked in the aftermath of the second Presidential debate, 'After Donald Trump, Will More Women Believe Their Own Stories?' (Dominus 2016). Answering optimistically, the journalist drew attention to women such as Natasha Stoynoff who no longer blame themselves for what the President did to them. The article argues:

> Maybe this presidential election, of all things, will be another milestone. Grueling and sordid or not, it has placed matters of sex, power and gender at the center of the national conversation, not off in the peripheral space typically reserved for women's issues in media. It is one thing to be a passive reader of the news about Cosby, or the trials endured by young women on college campuses; it is another for the public to consider their electoral choices in light of those kinds of issues.

The article continues: 'The stories emerging about Trump, as well as his own words, could give women a new way of seeing their own experiences with sexual assault going forward – as part of a pattern of male behaviour that has been noted, flagged and loudly denigrated' (Dominus 2016). And, in some ways, immediate events would seem to bear this out. The response to allegations against Trump, however, demonstrates the limitations of this speech. Women's speech about sexual violence by powerful men sat at the heart of the election. The women who spoke were judged and scrutinised by those who supported the men they spoke about, regardless of their political allegiances. Despite the testimony produced against him, Trump went on to win the election, and his support among female voters was comparable to other Republican candidates. Hashtag campaigns like #NotOkay that arose in response to Trump produced narratives and media attention but did not solve the political problem that Juanita Broaddrick poses for feminists. Keeping the complicated and convoluted events of October 2016 in mind, I now turn to some final reflections on narrative, politics and sexual violence, and to the question of developing a future-oriented politics that does not rely on a teleological logic.

Towards a Politics of Narratives

This book undertakes a critical survey of practices of speaking out since the 1970s, and particularly from the late 1980s onwards, following what I describe as a 'turning point' in public receptions of survivor narratives and the cultural authority of the discourse of speaking out. While this is presented primarily as an archive of the past and present, it is offered in the hope that this archive can 'provide materials through which future movements and activist practices can be imagined' out of the paradoxes and difficulties of the present (Rentschler and Thrift 2015, p. 242). I have argued against an understanding of speaking out as entirely oppositional or coterminous with feminist politics. I use Bakhtin (1981) to suggest instead that women's narratives, and the political practices around them, draw on and make use of a variety of discourses around sexual violence, including some that accept or promote hegemonic and normative understandings. I suggest that thinking of speaking out as simultaneously a form of politics and a genre of stories helps to articulate some of the strengths and weaknesses of this narrative-based politics. I posit that processes of generic inclusion and exclusion shape the political possibilities of speaking out and render it a genre dominated by white women's stories and understandings. I insist that the production of feminist expertise and processes of feminist judgement need to be understood as imbued with relations of power and, therefore, subject to critical scrutiny. Finally, I assert that rather than breaking the silence around rape, feminist and survivor speech is part of a cycle of 'speech, silence and refiguration' (Sielke 2002, p. 5). In this way, I contest the teleological assumptions that structure much public debate about speaking out. Instead, I explore the possibility of drawing on political and literary analysis to produce different practices and point to different futures.

Rather than offering a programmatic set of recommendations, I approach this question through a more direct reflection on the relationship between narrative and politics. I have argued that speaking out simultaneously narrativises politics and politicises narrative. To this point, however, I have not considered the relation or tension between the two in depth. Lyotard (1988) offers a way of thinking about the two centred on their differing potential to overcome *differends* such as those that render women's speech about violence unheard, denied or subject to corrosive doubt. He shares with Bakhtin (1981) a vision of the cultural and discursive landscape as heterogeneous and stratified in terms of discursive influence and power. These power struggles between discourses produce *differends* where certain narratives, experiences and interpretations are rendered unthinkable or unspeakable. Lyotard writes that both politics and narrative can be used to respond to or overcome *differends*, but they do so in different ways. Narrative 'retroactively organises' the heterogeneity of discourses and 'imposes an end' or a 'completion' that can naturalise the present state and foreclose the possibility of radical change (Lyotard 1988, p. 151). In contrast, politics recognises and maintains the 'multiplicity of genres, the diversity of ends' and raises the 'question of linkage'. 'Politics consists in the fact that language is not a language, but phrases, or that Being is not Being, but There Is's', contingent and changeable realities that can be contested (p. 138). If narrative closes a *differend* by imposing a single reality or story, politics, at its best, can force open the gap exposed by the *differend* so that the unheard cry of the victim can be turned not into the complaint of a plaintiff within the existing system, but a demand for something new altogether. Lyotard explains this distinction in relation to class politics, and the difference between discourses like religion that tell a story that naturalises the *differend* experienced by the poor and Marxism which expresses 'the silent feeling that signals a differend remains to be listened to' and offers the promise of producing something new from this politics (p. 171).

The difference between narrative and politics in relation to sexual violence would be between a response that concedes the inevitability of that violence but seeks to ameliorate it, and one which forces open the social, legal and cultural *differends* revealed by women's narratives to imagine a different world. This kind of imagining needs to, as Sharon Marcus (1992, pp. 388–389) writes, regard 'rape not as a fact to be accepted or opposed, tried or avenged, but as a process to be analysed and undermined as it occurs'. She argues that in order to 'refuse to recognise rape as the real fact of our lives', we might treat it as a '*linguistic* fact: to ask how the violence of rape is enabled by narratives, complexes and institutions which derive their strength not from outright, immutable, unbeatable force but rather from their power to structure our lives as imposing cultural scripts' (emphasis in original). This would produce an understanding of rape as 'subject to change' rather than inevitable and eternal, and of our speech as less about telling stories and more about rewriting and reshaping those stories.

It is essential to acknowledge that building a narrative politics in pursuit of an open and undetermined future involves risk and vulnerability. To enact a politics through and against the experience of sexual violence, I suggest, always entails vulnerability, but there is a form of comfort and safety in limiting the end of the story to what is known. Judith Butler (1997, pp. 161–162) has argued that when attempting a critical reflection on our politics we must not 'underestimate the force of the desire to foreclose futurity', and she acknowledges that there are often good reasons for this desire. An open and unpredictable future can be a terrifying prospect, particularly when, as in the case of widespread sexual violence, the stakes are so high. It means, among other things, allowing for the possibility of political failure and dead ends. It requires building a generic politics which seeks to construct solidarity between and among radically different and potentially unknowable experiences of sexual violence, and diverse understandings of and responses to these experiences. While the risks of this approach are real, there are, as I have shown, real risks to current feminist political and narrative practices. It is also undeniable that there is a widespread desire for a different and better future in relation to sex, violence and the connections between the two. The growing number of women's narratives of sexual violence that I discuss in this book documents and speaks to this desire.

For Wendy Brown (1995), contemporary feminist politics of narrative enact a tendency to attempt to achieve political change through extra-political means and discourses, and through making moral claims based on the truth of 'wounded identities'. This means asserting opposition to sexual violence as a moral truth or virtue and seeing women's stories of violence as having an inherent 'moral' meaning. Brown argues for the abandonment of this approach in favour of one that sees the truth of our stories as a product of political contestation. While Brown's approach has been criticised for not being cognisant enough of the risks of the political openness she calls for (e.g. Rentschler 2011), my analysis similarly demonstrates that the meaning of stories of sexual violence is not self-evident or fixed, but depends on the discourses through which they are told, heard and interpreted. The history of feminist discursive activism has not been to reveal the 'truth' of sexual violence as a moral wrong but to politically produce that truth. I agree with Brown that this continues to be the way in which the meaning and nature of the stories we tell about sexual violence might be changed. This means insisting that the stories we tell are meaningful, and our interpretations of them and their wider significance are valid, because that is the world we want to live in and the truth that we wish to construct, not because this truth sits in a realm of self-evident morality.

Returning to the discussion of the politicisation of survivor speech in the previous section, a politics of narrative cannot presume a natural connection between telling stories of sexual violence, having those stories heard and coming to specific understandings or interpretations of those narratives. It is a political demand to insist that women's stories of sexual violence must be given witness and a hearing on their own terms, and that survivors share the right to tell their story and to interpret it. This ethical insistence, however, will not automatically or necessarily produce a feminist politics, and it will certainly not produce a feminist politics capable of recognising and overcoming the multiple vectors of power and conflict that surround these stories. The broader political meanings and interpretations of rape are not shared by all survivors or all feminists, let alone the wider audiences to whom we tell our stories. Alcoff and Gray (1993) are right that survivor speech is always potentially transgressive, but it does not always enact this potential, and not all survivors make use of transgressive or oppositional discourses in order to make meaning or interpret their narratives (Naples 2003). These narratives may be structured through discourses that see them reproduce gendered or neoliberal understandings of personal responsibility, carceral assumptions about criminality, and racist and class-based discourses about the identities of sexual predators and their innocent victims. In Brown's language, wounded identities do not automatically result in radical politics, but a radical politics should demand that the experiences of those who are wounded are able to be heard and witnessed.

A final distinction between narrative and politics is that while the former focuses on the individual speaker, the latter opens the question of collective responses and responsibility. This latter approach constructs speaking out as a collective act of reciprocal speaking, listening and meaning-making rather than privileging the idea of a single heroic speaker. Adriana Cavarero (2000) argues that models of individual storytelling completely miss the political possibility inherent to feminist narrative practice, which is the production of reciprocal and collective biographies as opposed to the creation of autobiographies. Collective practices of listening, hearing, discussing and assimilating stories among ourselves and insisting that they receive a hearing in the world at large are essential to a feminist politics of narratives. These practices both insist that women and survivors of violence have lives that are narratable and that matter and make them matter through their collective and reciprocal production and telling.

For these reasons, the point of this book is not to argue for a less narrative-based politics, but for practices that conceive the relation between narrative and politics differently. The force of women's storytelling about violence, and the insistence that women be recognised as authors and protagonists of their own narratives, constitute some of the key legacies of feminist activism in this area. Maximising this force means not simply continuing to tell stories but seeking to tell them in ways that imagine a world in which we might not tell them anymore or not tell them as much. One aspect of this is building a narrative politics founded not in the 'law of genre', the foreclosure and drawing of boundaries and certain types of speech, but that makes use of the 'law of the law of genre' to see generic impurity and contamination as a political and narrative resource. If, for instance, we recognise that to say 'me too' produces a knowledge of sameness alongside the possibility of diversity and difference, what kinds of political practices might we construct? Recognising increasing numbers and varieties of stories as participating in the genre of speaking out would acknowledge the existence of a different kind of politics that exists already in the margins of officially recognised feminist stories. One example of this is the stories of black abolitionist feminists that insist on speaking of the violence of the carceral state in the same narratives as interpersonal violence rather than positioning the state as a protector or rescuer from interpersonal violence (Richie 2012). Another is the narratives told against rape in the civil rights movement documented by Danielle McGuire (2010), or in #BlackLivesMatter. What kind of vision of feminist narrative and feminist futures might we produce if #BlackLivesMatter was as central to the feminist story of violence as #MeToo?

I do not offer clear answers to these questions. Rather, I suggest that we need a practice of politically-engaged narrative and a politics that draws on the tools of generic and literary analysis to tell stories that seek to describe not only how things are but how they might be. This is part of the work of telling different stories to those that the world has demanded and expected of us, the story 'of us broken, the story of us never laughing out loud, never learning to enjoy sex, never being able to love or trust love again, the story in which all that survives is the flesh' (Allison 1996, pp. 71–72). We must, as Dorothy Allison insists, tell different stories, individually and collectively, to not tell that story and to produce a world in which it is no longer the story which is demanded and expected. This is the story of the world as we might desire it to be, a story in which we no longer need to tell the same stories of sexual violence. This kind of narrative politics is not the security of a unitary closure which is simultaneously the prison of a future that is already history. It is instead the embrace of an open and insecure future which is yet to be written but which insists that the story of a world without rape is possible, desirable and necessary.

Bibliography

Ahmed, S. (2000). Who Knows? Knowing Strangers and Strangerness. *Australian Feminist Studies, 15*(31), 49–68.

Akyel, E. (2014). #Direnkahkaha (Resist Laughter): 'Laughter Is a Revolutionary Action'. *Feminist Media Studies, 14*(6), 1093–1094.

Alcoff, L. M. (1991). The Problem of Speaking for Others. *Cultural Critique, 20*, 5–32.

Alcoff, L. M., & Gray, L. (1993). Survivor Discourse: Transgression or Recuperation? *Signs: Journal of Women in Culture and Society, 18*(2), 260–290.

Alexander, M. (2010). *The New Jim Crow: Mass Incarceration in an Age of Color-Blindness*. New York: The New Press.

Allen, W. (2014, February 7). Woody Allen Speaks Out. *New York Times* [Online]. Available from: https://www.nytimes.com/2014/02/09/opinion/sunday/woody-allen-speaks-out.html. Accessed 1 July 2018.

Allison, D. (1996). *Two or Three Things I Know for Sure*. London: Flamingo.

Anderson, P., & Wild, R. (2007). *Ampe Akelyernemane Meke Mekarle: 'Little Children Are Sacred'*. Report of the Northern Territory Board of Inquiry into the Protection of Aboriginal Children from Sexual Abuse. Darwin: Northern Territory Government.

Ang, I. (1995). I'm a Feminist But… 'Other' Women and Postnational Feminism. In B. Caine & R. Pringle (Eds.), *Transitions: New Australian Feminisms* (pp. 57–73). Sydney: Allen & Unwin.

Angelou, M. (1993). *I Know Why the Caged Bird Sings*. New York: Bantam Books.

Anonymous. (2015, June 4). One of the Kipnis Complainants Speaks Out. *Daily Nous* [Blog]. Available from: http://dailynous.com/2015/06/04/one-of-the-kipnis-complainants-speaks-out/. Accessed 4 June 2018.

Armstrong, L. (1978). *Kiss Daddy Goodnight: A Speak-Out on Incest*. New York: Hawthorn Books.

Armstrong, L. (1990). The Personal Is Apolitical. *Women's Review of Books, 7*(6), 1–4.

Armstrong, L. (1994). *Rocking the Cradle of Family Politics: What Happened When Women Said Incest*. Reading: Addison-Wesley.

Association of Internet Researchers. (2012). Ethical Decision-Making and Internet Research: Recommendations from the AoIR Ethics Working Committe (Version 2.0). Available from: http://www.aoir.org/reports/ethics2.pdf. Accessed 4 Sept 2018.

Astor, M. (2018, June 6). California Voters Remove Judge Aaron Persky, Who Gave a 6-Month Sentence for Sexual Assault. *New York Times* [Online]. Available from: https://www.nytimes.com/2018/06/06/us/politics/judge-persky-brock-turner-recall.html. Accessed 23 June 2018.

Baker, K. J. M. (2016a, June 3). Here's the Powerful Letter the Stanford Victim Read Aloud to Her Attacker. *Buzzfeed* [Online]. Available from: https://www.buzzfeed.com/katiejmbaker/heres-the-powerful-letter-the-stanford-victim-read-to-her-ra. Accessed 23 Mar 2018.

Baker, K. J. M. (2016b, August 15). Juanita Broaddrick Wants to Be Believed. *Buzzfeed* [Online]. Available from: https://www.buzzfeed.com/katiejmbaker/juanita-broaddrick-wants-to-be-believed. Accessed 22 June 2018.

Bakhtin, M. (1981). Discourse in the Novel. In M. Holquist (Ed.), *The Dialogic Imagination: Four Essays by M. M. Bakhtin* (pp. 259–422). Translated from the Russian by Michael Holquist. Austin: University of Texas Press.

Barbaro, M., & Twohey, M. (2016, May 14). Crossing the Line: How Donald Trump Behaved with Women in Private. *New York Times* [Online]. Available from: https://www.nytimes.com/2016/05/15/us/politics/donald-trump-women.html. Accessed 29 June 2018.

Barr, J. (1979). *Within a Dark Wood: The Personal Story of a Rape Victim*. New York: Doubleday.

Bash, D., & Kopan, T. (2016, October 6). 30 Former GOP Lawmakers Sign Anti-Trump Letter. *CNN Politics* [Online]. Available from: https://edition.cnn.com/2016/10/06/politics/republican-lawmakers-never-trump-letter/index.html. Accessed 30 June 2018.

BBC. (2016, October 10). US Election: Who Are Bill Clinton's Accusers Who Appeared with Trump? *BBC World News* [Online]. Available from: https://www.bbc.co.uk/news/election-us-2016-37612453. Accessed 23 June 2018.

BBC. (2017, January 5). Ealing Vicarage Rape Victim Jill Saward Dies. *BBC News* [Online]. Available from: https://www.bbc.co.uk/news/uk-england-38522714. Accessed 6 June 2018.

Behrendt, L. (1993). Aboriginal Women and the White Lies of the Feminist Movement: Implications for Aboriginal Women in Rights Discourse. *Australian Feminist Law Journal, 1*(1), 27–44.

Behrendt, L. (2007). The Emergency We Had to Have: The Intervention in Northern Territory Aboriginal Communities. In J. Altman & M. Hinkson (Eds.), *Coercive Reconciliation: Stabilise, Normalise, Exit Aboriginal Australia* (pp. 15–20). Melbourne: Arena Publications.

Bell, D. (1990). A Reply from Diane Bell. *Anthropological Forum, 6*(2), 158–165.

Bell, D. (1991a). Intraracial Rape Revisited: On Forging a Feminist Future Beyond Factions and Frightening Politics. *Women's Studies International Forum, 14*(5), 385–412.

Bell, D. (1991b). Letter to the Editor. *Women's Studies International Forum, 14*(5), 507–513.

Bell, D. (1996). Speaking of Things That Shouldn't Be Written: Cross-Cultural Excursions into the Land of Misrepresentations. In R. Klein & D. Bell (Eds.), *Radically Speaking: Feminism Reclaimed* (pp. 247–253). Melbourne: Spinifex Press.

Bell, D., & Nelson, T. N. (1989). Speaking About Rape Is Everyone's Business. *Women's Studies International Forum, 12*(4), 403–416.

Benedict, H. (1992). *Virgin or Vamp: How the Press Covers Sex Crimes*. New York: Oxford University Press.

Benjamin, W. (2002). The Storyteller: Observations on the Works of Nikolai Leskov. In H. Eiland & M. W. Jennings (Eds.), *Walter Benjamin: Selected Writings Volume 3 1935–1938* (pp. 143–166). Cambridge/London: The Belknap Press of Harvard University Press.

Bennett, C. (2000, June 8). Doubts About Dworkin. *The Guardian* [Online]. Available from: https://www.theguardian.com/books/2000/jun/08/society. Accessed 1 July 2018.

Berridge, S., & Portwood-Stacer, L. (Eds.). (2015). Feminism, Hashtags and Violence Against Women and Girls. *Feminist Media Studies, 15*(2), 341–358.

Bevacqua, M. (2000). *Rape on the Public Agenda: Feminism and the Politics of Sexual Assault*. Boston: Northeastern University Press.

Bindel, J. (2004, September 30). A Life Without Compromise. *The Guardian* [Online]. Available from: https://www.theguardian.com/books/2004/sep/30/gender.world. Accessed 1 July 2018.

Bletzer, K. V., & Koss, M. P. (2004). Narrative Constructions of Sexual Violence as Told by Female Rape Survivors in Three Populations of the Southwestern United States: Scripts of Coercion, Scripts of Consent. *Medical Anthropology, 23*(2), 113–156.

Bolter, J. D., & Grusin, R. (1999). *Remediation: Understanding New Media.* Cambridge: MIT Press.

Bowman, B. (2014, November 13). Bill Cosby Raped Me. Why Did It Take 30 Years for People to Believe My Story? *The Washington Post* [Online]. Available from: https://www.washingtonpost.com/posteverything/wp/2014/11/13/bill-cosby-raped-me-why-did-it-take-30-years-for-people-to-believe-my-story/. Accessed 23 Mar.

Bright, S. (2000). The Baffling Case of Andrea Dworkin. In *Inspired by Andrea: Essays on Lust, Aggression, Porn, & the Female Gaze That I Might Not Have Written If Not for Her.* New York: Self-Published.

Brigley Thompson, Z. (2017). Happiness (or Not) After Rape: Hysterics and Harpies in the Media Versus Killjoys in Black Women's Fiction. *Journal of Gender Studies, 26*(1), 66–77.

Brison, S. J. (2002). *Aftermath: Violence and the Remaking of a Self.* Princeton/Oxford: Princeton University Press.

Brockes, E. (2018, January 15). Me Too Founder Tarana Burke: 'You Have to Use Your Privilege to Serve Other People'. *The Guardian* [Online]. Available from: https://www.theguardian.com/world/2018/jan/15/me-too-founder-tarana-burke-women-sexual-assault. Accessed 14 June 2018.

Brooks, P. (2008). Narrative in and of the Law. In J. Phelan & P. J. Rabinowitz (Eds.), *A Companion to Narrative Theory* (pp. 415–426). Oxford: Wiley.

Brown, W. (1995). *States of Injury: Power and Freedom in Late Modernity.* Princeton: Princeton University Press.

Brown, W. (2005). *Edgework: Critical Essays on Knowledge and Politics.* Princeton/Oxford: Princeton University Press.

Brown, H., Kruse, B. H., Krieg, J., & Goodman, P. (1990, March 4). Did Series Rout Apathy or Just Arouse Racism? *The Des Moines Register,* p. 5C.

Brownmiller, S. (1976). *Against Our Will: Men, Women and Rape.* Melbourne: Penguin Books.

Brownmiller, S. (1999). *In Our Time: Memoir of a Revolution.* New York: The Dial Press.

Bumiller, K. (2008). *In an Abusive State: How Neoliberalism Appropriated the Feminist Movement Against Sexual Violence*. Durham: Duke University Press.

Burke, T. (2013). *The Me Too Movement: The Inception* [Online]. Just Be Inc. Available from: http://justbeinc.wixsite.com/justbeinc/the-me-too-movement-cmml. Accessed 11 June 2018.

Burke, T. (2017, December 6). #MeToo Founder Tarana Burke on What Needs to Happen After the Hashtag. *Glamour* [Online]. Available from: https://www.glamour.com/story/metoo-founder-tarana-burke-what-needs-to-happen-after-the-hashtag. Accessed 1 July 2018.

Butler, J. (1997). *Excitable Speech: A Politics of the Performative*. New York/London: Routledge.

Cadwalladr, C. (2014, March 16). Scarlett Johansson Interview: 'I Would Way Rather Not Have Middle Ground'. *The Guardian* [Online]. Available from: https://www.theguardian.com/film/2014/mar/16/scarlett-johansson-interview-middle-ground-under-the-skin-sodastream. Accessed 24 Mar 2018.

Campbell, J. (2008). *The Hero with a Thousand Faces*. Novato: New World Library.

Campbell, R., & Wasco, S. M. (2005). Understanding Rape and Sexual Assault: 20 Years of Progress and Future Directions. *Journal of Interpersonal Violence, 20*(1), 127–131.

Cavarero, A. (2000). *Relating Narratives: Storytelling and Selfhood*. Translated from the Italian by Paul A. Kottman. New York/London: Routledge.

Chesler, P. (1972). *Women & Madness*. New York: Avon Books.

Clark, R. (2016). 'Hope in a Hashtag': The Discursive Activism of #WhyIStayed. *Feminist Media Studies, 16*(5), 788–804.

Clark, A. E., & Pinto, A. (2016). *We Believe You: Survivors of Campus Sexual Assault Speak Out*. New York: Holt.

Clinton, H. R. (2017). *What Happened*. New York: Simon & Schuster.

CNN. (2018, January 15). Banfield Slams Ansari Accuser in Open Letter. *CNN* [Online]. Available from: https://edition.cnn.com/videos/us/2018/01/16/open-letter-to-aziz-ansari-sexual-assault-accuser-banfield.hln. Accessed 25 Mar 2018.

Committee to Recall Judge Persky. (2016). *Recall Aaron Persky* [Online]. Available from: https://www.recallaaronpersky.com/. Accessed 10 June 2018.

Connell, N., & Wilson, C. (Eds.). (1974). *Rape: The First Sourcebook for Women. By New York Radical Feminists*. New York: Plume Books.

Cooper, G. (1997, June 19). The Way You Dress, the Way You Walk. *Independent*, p. 2.

Corrigan, R. (2013). *Up Against a Wall: Rape Reform and the Failure of Success*. New York: New York University Press.

Crawley, K., & Simic, O. (2018, May 14). Telling Stories of Rape, Revenge and Redemption in the Age of the TED Talk. *Crime, Media, Culture* [Online]. https://doi.org/10.1177/1741659018771117.

Creative Coalition. (2017). *#KeepTellingPeople* [Online]. Available from: https://www.keeptellingpeople.org/. Accessed 17 June 2018.

Cuklanz, L. (1996). *Rape on Trial: How the Mass Media Construct Legal Reform and Social Change*. Philadelphia: University of Pennsylvania Press.

Cuklanz, L. (2000). *Rape on Prime Time: Television, Masculinity, and Sexual Violence*. Philadelphia: University of Pennsylvania Press.

Danica, E. (1988). *Don't: A Woman's Word*. Pittsburgh: Cleis.

Danica, E. (1996). *Beyond Don't: Dreaming Past the Dark*. Charlottetown: Gynergy.

Davies, S., & Holden, A. (1998). *When Worlds Collide: The Shari Davies Story*. Sydney: HarperCollins.

Davis, A. (1983). *Women, Race and Class*. New York: Vintage Books.

Derrida, J. (1992). The Law of Genre. In D. Attridge (Ed.), *Acts of Literature* (pp. 221–252). New York/London: Routledge.

Dobie, K. (2003). *The Only Girl in the Car*. London: Vintage.

Dockterman, E. (2014, March 14). Rape Survivors Talk About Why They Tweeted Their Stories. *Time* [Online]. Available from: http://time.com/25150/rape-victims-talk-about-tweeting-their-experiences-publicly/. Accessed 23 June 2018.

Doe, J. (2003). *The Story of Jane Doe: A Book About Rape*. Toronto: Random House Canada.

Doe, E. (2016, November 1). Stanford Sexual Assault Case Survivor Emily Doe Speaks Out. *Glamour* [Online]. Available from: https://www.glamour.com/story/women-of-the-year-emily-doe. Accessed 10 June 2018.

Dominus, S. (2016, October 13). After Donald Trump, Will More Women Believe Their Own Stories? *New York Times Magazine* [Online]. Available from: https://www.nytimes.com/2016/10/14/magazine/after-donald-trump-will-more-women-believe-their-own-stories.html. Accessed 14 June 2018.

Domonoske, C. (2016, October 11). One Tweet Unleashes a Torrent of Stories of Sexual Assault. *NPR* [Online]. Available from: https://www.npr.org/sections/thetwo-way/2016/10/11/497530709/one-tweet-unleashes-a-torrent-of-stories-of-sexual-assault. Accessed 11 June 2018.

Donofrio, B. (2013). *Astonished*. New York: Penguin.

Douglas, R. (2016). *On Being Raped*. Boston: Beacon Press.
Doyle, J. (2015). *Campus Sex, Campus Security*. New York: Semiotext(e).
Dworkin, A. (1997). *Life and Death*. New York: The Free Press.
Dworkin, A. (2000, June 5). The Day I Was Drugged and Raped. *New Statesman* [Online]. Available from: http://www.newstatesman.com/200006050009#. Accessed 16 Apr 2016.
Ehrlich, S. (2001). *Representing Rape: Language and Sexual Consent*. New York/London: Routledge.
English, B. (2002, March 12). Feminist Outsider's Work Finds Its Way Inside Ivy Walls. *Boston Globe*, p. E1.
Estrich, S. (1987). *Real Rape: How the Legal System Victimizes Women Who Say No*. Cambridge: Harvard University Press.
Estrich, S. (2001). *Sex & Power*. New York: Riverhead Books.
Ewick, P., & Sibley, S. S. (1995). Subversive Stories and Hegemonic Tales: Toward a Sociology of Narrative. *Law and Society Review, 29*(2), 197–226.
Farrow, D. (2014, February 1). An Open Letter from Dylan Farrow. *New York Times Blog* [Blog]. Available from: http://kristof.blogs.nytimes.com/2014/02/01/an-open-letter-from-dylan-farrow/. Accessed 16 Nov 2017.
Farrow, R. (2016, June 5). My Father, Woody Allen, and the Danger of Questions Unasked (Guest Column). *Hollywood Reporter* [Online]. Available from: https://www.hollywoodreporter.com/news/my-father-woody-allen-danger-892572. Accessed 24 Mar 2018.
Farrow, D. (2017, December 7). Why Has the #MeToo Revolution Spared Woody Allen? *LA Times* [Online]. Available from: http://www.latimes.com/opinion/op-ed/la-oe-farrow-woody-allen-me-too-20171207-story.html. Accessed 24 Mar.
Farrow, R. (2017, October 23). From Aggressive Overtures to Sexual Assault: Harvey Weinstein's Accusers Tell Their Stories. *New Yorker* [Online]. Available from: https://www.newyorker.com/news/news-desk/from-aggressive-overtures-to-sexual-assault-harvey-weinsteins-accusers-tell-their-stories. Accessed 21 Mar 2018.
Farrow, M. (2018, May 23). A Son Speaks Out. *Moses Farrow* [Blog]. Available from: https://mosesfarrow.blogspot.com/2018/05/a-son-speaks-out-by-moses-farrow.html. Accessed 1 July 2018.
Ferguson, F. (1987, Autumn). Rape and the Rise of the Novel. *Representations, 20*, 88–112.
Fiske, J. (1996). *Media Matters: Race and Gender in US Politics*. Minneapolis: University of Minnesota Press.

Foucault, M. (1998). *The Will to Knowledge: The History of Sexuality Volume I*. London: Penguin Books.
Francisco, P. W. (1999a, May 24). Out of the Darkness. *Salon.com* [Online]. Available from: http://www.salon.com/1999/05/24/rape/. Accessed 1 July 2018.
Francisco, P. W. (1999b). *Self Interview with Patricia Weaver Francisco* [Online]. Available from: http://www.tellingofrape.com/tellingfiles/interviews.html#anchor14868517. Accessed 14 Apr 2006.
Francisco, P. W. (1999c). *Telling: A Memoir of Rape and Recovery*. New York: HarperCollins.
Freedman, K. L. (2014). *One Hour in Paris: A True Story of Rape and Recovery*. Chicago: University of Chicago Press.
Garcia, S. E. (2017, October 20). The Woman Who Created #MeToo Long Before Hashtags. *New York Times* [Online]. Available from: https://www.nytimes.com/2017/10/20/us/me-too-movement-tarana-burke.html. Accessed 1 July 2018.
Garland, D. (2001). *The Culture of Control: Crime and Social Order in Contemporary Society*. Chicago: University of Chicago Press.
Gavey, N. (2005). *Just Sex? The Cultural Scaffolding of Rape*. New York/London: Routledge.
Gavey, N., & Schmidt, J. (2011). 'Trauma of Rape' Discourse: A Double-Edged Template for Everyday Understandings of the Impact of Rape? *Violence Against Women, 17*(4), 433–456.
Gay, R. (2017). *Hunger: A Memoir of (My) Body*. New York: Harper.
Geimer, S. (2013). *The Girl: A Life in the Shadow of Roman Polanski*. New York: Atria.
Gersen, J., & Suk, J. (2016). The Sex Bureaucracy. *California Law Review, 104*, 881–948.
Gibbons, F. (2000, August 16). Child Sex Attacks 'Merit Vengeance'. *The Guardian* [Online]. Available from: https://www.theguardian.com/uk/2000/aug/16/edinburgh2000.books. Accessed 1 July 2018.
Gilmore, J. (2017, January 9). The Great Legacy British Sexual Assault Activist Jill Saward Leaves Behind. *Sydney Morning Herald* [Online]. Available from: https://www.smh.com.au/lifestyle/the-great-legacy-that-uk-sexual-assault-activist-jill-saward-has-left-behind-20170109-gtny74.html. Accessed 16 June 2018.
Gilmore, L. (1994). *Autobiographics: A Feminist Theory of Women's Self-Representation*. Ithaca/London: Cornell University Press.

Gilmore, L. (2017). *Tainted Witness: Why We Doubt What Women Say About Their Lives*. New York: Columbia University Press.
Gracen, J. (2000, September 20). Andrea Dworkin in Agony. *Salon.com* [Online]. Available from: http://archive.salon.com/books/feature/2000/09/20/dworkin/. Accessed 16 May 2016.
Grant, A. (2010). *Words Can Describe*. London: Picador.
Graves, L. (2016, July 20). Jill Harth Speaks Out About Alleged Groping by Donald Trump. *The Guardian* [Online]. Available from: https://www.theguardian.com/us-news/2016/jul/20/donald-trump-sexual-assault-allegations-jill-harth-interview. Accessed 16 June 2018.
Gray-Rosendale, L. (2013). *College Girl: A Memoir*. Albany: State University of New York Press.
Greer, G. (1970). *The Female Eunuch*. London: MacGibbon & Kee.
Grewal, K. K. (2016). *Racialised Gang Rape and the Reinforcement of the Dominant Order: Discourses of Gender, Race and Nation*. New York/London: Routledge.
Grice, E. (2006, March 8). It's Not Whether You Can or Can't Forgive: It's Whether You Will or Won't. *The Telegraph*, p. 25.
Griffin, S. (1979). *Rape: The Power of Consciousness*. San Francisco: Harper & Row.
Grix, J. (1999). Law's Truth and Other Lies: Women, Sexual Assault and the Criminal Justice System. *Australian Feminist Law Journal, 12*(1), 83–93.
Haag, P. (1996). 'Putting Your Body on the Line': The Question of Violence, Victims, and the Legacies of Second-Wave Feminism. *Differences: A Journal of Feminist Cultural Studies, 8*(2), 23–67.
Hall, N. (1997, June 14). Rape Girl Says Some 'Ask for It'. *Daily Mirror*, p. 14.
Hall, L. K. (2017). *Caged Eyes: An Air Force Cadet's Story of Rape and Resilience*. New York: Beacon Press.
Halper, K. (2018, February 1). What Juanita Broaddrick Wants You to Know. *New York* [Online]. Available from: http://nymag.com/daily/intelligencer/2018/02/what-juanita-broaddrick-wants-you-to-know.html. Accessed 16 June 2018.
Harrison, J. (1997, June 18). I'm a Rape Victim Too, But You're So Wrong Jill…. *Daily Mail*, p. 22.
Harvey, D. (2005). *A Brief History of Neoliberalism*. Oxford: Oxford University Press.
Hayslip, L. L., with Wurts, J. (1989). *When Heaven and Earth Changed Places: A Vietnamese Woman's Journey from War to Peace*. New York: Penguin.

Hearn, J. (2018). You, Them, Us, We, Too? ...Online–Offline, Individual–Collective, Forgotten–Remembered, Harassment–Violence. *European Journal of Women's Studies, 25*(2), 228–235.

Heath, M., & Naffine, N. (1994). Men's Needs and Women's Desires: Feminist Dilemmas About Rape Law Reform. *Australian Feminist Law Journal, 3*(1), 30–52.

Heinzelman, S. S. (1990). Women's Petty Treason: Feminism, Narrative, and the Law. *Journal of Narrative Technique, 20*(2), 89–106.

Helliwell, C. (2000). 'It's Only a Penis': Rape, Feminism, and Difference. *Signs: Journal of Women in Culture and Society, 25*(3), 789–816.

Hemmings, C. (2011). *Why Stories Matter: The Political Grammar of Feminist Theory*. Durham: Duke University Press.

Herman, J. L. (1992). *Trauma and Recovery*. New York: Basic.

Hesford, W. (2004). Documenting Violations: Rhetorical Witnessing and the Spectacle of Distant Suffering. *Biography, 27*(1), 104–144.

Hesford, W., & Kozol, W. (2001). Introduction: Is There a 'Real' Crisis? In W. Hesford & W. Kozol (Eds.), *Haunting Violations: Feminist Criticism and the Crisis of the "Real"* (pp. 1–12). Urbana/Chicago: University of Illinois Press.

Higgins, L. A., & Silver, B. R. (1991). Introduction: Rereading Rape. In L. A. Higgins & B. R. Silver (Eds.), *Rape and Representation* (pp. 1–11). New York: Columbia University Press.

Hill, Z. (2017, October 18). A Black Woman Created the 'Me Too' Campaign Against Sexual Assault 10 Years Ago. *Ebony* [Online]. Available from: http://www.ebony.com/news-views/black-woman-me-too-movement-tarana-burke-alyssa-milano. Accessed 20 June 2018.

Holiday, B., with Dufty, W. (2006). *Lady Sings the Blues*. New York: Broadway Books.

hooks, b. (1994). *Outlaw Culture*. New York/London: Routledge.

Hoppe, T. (2016). Punishing Sex: Sex Offenders and the Missing Punitive Turn in Sexuality Studies. *Law & Social Inquiry, 41*(3), 573–594.

Horeck, T. (2004). *Public Rape: Representing Violation in Fiction and Film*. London/New York: Routledge.

Huggins, J., et al. (1991). Letter to the Editor. *Women's Studies International Forum, 14*(5), 506–507.

Incite! (2001). *Incite! and Critical Resistance Statement: Gender Violence and the Prison Industrial Complex*. Available from: http://www.incite-national.org/page/incite-critical-resistance-statement. Accessed 10 June 2018.

Jacobs, H. (2000). *Incidents in the Life of a Slave Girl: Written by Herself*. New York/Oxford: Oxford University Press.

Jane, E. A. (2014). 'Your a Ugly, Whorish, Slut': Understanding E-bile. *Feminist Media Studies, 14*(4), 531–546.
Jenefsky, C. (1998). *Without Apology: Andrea Dworkin's Art and Politics.* Boulder: Westview Press.
Johnson, L. M. (2014). *The Other Side: A Memoir.* Portland: TinHouse Books.
Joseph, L., with Mendenhall, D. B. (1998). *Little Girl Lost: One Woman's Journey Beyond Rape.* New York: Galilee.
Jurich, M. (1998). *Scheherazade's Sisters: Trickster Heroines and Their Stories in World Literature.* Westport: Greenwood Press.
Kalven, J. (1999). *Working with Available Light: A Family's World After Violence.* New York: W. W. Norton.
Kantor, J., & Twohey, M. (2017, October 5). Harvey Weinstein Paid Off Sexual Harassment Accusers for Decades. *New York Times* [Online]. Available from: https://www.nytimes.com/2017/10/05/us/harvey-weinstein-harassment-allegations.html. Accessed 15 June 2018.
Kaplan, A. (2015). *Still Room for Hope: A Survivor's Story of Sexual Assault, Forgiveness, and Freedom.* New York: Faith Words.
Karlsson, L. (2018, May 10). Towards a Language of Sexual Gray Zones: Feminist Collective Knowledge Building Through Autobiographical Multimedia Storytelling. *Feminist Media Studies.* https://doi.org/10.1080/14 680777.2018.1467944.
Kilby, J. (2018, April 22). Saving the Girl: A Creative Reading of Alice Sebold's *Lucky* and *The Lovely Bones. Feminist Theory.* https://doi.org/10.1177/1464700117752773.
Kipnis, L. (2015, February 27). Sexual Paranoia Strikes Academe. *Chronicle of Higher Education* [Online]. Available from: https://www.chronicle.com/article/Sexual-Paranoia-Strikes/190351. Accessed 19 June 2018.
Kipnis, L. (2017). *Unwanted Advances: Sexual Paranoia Comes to Campus.* New York: Harper Collins.
Kipnis, L. (2018a, January 13). Has #MeToo Gone Too Far, or Not Far Enough? The Answer Is Both. *The Guardian* [Online]. Available from: https://www.theguardian.com/commentisfree/2018/jan/13/has-me-too-catherine-deneuve-laura-kipnis. Accessed 19 June 2018.
Kipnis, L. (2018b, June 10). Should There Be a Future for Seduction? *New York* [Online]. Available from: https://www.thecut.com/2018/06/laura-kipnis-on-the-future-of-seduction.html. Accessed 19 June 2018.
Klein, R. (1991). Editorial. *Women's Studies International Forum, 14*(5), 505–506.
Kørra, M. (2015). *Kill the Silence: A Survivor's Life Reclaimed.* New York: Harmony Books.

Lacey, K. (2013). *Listening Publics: The Politics and Experience of Listening in the Media Age*. London: Polity.

Larbalestier, J. (1990). The Politics of Representation: Australian Aboriginal Women and Feminism. *Anthropological Forum, 6*(2), 143–157.

Larcombe, W. (2002a). Cautionary Tales and Telling Anxieties: The Story of the False Complainant. *Australian Feminist Law Journal, 16*(1), 95–108.

Larcombe, W. (2002b). The 'Ideal' Victim v Successful Rape Complainants: Not What You Might Expect. *Feminist Legal Studies, 10*(2), 131–148.

Larcombe, W. (2005). *Compelling Engagements: Feminism, Rape Law and Romance Fiction*. Sydney: The Federation Press.

Lauer, T. (1998). *Hours of Torture, Years of Silence: My Soul Was the Scene of the Crime*. Pacific Grove: Institute for Interpersonal Relations.

Lees, S. (1997). *Ruling Passions: Sexual Violence, Reputation and the Law*. Buckingham: Open University Press.

Leo, J. (2011). *Rape New York*. New York: The Feminist Press.

Levy, A. (2007). Foreword. In A. Dworkin (Ed.), *Intercourse* (Twentieth Anniversary ed., pp. xi–xxvii). New York: Basic Books.

Lewinsky, M. (2018, March). Monica Lewinsky: Emerging from 'The House of Gaslight' in the Age of #MeToo. *Vanity Fair* [Online]. Available from: https://www.vanityfair.com/news/2018/02/monica-lewinsky-in-the-age-of-metoo. Accessed 1 July 2018.

Lyotard, J.-F. (1988). *The Differend: Phrases in Dispute*. Minneapolis: University of Minnesota Press.

M., K. (2015, May 26). #YesAllWomen One Year Later. *The Toast* [Online]. Available from: http://the-toast.net/2015/05/26/yesallwomen-one-year-later/. Accessed 10 Jan 2016.

MacKinnon, C. (1989). *Toward a Feminist Theory of the State*. Cambridge: Harvard University Press.

Madigan, L., & Gamble, N. C. (1991). *The Second Rape: Society's Continued Betrayal of the Victim*. New York: Lexington Books.

Mai, M., with Cuny, M.-T. (2006). *In the Name of Honor: A Memoir*. New York: Washington Square Press.

Mallon, M. (2016, November 15). Stanford Sexual Assault Case Survivor Emily Doe Speaks Out at Glamour's Women of the Year Awards. *Glamour* [Online]. Available from: https://www.glamour.com/story/stanford-sexual-assault-case-survivor-emily-doe-speaks-out-at-glamours-women-of-the-year-awards. Accessed 16 June 2018.

Malone, N. (2015, July 26). 'I'm No Longer Afraid': 35 Women Tell Their Stories About Being Assaulted by Bill Cosby, and the Culture That Wouldn't Listen. *New York* [Online]. Available from: http://nymag.com/the-cut/2015/07/bill-cosbys-accusers-speak-out.html. Accessed 16 June 2018.

Mantilla, K. (2015). *Gendertrolling: How Misogyny Went Viral*. Santa Barbara: Praeger Press.

Marcus, S. (1992). Fighting Bodies, Fighting Words: A Theory and Politics of Rape Prevention. In J. Butler & J. Scott (Eds.), *Feminists Theorize the Political* (pp. 385–403). New York/London: Routledge.

Mardorossian, C. M. (2002). Toward a New Feminist Theory of Rape. *Signs: Journal of Women in Culture and Society, 27*(3), 743–774.

Mardorossian, C. M. (2014). *Framing the Rape Victim: Gender and Agency Reconsidered*. New Brunswick: Rutgers University Press.

Margolick, D. (1990, March 25). A Name, a Face and a Rape: Iowa Victim Tells Her Story. *New York Times*, p. 1.

Matoesian, G. M. (1993). *Reproducing Rape: Domination Through Talk in the Court-Room*. Cambridge: Polity Press.

Matoesian, G. M. (2001). *Law and the Language of Identity: Discourse in the William Kennedy Smith Rape TrialI*. Oxford/New York: Oxford University Press.

Mazza, E. (2014, October 31). #BeenRapedNeverReported Trending on Twitter as Women Share Stories of Sexual Violence. *Huffington Post* [Online]. Available from: https://www.huffingtonpost.co.uk/entry/beenrapedneverrep orted_n_6080054. Accessed 11 June 2018.

McCarthy, T. (1994). Victim Impact Statements – A Problematic Remedy. *Australian Feminist Law Journal, 3*(1), 175–195.

McCreary, P. (2004). *Out of the Shadows: A Rape Victim Examines Her Life In and Out of Mormonism*. New York: iUniverse, Inc.

McGillis, K. (1988, November 14). Memoir of a Brief Time in Hell. *People*, p. 154.

McGuire, D. L. (2010). *At the Dark End of the Street: Black Women, Rape and Resistance – A New History of the Civil Rights Movement from Rosa Parks to the Rise of Black Power*. New York: Vintage Books.

McKenzie-Mohr, S. (2014). Counter-Storying Rape: Women's Efforts Toward Liberatory Meaning Making. In S. McKenzie-Mohr & M. N. Lafrance (Eds.), *Women Voicing Resistance: Discursive and Narrative Explorations* (pp. 64–83). New York: Routledge.

McNaron, T., & Morgan, Y. (Eds.). (1982). *Voices in the Night: Women Speaking About Incest*. Minneapolis: Cleis.

McQuade, D. (2014, October 17). Hannibal Buress on Bill Cosby: 'You're a Rapist'. *Philadelphia* [Online]. Available from: https://www.phillymag.com/ticket/2014/10/17/hannibal-buress-bill-cosby-rapist/. Accessed 21 Mar 2018.

Megan, K. M., Heather, L. M., Amy, E. B., & Leija, S. G. (2018, January 1). 'I Was Grabbed by My Pussy and Its #NotOkay': A Twitter Backlash Against Donald Trump's Degrading Commentary. *Violence Against Women*. https://doi.org/10.1177/1077801217743340.

Meili, T. E. (2004). *I Am the Central Park Jogger: A Story of Hope and Possibility*. New York: Scribner.

Menchú, R. (1984). *I, Rigoberta Menchú: An Indian Woman in Guatemala*. Translated from the Spanish by Ann Wright. London/New York: Verso.

Mendes, K., Ringrose, J., & Keller, J. (2018). *Digital Feminist Activism: Women and Girls Fight Back Against Rape Culture*. Oxford: Oxford University Press.

Mitchell, P., Fraad, H., Murphy, P. A., Candib, L., Armstrong, L., Hoppe, S. T., Adams, C. J., Michel, S., & Rimmel, L. A. (1990). Letters. *The Women's Review of Books*, 7(8), 4–6.

Mohanty, C. T. (1992). Feminist Encounters: Locating the Politics of Experience. In M. Barrett & A. Phillips (Eds.), *Destabilizing Theory: Contemporary Feminist Debates* (pp. 74–92). Stanford: Stanford University Press.

Mohanty, C. T. (1997). Under Western Eyes: Feminist Scholarship and Colonial Discourses. In A. McClintock, A. Mufti, & E. Shohat (Eds.), *Dangerous Liaisons: Gender, Nation, Postcolonial Perspectives* (pp. 255–277). Minneapolis: University of Minnesota Press.

Monika Kørra Foundation. (2015). *Monika Kørra Foundation* [Online]. Available from: http://www.monikakorrafoundation.org/. Accessed 10 Oct 2016.

Moreton-Robinson, A. (2000). *Talkin' Up to the White Woman: Aboriginal Women and Feminism*. Brisbane: University of Queensland Press.

Namako, T. (2016, June 9). Joe Biden Writes an Open Letter to Stanford Survivor. *Buzzfeed* [Online]. Available from: https://www.buzzfeednews.com/article/tomnamako/joe-biden-writes-an-open-letter-to-stanford-survivor. Accessed 19 Mar 2018.

Nannup, A., Marsh, L., & Kinnane, S. (1992). *When the Pelican Laughed*. Perth: Fremantle Arts Centre Press.

Naples, N. A. (2003). Deconstructing and Locating Survivor Discourse: Dynamics of Narrative, Empowerment and Resistance for Survivors of Childhood Sexual Abuse. *Signs: Journal of Women in Culture and Society*, 28(4), 1151–1187.

Nelson, T. N. (1991). Letter to the Editor. *Women's Studies International Forum*, *14*(5), 507.
Newburn, T., & Jones, T. (2005). Symbolic Politics and Penal Populism: The Long Shadow of Willie Horton. *Crime Media Culture*, *1*(1), 72–87.
O'Shane, P. (1976, September). Is There Any Relevance in the Women's Movement for Aboriginal Women? *Refractory Girl*, *12*, 31–34.
Orr, D. (2005, April 16). Myth, Misogyny and Some Harsh Truths About the Gender Divide. *Independent* [Online]. Available from: http://www.independent.co.uk/opinion/commentators/deborah-orr/myth-misogyny-and-some-harsh-truths-about-the-gender-divide-489430.html. Accessed 16 Apr 2016.
Orth, M. (2014, February 7). 10 Undeniable Facts About the Woody Allen Sexual Abuse Allegation. *Vanity Fair* [Online]. Available from: https://www.vanityfair.com/news/2014/02/woody-allen-sex-abuse-10-facts. Accessed 25 Mar 2018.
Overholser, G. (1989, July 11). American Shame: The Stigma of Rape. *The Des Moines Register*, p. 6.
Overholser, G. (1990, February 25). Troubling, But Important, Series. *The Des Moines Register*, p. 19.
Pallotta, F. (2016, June 6). Why Ashleigh Banfield Read Stanford Rape Victim's Letter on CNN. *CNN* [Online]. Available from: http://money.cnn.com/2016/06/06/media/ashleigh-banfield-cnn-stanford-letter/index.html. Accessed 10 June 2018.
Payne, S. (1990). Aboriginal Women and the Criminal Justice System. *Aboriginal Law Bulletin*, *2*(46), 9–11.
Philadelphoff-Puren, N. (1997). Bodies/Ethics/Violence: A Review of *Heroines of Fortitude: The Experiences of Women as Victims of Sexual Assault and The Crimes (Rape) Act 1991 (NSW)*. *Australian Feminist Law Journal*, *9*(1), 134–142.
Philadelphoff-Puren, N. (2005). Contextualising Consent: The Problem of Rape and Romance. *Australian Feminist Studies*, *20*(46), 31–32.
Phillips, L. (1994). *Moving On: A Journey Through Sexual Assault*. Sydney: Sally Milner Publishing.
Phipps, A. (2016). Whose Personal Is More Political? Experience in Contemporary Feminist Politics. *Feminist Theory*, *17*(3), 303–321.
Pierce-Baker, C. (1998). *Surviving the Silence: Black Women's Stories of Rape*. New York/London: W. W. Norton and Company.
Plummer, K. (1995). *Telling Sexual Stories: Power, Change and Social Worlds*. New York/London: Routledge.

Polletta, F. (2006). *It Was Like a Fever: Storytelling in Protest and Politics*. Chicago: University of Chicago Press.
Porter, R. (1986). Rape – Does It Have a Historical Meaning? In S. Tomaselli & R. Porter (Eds.), *Rape* (pp. 216–236). Oxford: Basil Blackwell.
Portwood-Stacer, L., & Berridge, S. (Eds.). (2014). The Year in Feminist Hashtags. *Feminist Media Studies, 14*(6), 1090–1115.
Portwood-Stacer, L., & Berridge, S. (Eds.). (2015). Feminist Hashtags and Media Convergence. *Feminist Media Studies, 15*(1), 154–167.
R v Sherrin (No 2) [1979] 21 SASR 250.
Radway, J. A. (1991). *Reading the Romance: Women, Patriarchy and Popular Literature*. Chapel Hill: University of North Carolina Press.
Raine, N. V. (1994, October). Returns of the Day. *New York Times Magazine*.
Raine, N. V. (1998). *After Silence: Rape and My Journey Back*. New York: Three Rivers Press.
Rak, J. (2013). *Boom! Manufacturing Memoir for the Popular Market*. Waterloo: Wilfrid Laurier University Press.
Ramsey, M. (1995). *Where I Stopped: Remembering an Adolescent Rape*. San Diego/New York/London: Harcourt Brace & Company.
Rayburn, C. (2006). To Catch a Sex Thief: The Burden of Performance in Rape and Sexual Assault Trials. *Columbia Journal of Gender & Law, 15*(2), 436–483.
Razack, S. (1994). What Is to Be Gained by Looking White People in the Eye? Culture, Race, and Gender in Cases of Sexual Violence. *Signs: Journal of Women in Culture and Society, 19*(4), 894–922.
Read, B. (2018, February 22). Me Too Founder Tarana Burke: 'Watch Carefully Who Are Called "Leaders" of the Movement'. *Vogue* [Online]. Available from: https://www.vogue.com/article/me-too-tarana-burke-frustrations-mainstream-twitter-thread. Accessed 24 June 2018.
Rentschler, C. A. (2011). *Second Wounds: Victims' Rights and the Media in the US*. Durham: Duke University Press.
Rentschler, C. A. (2014). Rape Culture and the Feminist Politics of Social Media. *Girlhood Studies, 7*(1), 65–82.
Rentschler, C. A., & Thrift, S. (2015). Doing Feminism: Event, Archive, Techne. *Feminist Theory, 16*(3), 239–249.
Richie, B. E. (2012). *Arrested Justice: Black Women, Violence, and America's Prison Nation*. New York: NYU Press.
Roiphe, K. (1991, November 20). Date Rape Hysteria. *New York Times*, p. 27.
Roiphe, K. (1993). *The Morning After: Sex, Fear, and Feminism*. Boston: Black Bay Books.

Roiphe, K. (2018, March). The Other Whisper Network: How Twitter Feminism Is Bad for Women. *Harper's* [Online]. Available from: https://harpers.org/archive/2018/03/the-other-whisper-network-2/. Accessed 24 June 2018.

Rowland, R. (1991–1992). Letter to the Editor. *Anthropological Forum, 6*(3), 429–435.

Rush, F. (1980). *The Best Kept Secret.* New York: McGraw-Hill.

Russell, Y. (2016). Woman's Voice/Law's Logos: The Rape Trial and the Limits of Liberal Reform. *Australian Feminist Law Journal, 42*(2), 273–296.

Salter, M. (2013). Justice and Revenge in Online Counter-Publics: Emerging Responses to Sexual Violence in the Age of Social Media. *Crime, Media, Culture, 9*(3), 225–242.

Sanday, P. R. (1981). The Socio-Cultural Context of Rape: A Cross-Cultural Study. *Journal of Social Issues, 37*(4), 5–27.

Sanday, P. R. (1996). *A Woman Scorned: Acquaintance Rape on Trial.* New York: Doubleday.

Santiago, C., & Criss, D. (2017, October 17). An Activist, a Little Girl and the Heartbreaking Origin of 'Me Too'. *CNN* [Online]. Available from: https://edition.cnn.com/2017/10/17/us/me-too-tarana-burke-origin-trnd/index.html. Accessed 16 Mar 2018.

Saward, J. (2000, July 4). Rape – Why I Have to Give Up the Fight. *Daily Mail,* p. 26.

Saward, J., & Atkins, A. (1999, July 8). Date Rape. *Daily Mail,* pp. 52–53.

Saward, J., with Green, W. (1991). *Rape: My Story.* London: Pan Books.

Sayid, R. (2002, July 4). Offering Coffee Is a Euphemism for Sex. That's When to Say No; or Put Yes in Writing, Says Rape Victim. *Daily Mail,* p. 6.

Scherer, M. (1992). *Still Loved by the Sun: A Rape Survivor's Journal.* New York: Simon & Schuster.

Schorer, J. (1990a, March 1). It Couldn't Happen to Me: One Woman's Story – And Finally, the Trial Begins. *The Des Moines Register,* pp. 1, 8–9.

Schorer, J. (1990b, February 28). It Couldn't Happen to Me: One Woman's Story – Learning to Cope – With Pain and the Legal System. *The Des Moines Register,* pp. 1, 6.

Schorer, J. (1990c, February 27). It Couldn't Happen to Me: One Woman's Story – Months Drag On; No Trial: 'Is This Really Worth It?'. *The Des Moines Register,* pp. 1, 10.

Schorer, J. (1990d, February 25). It Couldn't Happen to Me: One Woman's Story – Staring Down the Cruel Stigma of Rape. *The Des Moines Register,* pp. 1, 6.

Schulhofer, S. (1998). *Unwanted Sex: The Culture of Intimidation and the Failure of Law*. Cambridge: Harvard University Press.
Scott, J. W. (1992). Experience. In J. Butler & J. W. Scott (Eds.), *Feminists Theorize the Political* (pp. 22–40). New York/London: Routledge.
Scott, J. W. (2004). Feminism's History. *Journal of Women's History, 16*(2), 10–29.
Sebold, A. (1999). *Lucky*. New York/Boston: Black Bay Books.
Seccuro, L. (2011). *Crash into Me: A Survivor's Search for Justice*. London: Bloomsbury.
Serisier, T. (2005). 'Remembering Anita': Rape and the Politics of Commemoration. *Australian Feminist Law Journal, 23*(1), 121–146.
Serisier, T. (2013). Who Was Andrea? Writing Oneself as a Feminist Icon. *Women: A Cultural Review, 24*(1), 26–44.
Serisier, T. (2015). 'How Can a Woman Who Has Been Raped Be Believed?' Andrea Dworkin, Sexual Violence and the Ethics of Belief. *Diegesis, 4*(1) [Online]. Available from: https://www.diegesis.uni-wuppertal.de/index.php/diegesis/article/view/191. Accessed 16 June 2018.
Shoard, C. (2018, May 13). Comparing Woody Allen to Polanski or Cosby Is Lazy and Dangerous. *The Guardian* [Online]. Available from: https://www.theguardian.com/commentisfree/2016/may/13/woody-allen-polanski-cosby-dangerous-cannes-ronan-farrow. Accessed 24 Mar 2018.
Sielke, S. (2002). *Reading Rape: Rhetoric of Sexual Violence in American Literature and Culture, 1790–1990*. Princeton/Oxford: Princeton University Press.
Sixty Minutes. (2017, October 23). On Trial. Channel 9 (Australia).
Smart, C. (1989). *Feminism and the Power of Law*. New York: Routledge.
Smart, C. (1998). The Woman of Legal Discourse. In K. Daly & L. Maher (Eds.), *Criminology at the Crossroads: Feminist Readings in Crime and Justice* (pp. 21–36). Oxford: Oxford University Press.
Smith, C. (2001). *Proud of Me: Speaking Out Against Sexual Violence and HIV*. Sandton: Penguin Books.
Smith, S., & Watson, J. (2010). *Reading Autobiography: A Guide for Interpreting Life Narratives*. Minneapolis: University of Minnesota Press.
Solnit, R. (2014, June 1). Our Words Are Our Weapons. *TomDispatch* [Online]. Available from: http://www.tomdispatch.com/blog/175850/. Accessed 11 June 2018.
Spivak, G. C. (1988). Can the Subaltern Speak? In C. Nelson & L. Grossberg (Eds.), *Marxism and the Interpretation of Culture* (pp. 271–313). New York: Macmillan.

Stern, J. (2010). *Denial: A Memoir of Terror*. New York: HarperCollins.
Stoynoff, N. (2016, October 12). Physically Attacked by Donald Trump – A PEOPLE Writer's Own Harrowing Story. *People* [Online]. Available from: https://people.com/politics/donald-trump-attacked-people-writer/. Accessed 16 June 2018.
Stringer, R. (2013). Vulnerability After Wounding: Feminism, Rape Law and the Differend. *SubStance, 42*(3), 148–168.
Sycamore, M. B., aka Mattilda (Ed.). (2004). *Dangerous Families: Queer Writing on Surviving*. New York: Harrington Park Press.
Taslitz, A. (1999). *Rape and the Culture of the Courtroom*. New York: NYU Press.
Telegraph. (2018, May 6). MeToo Movement Founder Tarana Burke Says Time for Talk Is over as She Calls for Action. *Telegraph* [Online]. Available from: https://www.telegraph.co.uk/news/2018/05/06/metoo-movement-founder-tarana-burke-says-time-talk-calls-action/. Accessed 16 June 2018.
Thompson, J. B. (2000). *Political Scandal: Power and Visibility in the Media Age*. Cambridge: Polity.
Time (1976, January 5). Women of the Year. *Time*.
Trinch, S. L. (2003). *Latinas Narratives of Domestic Abuse: Discrepant Versions of Violence*. Philadelphia: John Benjamins.
Trump, D. (2016, October 7). Statement. *Facebook* [Online]. Available from: https://www.facebook.com/DonaldTrump/videos/10157844642270725/. Accessed 23 June 2018.
Twohey, M., & Barbaro, M. (2016, October 12). Two Women Say Donald Trump Touched Them Inappropriately. *New York Times* [Online]. Available from: https://www.nytimes.com/2016/10/13/us/politics/donald-trump-women.html. Accessed 23 June 2018.
United States Senate Committee on the Judiciary. (1990). *Hearing on Legislation to Reduce the Growing Problem of Violent Crime Against Women, Second Session*. (Serial Number J-101-80). Washington, DC: U.S. Government Printing Office.
Van Godwin, P. (2000). *Diary of a Rape Victim: Breaking the Silence to Break Free*. Leawood: Leathers Publishing.
Veitch, J., & Boydell, A. (2017). Memories of Jill Saward. *Journal of Gender-Based Violence, 1*(1), 135–137.
Vernon, P. (2016, October 13). Q&A: Journalist Who Broke Trump Groping Story on Why Others Were Slow to Follow. *Colombia Journalism Review* [Online]. Available from: https://www.cjr.org/q_and_a/donald_trump_sexual_assault_allegations_lucia_graves.php. Accessed 23 June 2018.

Wagmeister, E. (2018, April 10). How Me Too Founder Tarana Burke Wants to Shift the Movement's Narrative. *Variety* [Online]. Available from: https://variety.com/2018/biz/news/tarana-burke-me-too-founder-sexual-violence-1202748012/. Accessed 1 July 2018.

Wagner, T. (2007). *The Making of Me: Finding My Future After Assault*. Sydney: Pan Macmillan.

Walden, C. (2018, March 7). 'It Could All Disappear': #MeToo Founder Tarana Burke on Where the Campaign Is Going Wrong. *Telegraph* [Online]. Available from: https://www.telegraph.co.uk/women/life/could-disappear-metoo-founder-tarana-burke-campaign-going-wrong/. Accessed 1 July 2018.

Waterhouse-Watson, D. (2013). *Athletes, Sexual Assault, and Trials by Media: Narrative Immunity*. New York/London: Routledge.

Way, K. (2018, January 14). I Went on a Date with Aziz Ansari. It Turned into the Worst Night of My Life. *Babe.net* [Online]. Available from: https://babe.net/2018/01/13/aziz-ansari-28355. Accessed 25 Mar 2018.

Weide, R. B. (2014, January 27). The Woody Allen Allegations: Not So Fast. *The Daily Beast* [Online]. Available from: https://www.thedailybeast.com/the-woody-allen-allegations-not-so-fast. Accessed 25 Mar 2018.

Weide, R. B. (2016, May 30). Hard Questions for Ronan Farrow – An Open Letter. *This Mortal Coil* [Blog]. Available from: https://ronanfarrowletter.wordpress.com/2016/05/30/hard-questions-for-ronan-farrow-an-open-letter/. Accessed 11 June 2018.

Weide, R. B. (2017, December 13). Q&A with Dylan Farrow. *This Mortal Coil* [Blog]. Available from: https://ronanfarrowletter.wordpress.com/2017/12/13/qa-with-dylan-farrow/. Accessed 25 Mar 2018.

White, H. (1980). The Value of Narrativity in the Representation of Reality. *Critical Inquiry*, 7(1), 5–27.

Williams, B. (2002). *Truth & Truthfulness: An Essay in Genealogy*. Princeton: Princeton University Press.

Winkler, C. (2002). *One Night: Realities of Rape*. Walnut Creek: AltaMira Press.

Winslow, E. (2016). *Jane Doe January: My Twenty-Year Search for Truth and Justice*. New York: William Morrow.

Winter, J. (2014, February 4). Don't Listen to Woody Allen's Biggest Defender. *Slate* [Online]. Available from: http://www.slate.com/articles/life/culturebox/2014/02/woody_allen_s_biggest_defender_robert_weide_s_attack_on_mia_farrow_and_her.html. Accessed 25 Mar 2018.

Wroe, M. (1990, September 17). Why Jill Wrote to God and Several Million Others. *The Independent*, p. 16.

Yang, G. (2016). Narrative Agency in Hashtag Activism: The Case of #BlackLivesMatter. *Media and Communication, 4*(4), 13–17.
Yeatman, A. (1993). Voice and Representation in the Politics of Difference. In S. Gunew & A. Yeatman (Eds.), *Feminism and the Politics of Difference* (pp. 228–245). Sydney: Allen & Unwin.
Young, S. (1997). *Changing the Wor(l)d: Discourse, Politics, and the Feminist Movement*. New York/London: Routledge.
Young, A. (1998). The Waste Land of the Law, the Wordless Song of the Rape Victim. *Melbourne University Law Review, 22*(2), 442–465.
Yúdice, G. (1991). Testimonio and Postmodernism. *Latin American Perspectives, 18*(3), 15–31.
YWCA Canada. (2016). *#NotOkay* [Online]. Available from: http://notokay.ca/. Accessed 7 Feb 2018.
Zacharek, S., Dockterman, E., & Sweetland Edwards, H. (2017, December 18). The Silence Breakers. *Time* [Online]. Available from: http://time.com/time-person-of-the-year-2017-silence-breakers/. Accessed 11 June 2018.
Ziegenmeyer, N., with Warren, L. (1992). *Taking Back My Life*. New York: Summit.

Index

NUMBERS AND SYMBOLS

#BeenRapedNeverReported, 94
#BlackLivesMatter, 215
#EachEveryWoman, 102
#EverydaySexism, 194
#KeepTellingPeople, Creative Coalition PSA video, 114–115, 195
#MeToo
  and #BlackLivesMatter, 215
  birth of movement, 94–96
  and Dylan Farrow's story, 108–110, 173
  and explosion of public speech around rape, 13
  and Grace-Aziz Ansari story, 111–113
  Kipnis' criticism of, 173–174
  and legacy of 2016 Presidential campaign, 208
  and political efficacy, 194, 195
  post-#MeToo initiatives, 113–116, 195
  Roiphe's criticism of, 174
  and role of collective story, 101, 102
  and role of personal stories, 4
  and validation of individual stories as part of collective story, 103
  See also 'Me Too' movement (2006)
#NotAllMen, 97
#NotOkay, 106, 112, 218–219, 235
#RapeHasNoUniform, 112–113
#YesAllWhiteWomen, 110, 114, 194
#YesAllWomen
  creation of, 94, 96–99
  and 'generic belonging' issue, 112
  going viral, 99
  Hillary Clinton's praise of, 207
  and racial/class issues, 98–99, 101–102

Index

#YesAllWomen (*cont.*)
  and role of collective story, 101, 194
  and role of personal stories, 4
  and validation of individual stories as part of collective story, 103
1001 Nights, Scheherazade character, 53

A

Aboriginal communities
  customary law and violence against women, 126–127
  Emergency Northern Territory Response ('the Intervention'), 122, 143–144
  sexual violence in, 18, 122 (*see also* Bell debate, indigenous stories and White feminist expertise)
Access Hollywood tape, *see* Trump, Donald
The Accused (film), 26, 27
The Age, 26
Ahmed, Sara, 121, 124, 125, 131, 138, 193
Akyel, E., 100
Alcoff, L. M., 27–28, 102, 187–188, 193, 213
Allen, Woody, 96, 103–107, 109–110
  'Comparing Woody Allen to Polanski or Cosby Is Lazy and Dangerous' (C. Shoard), 110
  'Why Has the #MeToo Movement Spared Woody Allen?' (Dylan Farrow), 108–109 (*see also* Farrow, Dylan)
Allison, Dorothy, 58, 62, 191–192, 215
'Anatomy of a Rape' (*It Ain't Me Babe* zine), 8
Anderson, P.
  '*Ampe Akelyernemane Meke Mekarle: Little Children Are Sacred*' (Anderson and Wild), 122
Anglophone Western feminism, 13–14
Ansari, Aziz
  story of Grace's date with and #MeToo, 111–113
Anthropological Forum, 120, 140, 142
Armstrong, Louise, 19, 185–189, 193
Association of Internet Researchers, 15
Australian feminism, 18, 119–121
  See also Bell debate, indigenous stories and White feminist expertise

B

Babe.net
  Grace-Aziz Ansari story, 111
Baker, Katie J. M., 204, 208–209
Bakhtin, M.
  authoritative discourse, 156
  competition between different discourses, 8, 16, 25, 88–89, 210, 211
  heteroglossia and consciousness, 65–66

Index

internally persuasive discourse, 64, 157
Banfield, Ashleigh, 70, 111–112
Barbaro, M.
 'Crossing the Line: How Donald Trump Behaved with Women in Private' (Barbaro and Twohey), 201, 203
Barr, Jennifer
 Within a Dark Wood, 45, 51, 55, 63–65
Barthes, R., 166
BBC
 Jill Saward documentary, 33
 Jill Saward's death, 35
Behrendt, Larissa, 143–144
Belief, *see* Judgement, genre and politics of belief; Online speech, collective stories and politics of belief
Bell, Diane
 Radically Speaking (Bell and Klein), 135, 142–143
 See also Bell debate, indigenous stories and White feminist expertise
Bell debate, indigenous stories and White feminist expertise
 chapter introduction and sources: Bell/Nelson 'Speaking about Rape is Everyone's Business' article, 119–120
 Bell's response to Huggins et al.'s contribution, 120
 Bell's response to Larbalestier's piece, 120
 Bell's retrospective piece on debate, 120–121, 142–143
 Huggins et al.'s/Larbalestier's responses to article, 120
 political backdrop of *Emergency Northern Territory Response*, 122
 chapter overview, 17–18, 121–122
 speaking out, with or for
  Bell's description of Nelson, 130
  case of Dennis Narjic, 126–127
  case of pack rape of Aboriginal girls, 126, 127
  co-authorship issue, 123–124
  meaning *vs.* shaping of speech, 122–123, 125
  Nelson's contributions in article, 121–126, 128–130
  Nelson's description of her relationship with Bell, 129, 131, 135–136
  reciprocal allegations of racism in debate, 130–131
  representational politics and Third World/raped woman as subaltern, 128–131
 'special voice' of feminists
  Bell on 'special voice' of feminists, 131–134, 138
  Bell's criticism of urban radical Aboriginal women, 135–139
  Bell's position on interracial vs. intraracial rape, 139
  Bell's position on race/class and gender, 138–140
  feminist 'knowers' and experience vs. expertise, 132–134
  feminist 'knowers' *vs.* the known, 134–136

Bell debate, indigenous stories and White feminist expertise (*cont.*)
   'Speaking about Rape' title debated, 135
   white academics as custodians of feminism, 138, 161, 193
   white feminists and discoursing about discourse
   Bell's accusation of distraction from real issues, 140–141
   Bell's accusation of 'white listing' and 'race card' playing, 143
   failure of listening, 192–193
   Hugging et al.'s objection to privileged white perspective, 143
   speaking out seen as inherently radical and accusation of silencing, 141–143, 177–178
   white feminists' need to interrogate knowledge production processes, 144
   See also Huggins, Jackie (et al.)
Benedict, Helen, 34
Benjamin, Walter
   'community of listeners' concept, 6, 17, 59, 192
Bennett, Catherine
   'Doubts About Dworkin' (*The Guardian*), 150–155
Biden, Joe
   open letter to Emily Doe, 70–71, 89
Black abolitionist feminists, 214

Blair Government
   and legislation on rape, 37–38
Bletzer, Keith V., 46
Book overview
   analysis of 'speaking out' against rape as narrative politics, 13
   focus on Anglophone Western feminism, 13–14
   interdisciplinarity and feminist theory, 14–15
   methodology and sources, 15
   Personal Statement, 19–21
   structure: case studies and focus on public reception, 15–16; chapter summaries, 16–19
   terminology issues, 15
Bowman, Barbara, 108
Boynton Robinson, Amelia, *see* Robinson, Amelia Boynton
Brecht, Bertolt
   'When Evildoing Comes Like Falling Rain' (poem), 181
Bright, Suzie, 152–153
Brigley Thompson, Z., 106
Brison, Susan J.
   Aftermath: Violence and the Remaking of a Self, 51–56, 59–60, 64, 65, 67, 181
Broaddrick, Juanita, 197, 199–201, 203–209
Brooks, P., 75
Brown, Wendy, 14, 18, 178, 189, 190, 212, 213
Brownmiller, Susan
   Against Our Will: Men, Women and Rape
   author's Personal Statement, 4–5, 19–20

definition of rape, 3
feminist politics and personal narratives, 3–4
Francisco's criticism, 63
NYRF speak-out and conference, 5–8, 11
'Police Blotter Rapist' and rape and race, 9–10
rape as belonging under feminist discourse, 8, 28, 160
ridicule faced by early feminist activists, 24
speaking out and feminism, 25
speaking out beyond feminist-defined spaces, 11–12
survivors' *vs.* feminists' storytelling, 10–12
In Our Time: Memoir of a Revolution, 5–8, 11
Time's 'Women of the Year' award, 3, 12, 93
West Village I (consciousness-raising group), 5, 7, 8, 99, 132
Bumiller, Kristen, 199
Burke, Tarana, 94–96, 98–99, 101, 102, 112–116, 195
Bush, George H. W., 31, 33
Butler, Judith, 212
Buzzfeed, 70, 73, 204

C
California state law
mandatory minimum sentences for sexual assault cases, 70–71
See also 'Emily Doe' case
Campbell, Joseph, 52, 53
Campbell, R., 198
Cavarero, Adriana, 61, 214
Central Park Jogger, *see* Meili, Trisha E.
Chesler, Phyllis
Women and Madness, 6
Chronicle of Higher Education
Kipnis' essay on 'sexual paranoia' in academia, 163
Civil rights movement
and narratives against rape, 214–215
Clark, Annie E., 48
Clark, R., 115
Class
and hashtag activism, 101–102
and race, 9, 84, 86–87, 90–91
and reproduction of silences by oppositional speech, 188–189
Clinton, Bill, 93, 197, 199–201, 222–205, 208, 223
Clinton, Hillary, 102, 199–103, 202–203, 224–226, 225–208
What Happened, 207
See also US Presidential election (2016)
CNN
Banfield's reading of Emily Doe's Victim Impact Statement, 70, 89
Banfield's reading of her own open letter to Grace, 111–112
Colonialism, *see* Neocolonialism, and Bell debate
'Community of listeners' concept (W. Benjamin), 6, 17, 59, 192

Consciousness-raising groups, 9, 10, 12, 24, 95–96, 145, 147, 198
  West Village I (New York), 5, 7–8, 99, 132
'Contextual privacy' concept, 15
Corrigan, Rose, 14, 198, 199, 208
Cosby, Bill, 95, 108–110, 115, 209
Creative Coalition
  #KeepTellingPeople PSA video, 114–115, 195
Criminal justice discourse
  and feminism, 8, 25, 28–31, 41, 48, 89
Criminal justice system
  law's suspicion of women's testimony, 73–74
  limits of legal reform and rape, 199
  and race and rape, 9, 32
  rape trial as theatre, 80
  rape trials as 'symbolic' trials, 34
  truth-telling and the law, 146
  undermining of women's narratives, 7–9
  undermining of women's testimony, 30
  victims' rights *vs.* offenders' rights, 29
  See also 'Emily Doe' case; Feminism
Crooks, Rachel, 201
Cuklanz, Lisa, 34, 80

D

Daily Mail
  Jill Saward's 2000 column, 37–38
  Jill Saward's 2002 interview, 40
  serialisation of Jill Saward's *Rape: My Story*, 33
Danica, Elly, 178–179, 181, 184, 185, 187, 188, 196
Date rape, 36, 37, 40, 148, 159, 160
Davies, Shari, 61
Davis, Angela, 9, 31, 86
Derrida, J.
  genre as enabling and constraining force, 9, 10, 44–45, 113, 145–146, 158, 172–173
  'law of genre' and 'law of the law of genre' concepts, 46–47, 101, 162, 214
  'marking' and 're-marking' concepts, 47, 100, 112
  principle of contamination and impurity, 162, 175
Des Moines Register
  serialisation of Nancy Ziegenmeyer's story, 24, 29, 31–33
'Differend' concept, *see* Lyotard, Jean-François
Discourse theories, *see* Bakhtin, M.; Foucault, M.
Dobie, Kathy
  The Only Girl in the Car, 47
Doe, Emily, *see* 'Emily Doe' case
Doe, Jane, 61
Dominus, S.,
  'After Donald Trump, Will More Women Believe Their Own Stories?' (*New York Times*), 209
Donofrio, Beverley, 47
Douglas, Raymond, 59
Dukakis, Michael, 27, 31
Dworkin, Andrea

Index   245

account of 'drug rape' experience, 149–150
account's failure to fulfil generic conventions, 153–156, 158, 173
in Bell's list of feminist authors, 125
Bennett's 'Doubts about Dworkin' piece, 150–155
Dworkin on her 'so-called' sisters' disbelief, 155
feminists' disbelief, 18, 147, 148, 152–153
Gracen's view of Dworkin's account, 150–154
Orr's criticism of Bennett's stance, 173–175

E

'Ealing Vicarage Rape' case, see Saward, Jill
'Emily Doe' case
chapter overview, 17, 71–72
details of case, 69
Doe's Victim Impact Statement (overview)
beginning and end of statement, 69
Hillary Clinton's praise of, 207
impact as 'extra-legal' document, 69–70
impact on California state law, 70–71
'lighthouse' passage, 70
reading of on CNN, 70, 89
feminists/survivors' criticisms of legal 'truths' of rape, 71
good witnesses and legal speech
catharsis from legal testimony, 79–80
Doe's calling for end to 'victim-blaming' in court, 81
Doe's statement's multiple addresses/registers, 80
feminism-inspired legal strategies, 82–85
positioning of defendant as 'rapist' within narrative, 85–87
public trial/conviction and wider audiences, 80–81
rape and race, 86–87
using law's dominant narratives/myths, 87–88
winning against victim-blaming, 81–82
speaking truth to law
Doe on court's deafness after reading her statement, 77–78
Doe on nightmare of after-the-rape bathroom scene, 72–73
Doe on nightmare of cross-examination at trial, 73–75, 77
Doe on Turner's defence narrative, 75–77
Doe's Glamour 'Woman of the Year' acceptance speech, 78
feminist criticisms of rape trials, 75
law's suspicion of women's testimony, 73–74
stereotypes used in court, 71, 76

'Emily Doe' case (*cont.*)
    validation of women's narrative via legal system, 78–79
    women's stories and legal grammars
        Doe's statement's broad appeal and narrow agenda, 89
        feminism, liberal grammar and the law, 88–89
        pluses and minuses of law's status as primary forum, 89–91
Estrich, Susan, 27, 30, 31, 204
Experience, politics of, 143

Farrow, Dylan
    as example of online speech and doubting women's stories, 96
    'Open Letter' re. sexual abuse by Woody Allen, 103–104
    opinion piece on #MeToo and Woody Allen, 108–109
    Weide's discrediting of Farrow's story, 114–118
    Weide's rebuttal of Farrow's 'Me Too' argument, 109–111
Farrow, Mia, 103–107
Farrow, Moses, 104
Farrow, Ronan, 104
Feminism
    1970s activism, 3, 9, 145
    Anglophone Western feminism, 13–14
    Australian feminism, 18, 119–121
    black abolitionist feminists, 214
    and hashtag activism, 99
    listening as feminist act, 193
    and personal narratives, 4
    racism within, 98
    radical feminism, 9, 153
    and rape
        'failures of success' in feminist politics of rape, 14, 198–199, 208
        feminism and survivor literature, 63–65
        feminism and survivors' storytelling, 10–12, 17–18, 57
        feminist discourse and popular culture, 26
        feminist expertise and experience of rape, 4–5, 19–21
        feminist theories, 14–15, 28
        survivors and feminist consciousness, 29, 41–42
    and rape and the law
        feminism-inspired legal strategies, 82–85
        feminism, liberal grammar and the law, 88–89
        feminism's ambivalent relationship to law, 71
        feminism vs. criminal justice discourse, 8, 16, 25, 28–31, 41, 48, 89
        feminist criticisms of legal 'truths' of rape, 71
        feminist criticisms of rape trials, 75, 80
    second-wave feminism, 4, 25, 64, 71, 177, 185
    and speaking-out, 6–7, 11–12, 25, 40–42, 93

and *Time*'s 'Silence Breakers' award, 93
See also Bell debate, indigenous stories and White feminist expertise; Consciousness-raising groups; Dworkin, Andrea; Judgement, genre and politics of belief; Kipnis, Laura; New York Radical Feminists (NYRF) collective; Roiphe, Katie
Fiske, John, 13
Foster, Jodie, 26, 27
Foucault, M.
'confessional' vs. political speech, 187
discourse, silence and power, 18, 189–190
'speaker's benefit' concept, 141–142, 178, 184–185, 189
Fox, Christine, 100–101
Francisco, Patricia Weaver
'Out of the Darkness' (article), 43, 45, 62
self-interview, 50
Telling: A Memoir of Rape and Recovery, 43, 47, 50, 54, 56, 63–64, 66, 80
Freedman, Karyn L.
One Hour in Paris: A True Story of Rape and Recovery, 55, 67

Gang rape, 47, 48, 81
Gavey, Nicola, 76
Gay, Roxane

Hunger: A Memoir of (My) Body, 49
Geimer, Samantha
The Girl: A Life Lived in the Shadow of Roman Polanski, 60, 62
Gender politics
and rape, 8, 28, 30
and Violence Against Women Act, 41 (*see also* Intersectional politics)
Genre, *see* Derrida, J.; Judgement, genre and politics of belief; Storytelling, genre and subjectivity
Ghomeshi, Jian, 2014 trial, 94
Gibbons, F., 150
Gilmore, Leigh, 7, 14, 15, 53, 82, 105, 109, 186
Glamour magazine, 77
'Woman of the Year' award to Emily Doe, 78
Grace
story of her date with Aziz Ansari and #MeToo, 111–113
Gracen, Julia, 150–154
Grant, Abi
Words Can Describe, 50, 56, 85–87
Gray, L., 27–28, 102, 187–188, 213
Gray-Rosendale, Laura
College Girl: A Memoir, 56, 60
Greer, Germaine, 6
Grewal, Kiran K., 57
Griffin, Susan
Rape: The Power of Consciousness, 54, 186–187
Grix, Julia, 71, 76

The Guardian
   'Comparing Woody Allen to Polanski or Cosby Is Lazy and Dangerous' (C. Shoard), 110
   'Doubts About Dworkin' (Catherine Bennett), 150–155
   Jill Harth's interview, 203
   Nancy Ziegenmeyer case, 26

Hale, Matthew, 73
Hall, Lynn K., 51
Harrison, Jemima, 36
Harth, Jill, 203
Hashtag activism, *see* Online speech, collective stories and politics of belief; *specific hashtags*
Heinzelman, Susan S., 87–91
Hemingway, Mariel, 110
Hemmings, Clare, 89
Heroism
   'hero's quest' narrative, 52–53
   hero's story, 61
   See also Storytelling, genre and subjectivity
Heteroglossia, 65–66
Higgins, Lynn A., 14, 128, 194
hooks, bell, 161
Horeck, Tanya, 3, 161, 186–187, 199
Horton, Willie, 31, 33
Howard Government
   Emergency Northern Territory Response ('the Intervention'), 122
Huggins, Jackie (et al.)
   criticisms of Bell/Nelson article
      Bell's use of relationship with Nelson for her work, 131–132, 134, 135
      co-authorship issue, 120, 123–125, 130
      example of white imperialism, 130
      gender, race and colonialism, 133, 137–138, 143
      real effects of speech about sexual violence, 121–122
      white custodianship of feminism, 138
   dismissed by Bell as well-educated urban Aboriginal women, 136–137
   Larbalestier's article in support of, 120
   See also Bell debate, indigenous stories and White feminist expertise

Intersectional politics
   and Bell debate, 139
   and hashtag activism, 98
Isla Vista shootings (California, 2014), 94, 97
It Ain't Me Babe (San Francisco zine), 'Anatomy of a Rape', 8

Jenefsky, C., 149
Johansson, Scarlet, 107
Johnson, Lacy M.
   The Other Side: A Memoir, 58–59, 62

Jones, Paula, 200
Joseph, L.
  Little Girl Lost: One Woman's Journey Beyond Rape, 51
Judgement, genre and politics of belief
  chapter overview, 18
  feminism and women as truth-tellers, 145
  feminist judgement and sincerity criterion, 146–147
  feminist judgment and authenticity criteria, 147–148
  genre construction and new modes of judging/disbelieving, 145–146, 148–149
  legal *vs.* feminist truth criteria, 146
  political implications of generic judgement, 172–175
  See also Dworkin, Andrea; Roiphe, Katie
Jurich, Marilyn, 52–53

K

Kalven, Jamie
  Working with Available Light: A Family's World After Violence, 43–44, 48, 67
Kaplan, Alisa
  Still Room for Hope: A Survivor's Story of Sexual Assault, Forgiveness, and Freedom, 51, 52
Karlsson, Lena, 99, 103, 110

Kipnis, Laura
  criticism of #MeToo, 173–174
  essay on 'sexual paranoia' in academia (*Chronicle of Higher Education*), 163
  Unwanted Advances: Sexual Paranoia Comes to Campus
  call for politics promoting women's agency, 199
  criticism of feminist generic/melodramatic framing, 18, 148, 158–159, 163, 165–169
  criticism of Title IX campus system, 162–163
  criticism of Title IX investigation of students' complaints, 163–165
  rewriting of students' stories and own generic preferences, 165–172
Klein, Renate
  Radically Speaking (Bell and Klein), 135, 142–143
  Women's Studies International Forum 1991 editorial, 142
Kørra, Monica
  Kill the Silence: A Survivor's Life Reclaimed, 50, 180, 183–184, 195–196
Koss, Mary P., 46
Kristof, Nicholas, 103

L

Lamott, Anne, 70
Larbalestier, Jan, 120, 122, 140, 141
Larcombe, Wendy, 84
Latin American *testimonio* genre, 49

Lauer, T.
  Hours of Torture, Years of Silence: My Soul Was the Scene of the Crime, 180
Law, *see* Criminal justice discourse; Criminal justice system; 'Emily Doe' case; Feminism
'Law and order' discourse, 12, 16, 25, 29
Leeds, Jessica, 201
Leo, Jana
  Rape New York, 54, 86, 87
Levy, A., 149, 154
Lewinsky, Monica, 208
Listening, *see* 'Community of listeners' concept (W. Benjamin); Silence and politics of listening
Lively, Blake, 109
Los Angeles Times
  'Why Has the #MeToo Movement Spared Woody Allen?' (Dylan Farrow), 108–109
Ludlow, Peter, 163–170
Lyotard, Jean-François
  'differend' concept, 18, 179–181, 194, 195
  and Armstrong's account, 185
  and Emily Doe case, 77–79, 89
  and Kørra's account, 184
  and Pines' story, 7
  and politics vs. narrative, 220–221
  and Raine's account, 182, 190–191
  and Sebold's account, 83, 86
  'referent/no referent' concept, 77, 78, 115, 180–181, 184

M

M., Kaye, 96–99, 101–102, 112
McCreary, P.
  Out of the Shadows: A Rape Victim Examines Her Life In and Out of Mormonism, 51
McGillis, Kelly, 26–27
McGuire, Danielle L., 49, 215
MacKinnon, Catharine, 125, 133
McNaron, Toni
  Voices in the Night (McNaron and Morgan, eds), 66
Mai, Mukhtar, 47–48
Marcus, Sharon, 14, 141, 211–212
Marxism, 211
Media, coverage of rape cases, 34
Meili, Trisha E.
  I Am the Central Park Jogger: A Story of Hope and Possibility, 47, 51, 186
Menchú, Rigoberta, 49
'Me Too' movement (2006), 94–95, 98–99, 102, 114
  See also #MeToo
Milano, Alyssa, 94–96, 99, 113, 114, 195
Mitchell, P., 186
Mohanty, Chandra T., 129–133, 139
Moreton-Robinson, Aileen, 128, 129, 135–136
Morgan, Yarrow
  Voices in the Night (McNaron and Morgan, eds), 66

N

Naples, Nancy A., 29
Narjic, Dennis, 126–127

'Narrative immunity' concept, 76, 85, 167
Narrative politics
  speaking out as a form of, 4, 13
  See also Politics of narrative; Public survivors and rape narratives; Storytelling, genre and subjectivity
National Organisation of Women, 26
Nelson, Topsy Napurrula
  Bell's description of, 130
  description of her relationship with Bell, 129, 131, 135–136
  response to Higgins et al.'s article, 120, 129
  'Speaking About Rape Is Everyone's Business' (Bell and Nelson), 119–120
  Nelson's contributions, 121–126, 128–130
  See also Bell debate, indigenous stories and White feminist expertise
Neocolonialism
  and Bell debate, 119–120, 122, 133
Neoliberalism, 37–41, 186
New Statesman
  Andrea Dworkin's 'drug rape' piece, 149–150, 155
New Yorker
  Harvey Weinstein story, 94, 104
New York magazine
  Bill Cosby story, 95
New York Radical Feminists (NYRF) collective
  Rape: The First Sourcebook for Women, 10
  speak-out and conference, 5–8, 11
New York Times
  'After Donald Trump, Will More Women Believe Their Own Stories?' (Dominus), 209
  Brownmiller's *Against Our Will* bestseller, 3
  'Crossing the Line: How Donald Trump Behaved with Women in Private' (Barbaro and Twohey), 201, 203
  Dylan Farrow's 'Open Letter' (Kristof's blog), 103–104
  Harvey Weinstein story, 94
  Katie Roiphe on feminists 'turning rape into fiction,' 148
  Nancy Ziegenmeyer case, 26, 32–33
NYRF, *see* New York Radical Feminists (NYRF) collective

Obama Administration, Title IX legislation, 162
Online speech, collective stories and politics of belief
  chapter introduction
    award to Silence Breakers, 93–94
    birth of 'Me Too' movement, 94–95
  chapter overview, 17, 95–96
  hashtags and collective stories
    construction of hashtag stories, 96–97
    creation of #YesAllWomen, 97–99

Online speech, collective stories and politics of belief (*cont.*)
  creation of pre-hashtag 'Me Too Movement,' 98–99
  feminist analysis of hashtags, 99
  generic commonality and repetition, 99–101
  genre and meaning of collective story, 101–102
  hashtags and race/racism within feminism, 98–99, 101–102
  hashtags and social class, 101–102
  online stories and generic judgements
    #MeToo and contestation of generic belonging, 109–113
    belief and 'semantic thickness' of generic belonging, 103, 108, 109
    belief and stories outside collective narrative, 103
    Dylan Farrow's 'Open Letter' re. sexual abuse by Woody Allen, 103–104
    Dylan Farrow's opinion piece on #MeToo and Woody Allen, 108–109
    Grace-Aziz Ansari story and #MeToo, 111–113
    Weide's discrediting of Farrow's story, 104–108
    Weide's rebuttal of Farrow's 'Me Too' argument, 109–111
    Weinstein and Cosby stories, 108, 110
  post-#MeToo
    Alyssa Milano's #KeepTellingPeople, 113–115
    hashtag activism and political efficacy issue, 194–195
    Tarana Burke's call for 'the work' after #MeToo, 115–116
  See also specific hashtags
Orr, Deborah, 151–153
Overholser, Geneva, 26–27, 32
Oxford, Kelly, 99–100, 195

P

Patriarchy, 8, 112, 131–139, 141, 147, 178, 185
Payne, Sharon, 126
Penal populism, 29, 31
People magazine, 27, 201, 203
Persky, Aaron, Judge, 71, 78–79
Personal narratives
  and feminist politics, 4 (*see also* Speaking out)
Personal Statements
  from author of this book, 19–21
  from Susan Brownmiller, 4–5, 19–20
Phillips, L.
  Moving On: A Journey Through Sexual Assault, 51
Phipps, Alison, 143
Pierce-Baker, Charlotte
  Surviving the Silence: Black Women's Stories of Rape, 43, 47–50, 53, 55, 79–80, 180
Pines, Sara, 5, 7, 10–11, 198
Pinto, Andrea, 48

Plummer, Ken, 13–14, 24
Polanski, Roman, 60, 107
  'Comparing Woody Allen to Polanski or Cosby Is Lazy and Dangerous' (C. Shoard), 110
Politics of experience, 143
Politics of narrative
  chapter overview, 19
  'failures of success' in feminist politics of rape, 198–199, 208
  generic impurity as political/narrative resource, 214–215
  individual narratives and collective listening, 213–214
  morality vs. truth as product of political contestation, 212–213
  narrative vs. politics and Lyotard's 'differend' concept, 214–215
  overview of critical survey of speaking out practices, 210
  potential transgression of survivor speech vs. radical politics, 213
  reshaping vs. telling stories, 211–212
  telling the story of a world without rape, 215
  See also US Presidential election (2016)
Polletta, Francesca, 78
Previn, Soon-Yi, 106
Public survivors and rape narratives
  chapter overview, 16
  See also Saward, Jill; Ziegenmeyer, Nancy

R v. Dennis Narjic, 126–127
R v. Sherrin, 74
Race
  and class, 9, 84, 86–87, 90–91
  and feminism, 98
  and hashtag activism, 98–99, 101
  and rape, 9–10, 31–33, 47–49, 84, 86–87, 90–91
  and reproduction of silences by oppositional speech, 188–189
  and victim *vs.* heroic survivor status, 57
  and Violence Against Women Act, 41
  See also Bell debate, indigenous stories and White feminist expertise; Black abolitionist feminists; Intersectional politics
Radical feminism, 9, 153
  See also New York Radical Feminists (NYRF) collective
Raine, Nancy Venable
  After Silence: Rape and My Journey Back, 19, 43, 180–183, 190–192, 194
  'Returns of the Day' (essay), 182
Ramsey, Martha
  Where I Stopped: Remembering an Adolescent Rape, 55, 58, 67
Rape
  as crime equivalent to murder, 24, 25
  date rape, 32, 33, 36, 148, 159, 160
  gang rape, 47, 48, 81
  and gender politics, 8, 28, 30
  'her rape/rapist' terminology issue, 15

Rape (*cont.*)
  inscription/erasure cycles in representations of rape, 194
  male rape victims/survivors, 59
  and popular culture, 26
  and race, 9–10, 31–33, 47–49, 84, 86–87, 90–91
  'real/stranger' vs. 'simple/acquaintance' rape and disbelief of women's stories, 103
  and rape memoirs, 48, 50
  and Roiphe, 160
  and Saward, 35–41
  and Ziegenmeyer, 30–32
  and slavery, 9
  See also Feminism
Rape memoirs, *see* Storytelling, genre and subjectivity
Rape: The First Sourcebook for Women (New York Radical Feminists), 10
Rentschler, C. A., 13, 210
Richie, Beth E., 199
Robinson, Amelia Boynton, 9
Rodger, Elliot, 94, 97
Roiphe, Katie
  criticism of #MeToo, 174
  The Morning After, criticism of 'rape-crisis' feminism, 147, 156, 161
  feminists 'turning rape into fiction,' 147, 148, 156
  generic feminist conventions vs. authenticity, 18, 147–148, 157–159, 161
  The Morning After, critique of Roiphe's acceptance of pressure in sex, 160
  Roiphe's impossible demand for genrelessness, 159, 161–162
  Roiphe's pre-feminist view of rape as 'private' matter, 159–160
  Roiphe's self-positioning as rightful custodian of feminism, 161
Rowland, Robyn, 120, 124, 140–143
Rush, Florence
  The Best Kept Secret, 6
Russell, Yvette, 199

S

Salter, Michael, 101
Saward, Jill (also known as 'Ealing Vicarage Rape' victim), 24–25, 33, 35
  activist career, 33, 35, 178
  Christian socially conservative framing, 25, 39–40
  conservative *vs.* feminist framing, 16, 25, 35, 38, 40–42
  Daily Mail 2002 interview, 40
  Daily Mail 'Rape-Why I Have to Give Up the Fight' column, 37–38
  media coverage of her case, 33, 34
  neoliberal framing, 37–41
  public speaking after validation of a conviction, 81
  Rape: My Story, 24, 33–35, 47
  'real' *vs.* 'simple' rape (or 'forced sexual entry'), 35–41
  speaking out *vs.* feminism, 25, 40–41

Scheherazade (*1001 Nights*), 53
Scherer, Migael, 85, 87, 192
Schorer, Jane, 26, 28, 29, 31, 32
Scott, Joan W., 64, 132, 147
Sebold, Alice, *Lucky*, 47, 60, 82–87, 193
Seccuro, Liz, *Crash into Me: A Survivor's Search for Justice*, 51, 55
Self-help discourse, 186
'Semantic thickness' concept, 103, 108, 109, 158
Shelton, Cathy, 200
Sherrin case, 74
Shoard, C., 'Comparing Woody Allen to Polanski or Cosby Is Lazy and Dangerous' (*The Guardian*), 110
Sielke, Sabine, 160, 194, 195, 199, 220
Silence and politics of listening
  chapter introduction
    arguments for breaking the silence, 177–178
    limitations of breaking the silence, 178–179
    silence as positive strategy, 178, 179
  chapter overview, 18–19, 179
  defining silence
    analysis of rape memoirs titles, 180
    social silencing as active force, 55, 180–184, 194
  silences of speaking out
    Armstrong's critique of 'breaking the silence' project, 19, 185–189, 193
    Danica's critique of 'breaking the silence' project, 178–179, 181, 184, 185, 187, 188, 194
    questioning automatic transgression of speaking out, 184–185, 187–188
    reproduction of silences by oppositional speech, 188–189
  types of silence and listening
    choosing silence and control over one's story, 191–192
    different types of silence, 190–191
    discourse, silence and power, 189–190
    listening, attentive silence and political solidarity, 192–193
  a world 'after silence'
    cycles of inscription/erasure in representations of rape, 194
    hashtag campaigns and political efficacy issue, 194–195
    politics for world without rape, 195–196
Silence Breakers, 12, 83–84, 204–205
Silver, Brenda R., 14, 128, 194
Sinatra, Frank, 107
Slavery, and rape, 9
Smart, Carol, 30, 90
Smith, Bobby Lee, 23, 31–32
Smith, Charlene
  Proud of Me: Speaking Out About Sexual Violence and HIV, 51, 54–57, 80–81

Smith, S., 59
Social media, *see* Online speech, collective stories and politics of belief; *specific hashtags*
Solnit, Rebecca, 99
Spacey, Kevin, 109–110
'Speaker's benefit' concept, *see* Foucault, M.
Speaking for, 56–57
Speaking out
  critical survey of practices of (overview), 220
  and feminism, 6–7, 11–12, 25, 40–42, 83
  as form of genre creation, 8
  as form of narrative politics, 4, 13
  and the law, 71
  silence as 'other' of speaking out, 177
  success of, 40–41
  success of and failure to end sexual violence, 12
  See also Online speech, collective stories and politics of belief; Politics of narrative; Silence and politics of listening; Storytelling, genre and subjectivity
Spivak, Gayatri C.
  'Can the Subaltern Speak?' (essay), 56, 128
Stereotypes (stock characters)
  and Alice Sebold's testimony, 83, 84
  and class/race difference, 86–87
  and Dworkin story, 153–155
  and Emily Doe trial, 71, 76
  and Kipnis' criticism of campus feminism, 163, 166–167
  and Roiphe's criticism of feminist generic conventions, 147–148, 157–161, 179
  and Saward's views on rape, 34, 36
  and Weide's discrediting of Dylan Farrow's story, 96–97
Stern, Jessica, 56–57
Stock characters, *see* Stereotypes (stock characters)
Stoltenberg, John, 149–150, 153
Storytelling, genre and subjectivity
  chapter introduction
    Francisco's praise of new literature on rape, 43–44
    paradoxical effects of rape memoir genre, 46–47
  chapter overview, 16–17
  constructing a genre
    defining rape memoirs and list of texts, 47–48
    Derrida's 'law of genre' theory, 46–47
    first published English-language rape memoir, 45
    flowering of genre from mid-1990s, 45–46
    politics of generic inclusion and exclusion, 49–50
    rape and race, 47–49
    rape in broader trauma narratives, 49
  heroine's quest for subjectivity
    analysis of titles, 50–51, 180
    feminine/feminist 'hero's quest' narrative, 52–53
    individual recovery narratives and speaking out politics, 51–52
    journey from victim to heroism, 53–56

silence and social denial, 55
speaking for and heroic subjectivity, 56–57
storytelling and hope of political change, 56, 57
survivors, feminist experts and race, 57
narrative vulnerability and storyteller's dilemma
'heroic victim' character and sense of self, 57–58
my story vs. web of stories, 58–59
negative impact of readers' expectations, 59–60
sense of being defined by 'rape victim' identity, 60–62
survivor literature politics and feminism
feminist criticisms of survivor narratives, 64
gap between survivors' and feminism's truths, 63–65
survivor literature's multiplicity of discursive frameworks, 65–66
transformative nature and limitations of creative authorship, 66–68
Stoynoff, Natasha, 201, 203, 209
Subalternity
and Western/feminist representational politics, 128–131, 136
Subjectivity, see Storytelling, genre and subjectivity
Survivors
survivor discourse, potentials and limitations of, 14
survivors' storytelling and feminist experts, 10–12, 17–18, 57

use of term, 15
See also Public survivors and rape narratives; Victims
Sycamore, Mattilda Bernstein, 48

Taslitz, Andrew, 76, 146
Taylor, Recy, 9
Terminology issues, 15
Testimonio genre, 49
Third World women and Western representational politics, 128–131
Thrift, S., 13, 210
Time magazine
'Person of the Year' award to Silence Breakers, 12, 93–94, 204–205
'Women of the Year' award to Brownmiller, 3, 12, 93
'Time's Up' campaign, 111
Title IX (USA), 162–165, 168, 169, 171
Toback, James, 109–110
Trump, Donald
Access Hollywood tape and #NotOkay, 94, 100, 195
and Hillary/Bill Clinton story, 197–198, 204–202, 205–204
Hillary Clinton's view on, 207
articles
'After Donald Trump, Will More Women Believe Their Own Stories?' (Dominus), 209
'Crossing the Line: How Donald Trump Behaved with Women in Private'

Trump, Donald (*cont.*)
    (Barbaro and Twohey), 201, 203
  Broaddrick's support for Trump, 205–207
  Weide on difference with Woody Allen, 109–110
  See also US Presidential election (2016)
Truth
  morality vs. truth as product of political contestation, 212–213
  truth-telling and feminist vs. legal genres, 145, 166
Turner, Brock
  conviction, 81, 89
  defence narrative, 75–77, 85
  Emily Doe's Victim Statement, 17, 69, 70, 72, 77, 78, 80
  See also 'Emily Doe' case
Twitter, *see specific hashtags*
Twohey, M.
  'Crossing the Line: How Donald Trump Behaved with Women in Private' (Barbaro and Twohey), 201, 203

U

US Congress
  reading of Emily Doe's Victim Impact Statement, 70
US Presidential election (2016)
  Broaddrick's allegations against Bill Clinton and her support for Trump, 197, 199–201, 203–209
  Hillary Clinton's feminist campaign and selective disbelief of survivors, 204–208
  Trump's *Access Hollywood* tape and Hillary/Bill Clinton story, 197–198, 200–203
  women's stories of violence as political tools for regressive ends, 201–202
  women's stories validated by men and along partisan political lines, 199, 203–205
  See also Politics of narrative
US Senate Judiciary Committee (Legislation to Reduce the Growing Problem of Violent Crime Against Women)
  Nancy Ziegenmeyer's testimony, 24, 28, 30, 31

V

Van Godwin, P.
  Diary of a Rape Victim: Breaking the Silence to Break Free, 180
Victim Impact Statements, 77, 85
  See also 'Emily Doe' case
Victims
  use of term, 15
  victim-blaming, 26, 34, 36, 39, 81–82, 94, 154–155
  victims' rights and neoliberalism, 37–41
  'victim's rights' discourse, 12, 25, 29, 30, 33 (*see also* Survivors)
Violence Against Women Act (US), 24, 30, 41

W

Wagner, Tegan
  The Making of Me: Finding My Future After Assault, 51, 54, 81–82
Walker, Alice, 156
Wasco, S. M., 198
Waterhouse-Watson, Deb, 76, 103
Watson, J., 59
Way, Katie, 111
Weide, Robert B., 104–111
Weinstein, Harvey, 84, 85, 104, 108–110, 115
West Village I (New York consciousness-raising group), 5, 7, 8, 99, 132
White, Hayden, 50
Wilde, R.
  '*Ampe Akelyernemane Meke Mekarle*: Little Children Are Sacred' (Anderson and Wild), 122
Willey, Kathleen, 200
Williams, Bernard, 146
Winkler, Cathy, 15, 55
Winslet, Kate, 107
Winslow, Emily
  Jane Doe January: My Twenty-Year Search for Truth and Justice, 51, 61, 86–87
Women's Review of Books, 186
Women's Studies International Forum (*WSIF*)
  Bell's and Nelson's 'Speaking About Rape Is Everyone's Business' article, 129, 177–178
  Huggins et al.'s response to article, 120
  Klein's 1991 editorial, 142

Y

Yeatman, Anna, 121, 135, 138, 161
'You Are Not Alone' day (Los Angeles), 43
Young, Alison, 75
Young, Stacey, 11, 88–89
Yúdice, G., 136

Z

Zacharek, S., 83–84
Ziegenmeyer, Nancy
  career as public rape survivor, 23–24, 178, 179
  comparison with 'Emily Doe' case, 71
  Des Moines Register serialisation of her story, 24–29, 31–33
  feminism and rape in popular culture, 26–27
  feminism *vs.* criminal justice discourse, 16, 28–31, 41
  feminist analysis and victim's rights, 25, 30
  her testimony to US Senate Judiciary Committee, 24, 28, 30, 31
  public speaking after validation of a conviction, 81
  rape and race, 31–33
  speaking out *vs.* feminism, 25, 40–41

GPSR Compliance

The European Union's (EU) General Product Safety Regulation (GPSR) is a set of rules that requires consumer products to be safe and our obligations to ensure this.

If you have any concerns about our products, you can contact us on

ProductSafety@springernature.com

In case Publisher is established outside the EU, the EU authorized representative is:

Springer Nature Customer Service Center GmbH
Europaplatz 3
69115 Heidelberg, Germany

www.ingramcontent.com/pod-product-compliance
Lightning Source LLC
LaVergne TN
LVHW020343260326
834688LV00045B/1500